3·7817963
BOU

D0261241

WITHDRAWN

1 8 SEP 2019

WELSH COLLEGE OF
MUSIC & DRAMA
LIBRARY

Developing Student Autonomy in Learning

Second Edition

Edited by David Boud

Kogan Page, London/Nichols Publishing Company, New York

3.7817943

D

Copyright © 1981, 1988 David Boud and named contributors

All rights reserved. No reproduction, copy or transmission of this publication
may be made without written permission.

No paragraph of this publication may be reproduced, copied or transmitted save
with written permission or in accordance with the provisions of the Copyright
Act 1956 (as amended), or under the terms of any licence permitting limited
copying issued by the Copyright Licensing Agency, 7 Ridgmount Street, London
WC1E 7AE.

Any person who does any unauthorised act in relation to this publication may be
liable to criminal prosecution and civil claims for damages.

First edition published in Great Britain by Kogan Page
and in the United States of America by Nichols Publishing Company in 1981

This second edition first published in Great Britain in 1988 by
Kogan Page Limited, 120 Pentonville Road, London NI 9JN

British Library Cataloguing in Publication Data
Developing student autonomy in learning — 2nd ed.
1. Independent study
2. Education, Higher
I. Boud, David.
378'.17943 LB1049

ISBN 185091 276 9

WITHDRAWN

18 SEP 2013

This second edition first published in the United States of America in 1988 by
Nichols Publishing Company, PO Box 96, New York NY 10024

Library of Congress Cataloging-in-Publication Data
Developing student autonomy in learning / edited by David Boud. — 2nd ed.
    p. cm.
  Bibliography: p.
  Includes index.
  ISBN 0-89397-291-6 : $32.50
  1. Independent study. 2. Study, Method of. 3. Individualized
instruction. I. Boud, David.
LB2395.2.D48 1988
371.3'94—dc 19   87-22315 CIP

Photoset in North Wales by
Derek Doyle & Associates, Mold, Clwyd
Printed and bound in Great Britain by
Billing & Sons Ltd, Worcester

Contents

Preface

Let me try to put this book in the context of its appearance at this particular time in the history of our civilization. Seeing it in this context may help you to perceive its significance – and I view this as a most significant book.

Prescient observers of our civilization – H.G. Wells, Aldous and Julian Huxley, Pierre Teilhard de Chardin, Bertrand de Jouvenal, George Orwell, Edgar Faure, Donald Schon, Alvin Toffler, to mention some of the most outstanding – have been trying to prepare us during much of this century for the emergence of a drastically different kind of civilization in the next century. They have convinced me that as we approach the 21st century we are facing a major turning point in human history. The assumptions and ideologies – about the nature of man, the distribution of power and wealth, the stability of knowledge and technology, and about many other things – on which past and present civilizations have been operating have become dysfunctional in a world of accelerating change. The axioms of the last century are becoming the myths of the next century. And a society that is operating on the basis of myths is in deep trouble.

The set of assumptions, ideologies and myths to which this book is directed concerns the purpose and nature of education – or, to be more accurate, of learning. Traditional education has been based on the premise that the central purpose of education is to produce knowledgeable persons. Often this purpose has been couched in the term 'socialization', by which is meant providing individuals with the concepts, values, and skills required to function reasonably well in the world as it is now. Accordingly, educational systems consisting of primary schools, secondary schools, technical institutes, and colleges and universities were established. Individuals were permitted to 'graduate' into life at any level prepared to function in society in roles for which that level of education had equipped them. Learning was perceived as being 'terminal' almost any where along the line.

This assumption about the purpose of education may have been appropriate in a world of relative stability, in which people could function reasonably well for the rest of their lives on the basis of what they had learned in their youth. But this assumption is a myth in a world in which the half-life of a fact or a technical skill or a value or an attitude is shrinking year by year. People whose personal equipment became fixed at 16 or 20 or 25 will largely obsolete within a few years – or, in some areas of life, within months. This is the great risk of continuing to operate on this myth of socialization – the impending obsolescence of man.

The new assumption about the purpose of education, to which the authors of this book subscribe, is that it is to produce autonomous *lifelong* learners. As Edgar Faure and his associates proclaim in their seminal book, *Learning To Be* (1972), if lifelong learning is to be the organizing principle for all of education,

4

the primary mission of education for children and youth must be the development of the skills of self-directed inquiry rather than the inculcation of subject-matter content. The test of the readiness of students to leave formal schooling would be demonstration of the mastery of the skills of autonomous learning. What a different curricular structure and what a different set of teaching-learning strategies this would require. There are signs, though, that islands of primary, secondary, and higher education institutions are beginning to experiment with ways of doing this. Being an optimist, it is my hope that the generation of my grandchildren will emerge from schooling as highly skilful autonomous learners so that the tertiary educators of that era will be primarily educational brokers with responsibility mainly for linking autonomous learners with appropriate learning resources.

Meantime we are faced with the reality that most people seeking higher education have learned only the skills of learning by being taught. They do not know how to diagnose their own needs for learning, for formulating their own learning objectives, identifying a variety of learning resources and planning strategies for taking the initiative in using those resources, assessing their own learning, and having their assessments validated. The 21st century will not wait for my grandchildren to have acquired these skills; survival under its mercurial conditions will require that this generation of adults has those skills. Thus there is an urgent need for all programmes of higher education between now and the end of the century to be geared to developing the skills of autonomous learning at the front end of their sequence of learning experiences and that subsequent units of the sequence be designed as self-directed learning activities. This is to say that the new emphasis in higher education must be on the *process of learning*, with the *acquisition of content* (rather than the transmission of content) being a natural (but not pre-programmed) result.

To reorient higher education around the world in this direction is a tremendous challenge. It is a concept that is foreign to most educators. It has not been part of their training (ie socialization). It requires a redefinition of their role away from that of transmitter and controller of instruction to that of facilitator and resource person to self-directed learners. It is frightening. They do not know how to do it.

For such a drastic transition to occur, therefore, teachers in higher education throughout the world need (1) to know that there is a respectable (preferably research-based) rationale for autonomous learning, (2) to know that its benefits have been successfully demonstrated in practice, and (3) to have specific guidelines and techniques for implementing it. These are precisely the things that this book gives them.

Returning to my opening statements, I would like to emphasize that I do not view what we are talking about here as a passing fad or a cosmetic improvement in education. I am convinced that we are talking about a fundamental restructuring of our way of thinking about the purpose and nature of education. We might say that we are now beginning to perceive that the purpose of education is *learning*. And we are beginning to realize that frequently *teaching*

5

interferes with learning. As Allen Tough has demonstrated (in his *Adult's Learning Projects* [1971]), when adults undertake to learn on their own they tend to follow a sequence of steps, move at a pace, make use of a variety of resources, exhibit a style, and assess their learning in ways that are uniquely their own. If we want to facilitate their learning, we 'teachers' will follow the flow of their natural process rather than impose our teacher-made sequence on them.

I am certain that the next two decades are going to be the most innovative, revolutionary, full of ferment, and painful but exciting in the history of education.

Malcolm S. Knowles
Professor Emeritus
North Caroline State University

Introduction to the Second Edition

David Boud,
Tertiary Education Research Centre, University of New South Wales

What is this book about?

This book is about a very important goal of education and how it can be translated into practice. It concerns ways in which teachers in higher education can enable students to become more autonomous in their learning; that is, assist students to learn more effectively without the constant presence or intervention of a teacher.

Few people would dispute the central theme of this book, that the role of teachers is not just to transmit knowledge but also to help students take increasing responsibility for their own learning. This idea has received a great deal of token support but has rarely received the depth of consideration exhibited in the contributions presented here.

Many of those who agree, in principle, that one important aim of education should be to produce students who will eventually be capable of functioning independently of their teachers and their set texts, are at a loss when it comes to organizing their courses to achieve this end. 'Students don't want to be autonomous'; 'The institution isn't set up for this'; 'What about the problem of assessment?' are some of the common responses to the question: 'If you believe this to be important, why aren't you doing something about it?' In this book, teachers in higher education from different disciplines and from different institutional settings show how they are attempting to promote autonomy in learning by describing their experiences of introducing alternatives to the traditional modes of teaching and course design. They provide personal accounts of their experiences rather than exhortations about what should be done. It is not intended to be a recipe for how-to-do-it but rather a source of information, encouragement and even inspiration for others who wish to pursue the goal of increasing student autonomy but are not quite sure whether it is possible or, if it is, how they might start.

Many terms have been used to describe approaches to developing student autonomy in higher education: independent study, self-directed learning, student-initiated learning and project-orientation are a few. Some of these have been used to refer to particular practices or to specific contexts and have special connotations for some people. The theme of this book, however, encompasses all these approaches and examines them with respect to their common element: the goals of developing independence and interdependence, self-directedness, and responsibility for learning.

Although the focus will not be on teaching methods *per se*, but on strategies for fostering learning within the context of particular courses, various methods will be described. These include the use of learning contracts in which students prepare a formal plan for their learning and its evaluation which is validated by a staff member; one-to-one learning in which students work in pairs to facilitate each other's learning; student-planned courses in which students work on their own and in groups to initiate their own projects and put them into practice; peer support systems in which newly arrived students are assisted in problems of personal and academic adjustment by students with longer experience of the institution; and collaborative assessment in which staff and students cooperate in establishing criteria for student assessment and make judgements on the basis of these. Each of these approaches is described in a particular context from the point of view of the teacher using the approach.

Why should we be concerned about creating opportunities for students to develop and exercise autonomy in learning? The reasons emphasized in this book are not primarily theoretical and philosophical but practical. Independence in learning within an educational institution may or may not be an ideal towards which an individual may strive; it is, nevertheless, a vital requisite for someone to be able to function effectively in modern society. Those acting in responsible positions need to be able to plan their own learning and draw upon a variety of resources to assist them in putting their learning plan into action. They need to use the experience and expertise of others, but it is their own responsibility to ensure that the answer needed is found.

If people outside educational institutions do, by force of circumstance, act more or less as autonomous learners, and there is evidence to suggest that they do (Tough, 1971: 1979 edition), then the activities within educational institutions should be structured in such a way that they prepare students for 'learning after school' (lifelong learning) and assist them to develop the skills that they will need in order to exercise responsibility for learning effectively. If students enter these institutions with a very limited capability of being independent learners, one of the important roles of colleges and universities should be to provide the circumstances in which they can develop this capability. Unfortunately, at present, the assumption of most institutions is that students should be able to satisfactorily conduct their own learning. They are dismayed when they find evidence to the contrary, but provide little in the way of training in the skills which are needed, focusing instead on the presentation of new subjects and increasingly sophisticated problems.

The assumption of the contributors to this volume is that if a skill is as important as that of autonomy in learning, then it is the responsibility of teachers in higher education to do something about creating the conditions in which it can flourish. They believe that it is the responsibility of all teachers to ensure that they construct their courses to foster autonomy and that this goal is compatible with the discipline-centred goals which often predominate. No matter what the professional background of the teacher, and irrespective of whether he or she has had any formal educational training, it is possible to design and conduct courses on this basis.

The new edition

Since 1981, when the first edition of this book was published, there have been many changes in the world of higher education. At a personal level we have sadly lost one of our contributors, Jane Abercrombie, who died in 1984. She was a friend and a consultant to me and I will miss her warmly supportive and insightful advice. She was one of the British pioneers in the area of student autonomy, and her book *The Anatomy of Judgement*, first published in 1960, will remain one of the seminal texts which will continue to stimulate our thinking. On the world scene we have also lost the immensely influential figure of Carl Rogers who died last year. His book *Freedom to Learn* (1969) has probably had more impact on the attitudes of teachers at all levels than any other book written. Rogers' commitment to a person-centred approach shone through all his writing. He was one of the few educationalists, like Jane Abercrombie, whose writing and practice manifested not only a commitment to the values of student autonomy but also a deep care for individuals. Rogers wrote simply but with such conviction that his work demanded that we consider our own values and attitudes and ask ourselves whether our own practice as teachers measures up to what we hold to be true. One of his last projects was a thorough revision of his 1969 book, which has been published as *Freedom to Learn in the 80s* (1983).

Although important individuals are no longer with us, there have been a considerable number of developments in the area of student autonomy in higher education in the past six years and these are reflected in this revised edition. There has been more research conducted both of a conceptual and an empirical kind to provide a more secure underpinning for many of the principles which had been adopted almost intuitively earlier. There have been many attempts to involve students more deeply in learning, both in terms of what and how they study. And, generally, there is a more sophisticated appreciation of the importance of developing student autonomy and a more realistic understanding of what might be achieved within the constraints of conventional educational institutions. This does not mean that the number of highly innovative approaches has declined, but rather that it is easier now to point to modest examples of courses that emphasize autonomy than it was before. At a policy level it was encouraging to see that the Council for Educational Technology in the UK, the national body looking to the future in education, adopted the theme of increasing learner autonomy as its centrepiece for its five-year plan for 1985-1990.

These changes are reflected in this book. There are eight new chapters and many revisions to existing ones to bring them up to date and to include new information. Five chapters have been removed to make room for the new ones. There is a greater emphasis on research, although there is still a shortage of appropriate research focused on the problems we are considering here. There are more examples of innovative practice, particularly in the more technical and scientific areas: Cowan's work (Chapter 12) is within the context of an engineering course, and Bawden in Chapter 14 describes his work on agriculture education.

The climate of higher education has also changed in the past six years. 1981 was a time of cuts after a long static period. In different countries cuts may have been more or less severe, and the exact dates may have varied somewhat. However, the common feature was that the time was not ripe for innovation: teachers were hanging on to what they had achieved, and they had not come to grips with the fact that many of them could not sustain their existing practices. Since the shock of that period, there has been a period of adjustment. This has taken the form of either consolidating traditional courses with less resources, for example reducing staff-student contact, and placing more emphasis on lecturing; or, less commonly, it has led to a reappraisal of the purposes of higher education and the ways in which it is conducted. In the past, new developments have usually occurred in new institutions, but now, if they are to happen at all, they must take place in existing colleges and universities.

The climate of the times led one of the few negative reviewers of the first edition to decry its arguments and suggestions as 'too radical and too strident to have much impact on the mainstream of academic practice' (Fleming and Rutherford, 1984). Although the ideas are even more closely argued now, it remains to be seen if there are sufficient numbers of concerned people in post-secondary education to realise that if we cannot accept the need for rethinking and change at this point in history, we are likely to see a narrowly utilitarian model of education forced on us by the weight of circumstance. The time has come for a resurgence of endeavour in education to promote its core values of the development of intellectual independence, personal initiative and working together. This is a commitment which the contributors to this volume all share.

The book is composed of two parts. The first part provides the reader with a general orientation to the issues which will be illustrated later in practical detail. This section has been totally revised. The first three chapters in this section should be considered together as a basic introduction to the area. In Chapter 1, I clarify some of the ideas that are used in discussing autonomy and survey some of the key issues that have been canvassed in recent years concerning the ideal of autonomy and how it might be translated into practice. Some of the approaches used in courses which encourage autonomy are discussed, and research related to the theme is presented. In Chapter 2, Joy Higgs, from her experience as a teacher and researcher in the area of autonomous methods, examines ways in which courses can be designed with an emphasis on student autonomy. Her chapter provides a useful starting point for those who wish to plan learning activities to promote autonomous learning, and covers some of the same ground as Chapter 1, but from a practical perspective. Phil Candy's major new contribution in Chapter 3 complements the two others in pointing to the ways in which autonomy can be fostered with respect to the specific subject being studied. He takes the view that the development of autonomy includes the ability not only to organize one's own learning, but also to form one's own judgements, to decide on a point of view, and to be able to defend one's position in a given area of knowledge. This aspect of intellectual autonomy provides the bridge between older notions of independence and intellectual rigour and the autonomous methods which have grown in prominence during the past twenty years. Candy stresses that the attainment of autonomy in learning is not a universal, content-free accomplishment, but is subject-dependent.

Assessment practices are often the major barrier to developing increasing student responsibility: if students always look to others for judgements of their competence, how can they develop their ability to assess their own learning? John Heron, in Chapter 4, argues that the transactions between students and teachers are critically affected by the balance of power: where it rests and how it is used determines the quality of learning. Assessment is the clearest example of this power in action, and he advocates the use of collaborative forms of assessment to overcome the problem of authority while still meeting the need for a certificate of intellectual competence.

The use of new technologies in education has the potential to revolutionize learning, but will it lead to more efficient forms of dependency-producing instruction, or will it act to liberate learners not only from the classroom but also from the rigidities of externally defined learning activities? So much has been claimed by proponents of computer-assisted learning and other technological innovations that it has been wise to treat such developments with a degree of scepticism. Chris Knapper in Chapter 5 is neither a one-eyed enthusiast nor a sceptic. He provides a balanced evaluation of the possibilities of many of the new computer-based technologies in terms of their ability to meet criteria for lifelong learning, which he sees as largely synonymous with autonomy in learning. He concludes that, if treated appropriately, many of them can be successful used in pursuing these goals.

Part 2 comprises the bulk of the book and consists of case studies in which practising teachers in universities and colleges describe the ways in which they have confronted the issues raised in Part 1. Examples have been drawn from many disciplines: history, engineering, medicine, the professions allied to health, agriculture, psychology and education; from many parts of the world: England, Scotland, Australia, Canada and Switzerland; and all describe courses which require formal accreditation of student performance.

Student reticence and resistance to taking responsibility for learning are likely to be among the first problems a teacher will meet. Many existing courses unconsciously encourage dependence and, if a teacher who wishes to foster independence finds him or herself immersed in such an environment, problems can and do arise. In Chapter 6, John Powell gives a personal account of his own struggle against these forces as he deliberately tried to reduce his own control over his course and give it to his students. In Chapter 7, Harry Stanton identifies the main problem as being one of students' lack of confidence in handling a more open-ended approach to learning. His solution to this was to incorporate training in enhancing self-confidence as an early part of his course.

Students can learn as much, or even more, from their peers as from their teachers, but the help students can give to each other is a severely under-utilized resource in higher education. It is recognized that it may occur informally, but it appears to be assumed that it is not really the concern of teachers to involve themselves in this rather unstructured activity. That there is enormous potential in peer learning is clearly demonstrated by David Potts in Chapter 8. His course is structured around the basic principle of students helping each other to learn, with the teacher providing the environment and materials needed. On a broader scale, Marcel Goldschmid in Chapter 9 considers the problem of inducting students into what is to them a strange and new institution and how staff are able to foster student support activities which then become self-sufficient.

Medicine and health care are some of the most sensitive areas in which to make changes towards autonomous learning. Graduates must possess a high level of competence when lives are at risk. This does not, however, prevent this area of higher education being one of those in which the greatest steps have been taken in recent years towards developing self-directed learning. The Faculty of Health Sciences at McMaster University in Canada has been one of the leaders of this trend and is represented in both Chapters 10 and 11. In Chapter 10, Barbara Ferrier and two of her former students, Michael Marrin and Jeffrey Seidman, describe their experiences of participating in a self-directed course in medicine, and in the totally new Chapter 11, Catherine Tompkins and Mary-Jean McGraw describe the use of learning contracts which have become one of the most widely used devices for organizing self-directed learning worldwide.

The use of learning contracts is one way of involving students more actively in their own assessment; another is provided by John Cowan in a new chapter (12). He takes the idea of student self-assessment perhaps as far as it will go in a traditional institution by getting students to grade their own work in a structural engineering course. He describes how he has come to adopt his particular view on assessment and how it operates in this course.

The final case studies move away from developing autonomy within part of a defined course of study to student involvement in the design and conduct of entire undergraduate programmes. John Stephenson in a new chapter (13) describes the most well known example in Britain of a course of independent studies, that at North East London Polytechnic, and focuses on its successes in helping students who would not normally be served well by the higher education system. He points out that independent study can be accommodated in a conventional institution and that it can be conducted within normal funding levels. The penultimate chapter focuses on probably the most innovative course in Australian higher education, which also exists in a conventional higher education institution: Hawkesbury Agricultural College. Richard Bawden describes how he introduced changes which revolutionized an existing faculty with existing staff in a college with a hundred-year tradition. The theme of this chapter is leadership, and it leaves us on an optimistic note. Worthwhile educational change is possible, though it does not come easily. It requires us to have a view that things do not have to be as they are, to have the commitment to pursue this view and to develop the skills which we need to get it implemented. These are not the skills which many teachers presently have, but if we believe our students can develop through autonomous learning, there is no reason why we should not apply this principle to ourselves and develop the skills we need to bring about educational change. We are all learners too.

Finally in Chapter 15 Malcolm Cornwall brings us back to the conventional institutions with which we will all be familiar to look at some of the arguments about independent learning which have been touched upon earlier. What can be done within the contexts in which most of us operate? Can independent learning fit in to existing institutions? How can we address the legitimate concerns, and the fears, of our colleagues? He is realistic in his appraisal and offers some practical advice on how we might approach the problem.

Developing student autonomy is a challenge to us all. If we cannot meet this challenge we should probably give up any claims to be providing a *higher* education.

Footnote: use of language

All new contributions to this edition have been written to be gender-inclusive following the style preferred by each author. However, a few chapters reprinted from the first edition still retain the language adopted by their authors at that time.

Part I
Issues

Chapter 1

Moving Towards Autonomy

David Boud

Introduction

Autonomy is a term that is used in many different ways in education. What do people mean when they talk about student autonomy? What are autonomous learning methods? The notion of autonomy in learning is a many-faceted one and is subject to much debate. The aim of this chapter is to throw some light on the ways in which both philosophers and teachers use the word 'autonomy' in order to identify the key issues for someone who wishes to promote the idea of autonomy or autonomous learning with their students. In addition to clarifying some of these ideas, I will also examine research on student learning which identifies aspects of teaching and course design that appear to do most to promote or inhibit autonomy in learning.

The notion of autonomy encompasses three groups of educational ideas. First, it is a goal of education, an ideal of individual behaviour to which students or teachers may wish to aspire: teachers assist students to attain this goal. Secondly, it is a term used to describe an approach to educational practice, a way of conducting courses which emphasizes student independence and responsibility for decision-making. Thirdly, it it also an integral part of learning of any kind. No learner can be effective in more than a very limited area if he or she cannot make decisions for themselves about what they should be learning and how they should be learning it: teachers cannot, and do not wish to, guide every aspect of the process of learning.

These three aspects of autonomy are usually treated quite separately in discussions of teaching and learning, and each of these areas has come to be influenced by different groups. Philosophers of education have dominated discussions of autonomy as a goal for education, innovative teachers have influenced practices which aim to give students responsibility for what and how they learn, and researchers interested in student learning have recently begun to consider the structure of knowledge in different disciplinary areas and how students need to exercise autonomy in coming to understand and utilize this knowledge. So far there has not been much cross-fertilization of ideas between groups: philosophers have not given serious attention to what teachers are actually doing; practitioners could benefit from clearer thinking about what they are and are not trying to achieve; and researchers need to broaden their view from some of the relatively simple learning tasks with which they have become preoccupied. I cannot in a brief chapter do more than point to some of the issues which need to be examined, but by setting discussions of these three areas beside each other in the first part of this book I hope to provide a foundation for thinking about the case studies on autonomous learning approaches which form the main section.

This chapter considers the first two of these areas – autonomy as a goal and the use of autonomous methods in courses in higher education – and also introduces some of the research that has been conducted in recent years on student learning. Joy Higgs in Chapter 2 discusses how to plan learning activities using autonomous approaches, and Philip Candy takes the third area – autonomy with respect to subject-matter – as the main theme for Chapter 3 and focuses on what he calls epistemological autonomy. John Heron in Chapter 4 elaborates on issues concerning the forms of assessment which are compatible with ideas of autonomy in learning.

Before considering any educational practices designed to promote autonomy in learning, it is first necessary to clarify what it is that we are discussing. What is meant by autonomy? What does it mean to pursue the goal of autonomy in learning?

Autonomy as a goal of eduction

The most common notion of autonomy is as a goal of education: what can be referred to as the goal of *individual autonomy*. A fundamental purpose of education is assumed to be to develop in individuals the ability to make their own decisions about what they think and do.

The concept of autonomy can be traced back to Ancient Greece and to a political context. It was concerned with the property of a state to be self-ruling or self-governing. Its educational usage, by analogy, refers to the capacity of an individual to be an independent agent, not governed by others. R.F. Dearden defines it thus:

> A person is autonomous to the degree, and it is very much a matter of degree, that what he thinks and does, at least in important areas of his life, are determined by himself. That is to say, it cannot be explained why these are his beliefs and actions without referring to his own activity of mind. This determination of what one is to think and do is made possible by the bringing to bear of relevant considerations in such activities of mind as those of choosing, deciding, deliberating, reflecting, planning and judging. (Dearden, 1972, p 461)

Benjamin Gibbs elaborates on this:

> an autonomous individual must have both independence from external authority and mastery of himself and his powers. He must be free from the dictates and interference of other people, and free also from disabling conflicts or lack of coordination between the elements of his own personality. He must have the

freedom to act and work as he chooses, and he must be capable of formulating and following a rule, pattern or policy of acting and working. (Gibbs, 1979 p 119)

In a later paper Dearden gives a further description of the qualities which could be observed in a person who would be thought of as autonomous:

(i) wondering and asking, with a sense of the right to ask, what the justification is for various things which it would be quite natural to take for granted;
(ii) refusing agreement or compliance with what others put to him when this seems critically unacceptable;
(iii) defining what he really wants, or what is really in his interests, as distinct from what may be conventionally so regarded;
(iv) conceiving of goals, policies and plans of his own, and forming purposes and intentions of his own independently of any pressure to do so from others;
(v) choosing amongst alternatives in ways which could exhibit that choice as the deliberate outcome of his own ideas or purposes;
(vi) forming his own opinion on a variety of topics that interest him;
(vii) governing his actions and attitudes in the light of the previous sort of activity.
In short, the autonomous man has a mind of his own and acts according to it. (Dearden, 1975, p 7)

These definitions encompass the important distinction made by Riesman (1950) between self-direction, other-direction and inner-direction. The autonomous person must be free not only from direction by others external to himself, but also from his or her own inner compulsions and rigidities. Autonomy is more than acting on one's own. It implies a responsiveness to one's environment and the ability to make creative and unique responses to situations as they arise rather than patterned and stereotypical responses from one's past (Jackins, 1965).

Individual autonomy is also context dependent. Chené defines autonomy as

one's ability to be free in regard to established rules or norms, to set the goals of one's actions and to judge its value (Chené, 1983, p 39)

and she points out that

the existence of norms is a necessary part of autonomy. On the one hand, norms set the boundaries; on the other, they allow the judging of values. Furthermore, autonomy cannot be separated from the valued. (Chené, 1983, p 39)

In other words individual autonomy is shaped by and relates to the situations in which it is manifest. What would be regarded as autonomous in one setting judged against one set of values might not be so regarded in another. At a simple level, the approach adopted by someone meeting a body of knowledge for the first time might be regarded as autonomous whereas it would be considered merely the following of a convention if exhibited by someone expert in the area.

Philosophers of education in the rational-liberal-democratic tradition have tended to treat autonomy as if it were something good which can hardly be questioned. As Dunlop puts it

> all promoters of autonomy [as a goal of education] have openly or implicitly appealed to things that lay beyond all local ideological allegiance, such as the value of faithful conscientious dissent and the disvalue of undiscriminating conformity. (Dunlop, 1986, p 153)

As long as autonomy remains as an abstract concept divorced from any particular situation it can be an ideal to which we can aspire but it is not something which we can realistically expect to emerge from any given course. However, even at this level these views have been challenged, by Phillips (1975), who finds difficulty in distinguishing an autonomous person of the type defined by Dearden and a person lacking in autonomy, and also by Crittenden (1978). Some writers on moral education have also started to have some qualms about unreservedly accepting autonomy as a prime goal (Dearden, 1984), and Dunlop (1986) questions whether the education of the emotions is compatible with the promotion of autonomy. He cautions us wisely not to be obsessed with the goal of individual autonomy to the exclusion of others. We are emotional and social animals and the exercise of our autonomy needs to be tempered by our sensibilities to ourselves and to others.

While there are important movements on the philosophical front, most teachers cannot afford to wait for further clarification before they act. Undeniably, independence and autonomy are highly rated goals of teachers and it is encouraging to note that this view is shared by students. In a study of the university experience of a cross section of students at the University of Melbourne, Little (1970) found that, of all the possible aims provided, the one stating that 'the university should develop in its students habits of independent intellectual inquiry' was rated most important. As a practical matter, it is necessary for teachers to act on what seem to them to be reasonable assumptions about autonomy in learning and perhaps reflect later on the action they take in the light of the philosophers' concerns.

Autonomy as an approach to education

While philosophers have been grappling with the autonomous individual, many teachers in all areas of education and training have been pursuing practices which have come to be classified under the rubric of autonomous learning. Are these teachers pursuing the same goal of the autonomous individual as has been described above, or do they have different intentions? Certainly many of them hold a notion of the autonomous individual which they are trying to promote. However, many teachers who accept the goal of the autonomous individual would not be associated with what we are calling autonomous methods, and many of those who are using autonomous methods would not have a clear notion of the type of person they are hoping to develop through their courses.

There is no automatic link between the goal of autonomy and the ways in which it might be pursued. Using the term independence which is often used as a synonym for autonomy, Dressel and Thompson in one of the few surveys of independent study in the United States note:

> At the heart of the problem of definition is the fact that independence has not been defined adequately in an academic context. It has come to mean independent of classes, independent of other students, or independent of faculty. Acceptance of any one or even all of these as essential would be missing the most important aspect of the whole process which is that the student becomes capable of self-directed study. (Dressel and Thompson, 1973, p 3)

That is, there has been a failure to discriminate between independent study as a learning experience and as a capability to be developed (Dittman, 1976). As Lewis says

> To approve 'autonomy' as an ideal for students is one thing: to commend 'autonomous' methods of learning is another – however 'autonomy' is defined. If, for the purposes of argument, we gloss it as independence, it is not quite obvious that independent methods of learning promote independence – auxiliary causal relationships must be established. (Lewis, 1978, p 152)

We should be careful in following this path too far. Although it may be in doubt that independent methods of learning themselves promote independence, it is certainly unlikely that dependent, teacher-dominated methods would do so. We must therefore look at methods which claim to foster autonomy through autonomous ways of working to see if they in fact do so. As Candy points out:

> It is clear that a person may be exposed to so-called autonomous methods of learning, without internalizing the values of autonomy, or necessarily being enabled to think and act autonomously (Campbell, 1964; Torbert, 1978). Conversely, it may be possible to develop autonomy without recourse to autonomous methods. If, for instance, autonomy is defined as the ability and willingness to approach situations with an open mind, to suspend critical judgement and to act in accordance with rules and principles which are the product of the autonomous person's own endeavours and experience, then, paradoxically, as Dearden argues, it might be precisely a student's upbringing and previous educational experience, with relatively little freedom, which does develop autonomy (Dearden, 1972, p 452). (Candy, 1987a, pp 167-8)

Whatever our views on the desirability of pursuing the goal of the individual autonomous learner, it cannot be denied that some of the attributes of the autonomous learner are required by anyone if they are to be effective learners in higher education, or indeed anywhere else. It is not likely that students who are dependent on their teachers are going to be as effective in the world of learning or subsequent employment as those who have developed strategies which enable them to find and use their own resources for learning. Similarly, if students are denied opportunities to participate in decision-making about their learning, they are less likely to develop the skills they need in order to plan and organize for life-long learning which depend on their decisions about their learning needs and activities.

This domain of what might be called *practical autonomy* is the one to which most attention has been given by practitioners in recent years. It involves providing students with opportunities to exercise significant degrees of decision-making with respect to the content and organization of courses. As far as particular approaches to promoting autonomy in learning are concerned, there are problems of terminology. Candy (1987a,b) has identified thirty different terms which have been used in this area including: independent learning, learner-controlled instruction, non-traditional learning, open learning, participatory learning, self-directed learning, self-organized learning, self-planned learning, self-study and self-teaching.

> This proliferation of terms would be difficult enough if they were all exact synonyms, but the problem is made worse by the fact that different authors use the same term to mean different things, and sometimes they use different terms to mean the same thing, and the only way to tell the difference is to delve beneath the surface to what is actually meant in any particular situation. (Candy, 1987a, p 160)

Some of these methods focus on teaching, some on learning. Some emphasize the acquisition of particular skills, some the development of ways of organizing learning. Some are highly structured by teachers, in others students create their own structures. All of them include as a goal that students take greater responsibility for their own learning. No absolute standard of autonomy is manifest in any of them; what is important is the *direction of change – towards student self-reliance* – not the magnitude of it. In some approaches this aspect predominates; in others it is of subsidiary concern. A definition which stresses practical autonomy is that of Gibbons *et al* (1980):

> In self-education, the individual masters all the activities usually conducted by the teacher: selecting goals, selecting content, selecting and organizing learning experiences, managing one's time and effort, evaluating progress and redesigning one's strategies for greater effect. In addition, the student of self-directed learning, must have the initiative to launch these processes as well as the personal motivation to continue learning, even when there is no pressure, guidance, or extrinsic reward. In self-directed education the student has the major responsibility for the purposes and methods of learning as well as the achievement of learning involved. (Gibbons *et al*, 1980, pp 51-2)

Rather than become distracted by descriptions of the variety of approaches (many of them are discussed elsewhere in the book) it might be more helpful to focus on some of the key issues and point to some of the trends that are emerging. All of the following remarks need to be prefaced by the observation that in any specific teaching or learning situation priority may be given by the teacher or the learner to some facet of it other than issues of autonomy. Autonomy can only be exercised on an occasion where something is being learned, and on many occasions the demands of the situation dominate. For example, safety issues will usually override autonomy issues. Likewise, an objective mutually accepted by teacher and student, say to pass the external examination, may also be given first priority in any given class. This does not mean that in such situations autonomous approaches must be rejected, simply that they are tempered by exigencies. As will become apparent later, situational constraints such as assessment procedures can inhibit the pursuit of autonomy in learning or help facilitate it.

The main characteristic of autonomy as an approach to learning is that students take some significant responsibility for their own learning over and above responding to instruction. Such an approach might involve students taking the initiative in any or all of the following:

- identifying learning needs,
- setting goals,
- planning learning activities,
- finding resources needed for learning,
- working collaboratively with others,
- selecting learning projects,
- creating 'problems' to tackle,
- choosing where and when they will learn,
- using teachers as guides and counsellors rather than instructors,
- opting to undertake additional non teacher-directed work, such as learning through independent (structured) learning materials,
- determining criteria to apply to their work,
- engaging in self-assessment,
- learning outside the confines of the educational institution, for example in a work setting,
- deciding when learning is complete,
- reflecting on their learning processes,
- making significant decisions about any of these matters, that is, decisions with which they will have to live.

Different approaches place the emphasis on different subsets of these activities and the extent to which students have ultimate responsibility for decision-making, for example on assessment, also varies. There is a continuum of approaches. Any given teaching and learning practice, whether or not it is identified with autonomy, can be judged by the extent to which it promotes aspects of autonomous learning. At one end of the spectrum are those highly didactic presentations in which students are relatively passive and where they have little opportunity to practise the skills needed in exercising independence in learning. At the other there are approaches in which all decisions are made by learners, and teachers are only involved as and when they are requested by the learners. (See Figure 1.) Most of the commonly used teaching and learning methods fall between these two extremes.

Highly didactic/
students make few decisions
about learning

Highly responsive/
students make most
decisions about
learning

Figure 1 *Spectrum of approaches*

Students will vary in their readiness to benefit from any given approach partly as a result of their prior educational experiences and partly as a result of their reasons for learning. Students often need considerable learning skills to be able to make full use of the opportunities that are available to them. At the low-autonomy end of the spectrum, students need to possess certain skills in learning if they are to be able to go 'beyond the information given' and do more than regurgitate and reproduce low-level cognitive knowledge. Similarly, at the highly autonomous end, students need to have developed skills in self-organization to be able to operate effectively in such an open environment. The ability to function well in a typical teacher-centred school environment does not necessarily transfer to other situations. Students also take time to adapt to a new learning regime and sometimes resist and are initially critical of approaches with which they are unfamiliar (see Martin, 1987, for an example of students entering a teacher-directed university environment from a school which emphasized autonomy).

The extent to which teachers and learners will create an environment that emphasizes autonomous learning depends on a number of factors. These include the prior experience of both groups in such situations, the educational values of the teachers, and the external constraints with which they are faced. The traditions of educational institutions normally mean that teachers are responsible for initiating an autonomous approach. This leads to a paradox expressed by Little:

> There is no escape from the paradox of leadership – the requirement that men should be *led* to freedom, that students be taught the autonomous style. (Little, 1975, p 260)

It is not necessarily desirable that teachers construct courses which always allow for the maximum exercise of autonomy on the part of students. If students have little experience of making decisions about structuring their learning on such a scale, the activity may be counterproductive and the course may simply give the appearance of promoting autonomy while actually inhibiting it. The criteria which should be used are that students ultimately become more effective learners and are more able to respond to the variety of environments with which they will be faced during their lives. In a static, unchanging society there may be less need for an emphasis on autonomous approaches than there is in one in which learners need to adapt to frequent change and need to learn new forms of knowledge and how to use that knowledge. Hence, the main impetus towards educational developments of the type discussed in this book is the rapidly changing nature of the world which graduates have to face.

Teaching approaches for the development of autonomy

Although many names have been used to describe approaches to autonomous learning, there are three main classes of approach which have been adopted. Each has a particular emphasis and has characteristic methods associated with it.

1. The individual-centred approach

This is characterized by a focus on individual learners and their needs. Teachers, co-learners and other resources for learning are enlisted to facilitate the attainment of the goals of the individual as defined by the individual. Groups of learners may provide general support but they do not generally have a specific role or commitment to any project other than their own.

A typical example of an approach in this category is that using a learning contract. In the first part of a course using learning contracts, students are first introduced to the idea of a learning contract and learn something about how they can draw upon the resources of others. They then prepare individual contracts which specify learning goals, activities in which they will engage, criteria for judging their performance and how the contract will be assessed. These draft contracts are negotiated with a teacher and, after modification, the agreed contract provides the specification for learning. Many other people may be involved in the learning activites, but they are usually contacted by the particular learner in response to a particular need they have identified.

The use of learning contracts has been extensively discussed by Knowles (1975) and Knowles and his associates (1986) and is further examined in this book by Catherine Tompkins and Mary-Jean McGraw in Chapter 11 who discuss some of the many variations on the theme of contracts in learning.

2. The group-centred approach

This cluster of approaches is characterized by a focus on the needs of a particular group of learners and a strong commitment to group learning and group processes. Individuals pursue their own learning needs within the context of the group, referring to others for support and feedback and for validation of the enterprise. Much learning occurs from interactions between group members. There is an emphasis on democratic decision-making and the consideration of different points of view within the group. The development of the group itself is often a focus for learning, with the aim being for the group to strive towards a relationship among its members that allows individuals to engage in their own learning with the tangible support of others. Interdependence is highly valued.

One example of a group-centred approach is Heron's peer learning community,

> A peer learning community is based on two fundamental principles of parity: equality of consideration and equality of opportunity. First, the needs and interests, skills and resources which each person – whether staff or student – brings to the community are equally worthy of consideration. Second, it is equally open to anyone – whether staff or student – to contribute to or intervene in the course process at any time in any manner which he judges to be appropriate. (Heron, 1974, p 2)

Heron points out that these principles do not imply that all contributions made by individuals or the skills and resources which each brings are of equal value from the point of view of fulfilling course objectives. However, equal attention must be given to a consideration of what different individuals want to get from the course and bring to the course; and equal opportunity must be given to different individuals to make their needs felt, to exercise their judgement on course events and to exercise whatever skills and resources they do bring to the course.

Another example of a group-centred approach which used a peer learning community approach within the constraints of one subject in a formal postgraduate programme in science education is described by Boud and Prosser (1979). In this, aims, activities and assessment procedures were all negotiated between staff and students and the course was conducted cooperatively, drawing upon the skills and expertise of both groups. Curriculum negotiation is a common theme in group-centred approaches, and two examples of how this works in practice are given by Millar *et al* (1986) in the training of adult educators, and Harber and Meighan in teacher training (Harber and Meighan, 1986; Meighan and Harber, 1986).

To illustrate how courses of this kind might be conducted it is interesting to note the principles of procedure in a specimen contract for a democratic learning cooperative used by Meighan and Harber (1986):

> (a) that we adopt a self-conscious research approach to our own teaching-learning situation;
> (b) that we seek to examine and practise in our teaching-learning different strategies and roles: e.g. inquiry-discovery strategy, neutral chairman;
> (c) that while the focus of much of our work will be individual, we should share our own work with the group, for our mutual benefit, and
> (d) that we should therefore accept responsibility for the work *as a group*;
> (e) within that group-responsibility we should seek to understand through mutual self-criticism;
> (f) that we see our primary aim to be competent, not right;

(g) that the ... tutors should be seen as a resource for the group, and that any seminars with their 'instructional input' should be chaired by members of the group;
(h) that the group should decide ... [who] ... to invite ... to [contribute], or how it will spend its time;
(i) that the 'contract' should be reviewed regularly;
(j) each course member (including the tutors) will undertake to write a short evaluation of the group's work to be circulated to each member regularly;
(k) that we use the experiences of previous courses as a source of ideas for course content;
(l) that a group logbook be kept of work completed, planning decisions and session papers;
(m) that each session shall have a chairperson, a secretary and a contributor(s) or leader(s) or organiser(s). (p 165)

Meighan and Harber (1986) stress that it is important that students opt in to such an approach rather than it being required of them to accept it.

3. The project-centred approach

In this group of approaches the particular learning project and its outcome are often as important or more important than the individuals or the group which is working on it. The project gives meaning to and characterizes the enterprise. The goals of the particular learning situation are central and often override the special interests of individuals or groups. There is typically a strong practical or relevance orientation defined in terms external to the learners directly involved. The needs and interests of this group are considered, but these influence the details of the enterprise rather than the main activities. In practice, elements of both the first two classes of approach may be included.

Learning through projects is one of the most common activities in courses in all disciplines. Morgan defines such a form of learning as:

an activity in which students develop an understanding of a topic through some kind of involvement in an actual (or simulated) real-life problem or issue *and* in which they have some degree of responsibility in designing their learning activities. (Morgan, 1983, p 66)

Problem-based learning is an approach that is gaining considerable ground in courses which train students for the professions. The basic idea that underlies problem-based learning is that:

the starting point for learning should be a problem, a query or a puzzle that the learner wishes to solve. Organized forms of knowledge, academic disciplines, are only introduced when the demands of the problem require them. (Boud 1985, p 13)

A typical series of stages in a problem-based learning approach is given by Barrows and Tamblyn (1980):

> 1. The problem is encountered first in the learning sequence, before any preparation or study has occurred.
> 2. The problem situation is presented to the student in the same way it would present itself in reality.
> 3. The student works with the problem in a manner that permits his ability to reason and apply knowledge to be challenged and evaluated, appropriate to his level of learning.
> 4. Needed areas of learning are identified in the process of work with the problem and used as a guide to individualised study.
> 5. The skills and knowledge acquired by this study are applied back to the problem, to evaluate the effectiveness of learning and to reinforce learning.
> 6. The learning that has occurred in work with the problem and in individualised study is summarised and integrated into the student's existing knowledge and skills.
> (Barrows and Tamblyn, 1980)

Students exercise considerable initiative and engage in individual learning in association with the problem, but it is the problem itself which ultimately defines the area of learning.

Project-orientation is an approach which also derives from concerns about the inappropriately academic nature of some courses in higher education, but it takes a more politicized form than problem-based learning (Cornwall *et al*, 1977). Like problem-based learning, project-orientation starts from the consideration of a problem in a given context. However, the kinds of problem used are usually larger in scale, and, instead of providing the initial impetus for learning, these problems shape the entire educational experience for an extended period of time and include considerations of the technical, social and political context. Examples have included a study of the scientific, environmental and political considerations of the siting of a nuclear power station, and a study of the microbiological and industrial relations implications of lubrication-oil contamination in a factory. Problems are real ones and are not specially contrived for teaching purposes.

It is important to stress that the individual-centred, the group-centred and the project-centred are three general ways of viewing the promotion of autonomy and any particular approach may involve a combination of the others. They are not rigid distinctions but they do provide the characteristic flavour to a particular learning experience: is it one that focuses on the individual, the group or the project?

Interdependence

The aim of autonomous learning, no matter which approach is adopted, is not normally for students simply to become learners who are individualistic or work on their own. Autonomous approaches do not imply treating learners in isolation from one another. What is usually sought is that students become interdependent learners, working with and helping each other (Cornwall, 1979; Goldschmid and Goldschmid, 1976; and also Chapters 8, 9 and 14). Autonomy cannot be pursued in a vacuum: it does not necessitate isolation from the ideas and experience of others. Its exercise has a social context:

> Mature autonomy requires both emotional independence – freedom from continual and pressing needs for reassurance and approval – and instrumental independence, the ability to carry on activities and cope with problems without seeking help from others and the ability to be mobile in relation to one's needs. Simultaneously, the individual must accept interdependence, recognizing that one cannot receive benefits from a social structure without contributing to it, that personal rights have a corollary social responsibility. (Chickering, 1969)

Even with independence as the goal there is an unavoidable dependence at one level on authorities for information and guidance. *Inter*dependence is therefore an essential component of autonomy in action. The shift to interdependence is often portrayed as a process starting from dependency and moving progressively through counterdependence and independence to interdependence (see Figure 2). In this view independence, meaning independence from a teacher or authority figure, is a stage through which learners need to pass in any given context to reach a more mature form of relationship which places them in the world and interrelating to it rather than being apart from it.

Interdependence
↗
Dependence → Counterdependence → Independence

Figure 2 *Stages of development in learning*

At the micro-developmental level, Brundage and MacKeracher (1980) have produced a synthesis of the various models describing the stages through which students move during their learning activities. These apply both to individual learners and to learners working in groups. They can be regarded as stages through which students pass as they develop autonomy with respect to a given project:

> *Entry stage*: This stage is triggered when a learner enters a situation which has a high degree of novelty, uncertainty, or lack of familiarity, which involves him in personal stress, or in which he perceives a threat to himself. He may perceive himself as disoriented within the situation, may defend himself by using inappropriate behaviour, may feel inhibited in his interpersonal relationships, may act as an observer without making a personal commitment to participate, may appear as if he were dependent or counter-dependent, and may communicate largely through monologue. The learner in the entry stage tends to rely on external standards to guide his behaviour and to make assumptions about his current situation based on

29

past experience which may or may not be appropriate. In the entry stage teachers or others can best support the learner by creating a reliable environment which operates on the basis of standardized and explicit behavioural norms and in which the consequences of behaviour are known.

Reactive stage: A learner moves out of the entry stage and into the reactive stage when he develops a sense of himself as being an individual who is capable of acting independently within the situation or when he perceives the environment as having become unreliable and unsupportive. The learner may perceive himself as autonomous and independent of the control of others, may work to develop a high degree of self-understanding, and may wish to carry out individual activities within a group setting. Learners in the reactive stage often express negative feelings, engage in conflicts and arguments with others, and express the feeling that the group is disorganized and confused. The learner in the reactive stage is best supported by teachers or others who encourage expressions of individual feelings and opinions and who do not demand strict adherence to standardized behavioural norms.

Proactive stage: When the learner feels confident about himself as an accepted and acceptable member of the group or actor within the situation, he moves on to discover and eventually accept the individuality of others involved. The learner in the proactive stage tends to perceive himself as involved in activities leading to mutuality, cooperation, and negotiation with others in the situation, as searching for an understanding of others in relation to self, and as developing shared norms and values for behaviour within the group. Learners generally use fewer individual activities and engage in fewer arguments. They are increasingly likely to use group activities and engage in dialogues. The proactive stage is often highly productive for the entire group. The learner in the proactive stage is best supported by teachers or others who accept and encourage cooperative and collaborative behaviour in preference to individual performance or competition and who can provide descriptive and immediate feedback about individual behaviour in relation to established objectives.

Integrative stage: When the learner can distinguish between individual others, he moves on to integrate the perspective of others with his own. As a result of integrating activities, he develops a sense of balance between himself and others and between working at group or individual tasks and maintaining interpersonal relationships with others. The learner may integrate perspectives which involve multiple standards of behaviour, multiple interpretations of experience, and multiple sources of information. The learner in the integrative stage is best supported by teachers or others who encourage him to develop internal standards to guide personal behaviour, who openly share information about themselves and their feelings and values, who willingly act as co-learners and value the role of learner for themselves, and who can value and accept individual performance and group activities simultaneously.

In terms of adult learning, these theories suggest that all adults, when they enter a new learning experience, begin with dependent-type behaviours and move first to independent behaviour and then to interdependent behaviour during the course of the learning activities. The progression can be facilitated by a teacher who is prepared to provide some structure and direction at the beginning of the learning activities; to move then to encouraging individual activities; and finally to provide opportunities for interdependent activities within the group and for integrative processes for individuals. (Adams, 1974; Kubler-Ross, 1970, Tuckman, 1965; Hunt and Sullivan, 1974; Gibb, 1964; Schutz, 1967). (Brundage and MacKeracher, 1980, pp 54-55)

It is recognized that teachers can trap learning groups in the early stages of development and block the transition of the group from one stage to another (see, for example, Watson *et al*, 1981). They can also, by appropriate interventions, facilitate progression and assist the group and its members to move from dependence to independence and interdependence. It is interesting to note that the final stage, called 'integrative' by Brundage and MacKeracher, is very similar to those described by many others. It is called 'equilibrium' by Taylor (1986, 1987), the 'community of inquiry' by Torbert (1976), the 'peer learning community' by Heron (1974), the 'learning community' by Boydell (1976), and the 'experimenting community' by Bilorusky and Butler (1975). All of these teachers aspire to a state in which students are freely interacting with each other, the teacher and others on jointly planned projects and individual projects and are responding to their own needs and those of others in a cooperative and supportive manner.

There has been an increasing literature over the past fifteen years describing various approaches to the pursuit of autonomy in learning ranging from simple and moving descriptions of what one individual has attempted to do in his or her own teaching (for example, Levitan, 1981, and others in Rogers, 1983) to highly readable descriptions of the rewards, dilemmas and frustrations of particular programmes (notably Meisler, 1984). While these are important documents describing practice and individuals' response to it, they do not aspire to examine the issues analytically. Interestingly there has been a steady output of work which begins the task of examining particular aspects of teaching and learning in higher education to uncover the basic issues that influence how students learn. Some of this has been conducted within the context of courses which explicitly attempt to promote autonomous learning; other research in more traditional settings has started to map the crucial barriers to effective learning and how students respond to them.

What does research have to say about student autonomy?

The simple answer to this question is: surprisingly little research addresses autonomy directly, considering how central an educational concept it is. However, in recent years there has been a steady output of research which is relevant to our concerns. Much of this is discussed in particular chapters later, where it is appropriate, but it might be helpful to introduce some of it here and suggest the ways in which it illuminates the area of concern of this book. In a way all the work referred to in this chapter is research of a kind – some of it systematic, some opportunistic, some empirical and some reflective. In this section we will consider findings from some of the more systematically planned research which examines what students actually do in real learning situations in courses in higher education.

Different types of research have been conducted on different approaches to autonomy. Research on teaching methods in higher education has demonstrated that it is usually inappropriate to adopt measures which compare one method with another as one approach seldom pursues the same objectives as another and, even when they do, they often have such differences in strategy or emphasis that direct comparisons are rendered invalid. This applies as much to autonomous approaches as it does to any other teaching methods, and it is particularly invalid to compare an approach which is designed to promote autonomy with one designed for entirely some other purpose. This is not to say that useful information cannot be derived from studies which measure the impact of different methods, but often a research technique which purports to measure learning in a situation in which, for example, the syllabus is defined by a teacher cannot be applied when the very characteristic of student learning which is valued is that of the ability of students to define a syllabus for themselves.

Research for situation improvement

One grouping of research studies is that which can be referred to as research for situation improvement. Many educational innovators have mounted studies designed to improve the practices in which they were engaged. Their aim was not to uncover generalizations about student learning or the effects of assessment, but to contribute towards creating more effective learning experiences for students. Thus, each major innovation in higher education has spawned a literature of its own. The medical schools at McMaster and Newcastle, for example, have generated large numbers of journal papers which not only describe their practices but also report experiments and case studies of approaches which they have introduced to improve the quality of education they offer. An example of an evaluation study which follows graduates who had undertaken independent study courses at medical school into their professional career is that of Blumberg *et al* (1982). In some innovative schools research for course improvement has extended into studies which look more broadly at educational issues, such as the work on student learning in problem-based courses by Newble and Clarke (1986).

The term 'situation improvement' to describe studies of this kind comes from the work at Hawkesbury Agricultural College (Bawden and Valentine, 1984, and also see Chapter 14). These authors conceive of agricultural education partly as situation improvement and apply the same concept to their own studies of courses. Many of the contributors to this book have undertaken research and evaluation for situation improvement, and there are considerable bibliographies available from Independent Studies at North East London Polytechnic (discussed in Chapter 13), civil engineering at Heriot-Watt University (discussed in Chapter 12), medical sciences at McMaster (discussed in Chapter 10) and Hawkesbury Agriculture College.

There are no clear-cut distinctions between research for situation improvement and other kinds. Some studies undertaken for purposes of situation improvement lead to more fundamental investigations of particular phenomena, and the results of basic studies of student learning are commonly applied to a problem which has arisen in a particular course. A variety of methodologies have been used, and it has proved fruitful, when examining issues concerning autonomy, to adopt research strategies which respect the phenomena being investigated and do not attempt to impose external control when the very thing being studied is the way in which students exert control over their learning.

Research on student learning

The second main category of studies are those which research student learning and related issues. Much research on student learning has focused on the effects of instruction of one kind or another. Many studies deliberately controlled for and eliminated opportunities for students to act autonomously. However, with the rise of research methodologies which began to adopt a learner's perspective and to separate learning from instruction, issues related to autonomy started to appear.

Two types of study are of interest. The main one is on students' experiences of academic learning, particularly following the phenomenography of Marton (1981) and studies which emphasize the experiences of students, such as those by Entwistle and Ramsden (1983). Another is on adults' experience of learning in a variety of formal and informal contexts. As the latter have recently been considered in a companion to this volume (Boud and Griffin 1987 – see especially Maclean 1987, Hodgson and Reynolds 1987, Candy 1987a, Taylor 1987, and Davie 1987), this section will focus on the former.

Approaches to learning

One of the most useful concepts to appear in the area of student learning has been that of approaches to learning. In a way similar to that in which we have described teacher approaches to developing autonomy, Marton and his colleagues in Gothenburg developed the notion of an approach to learning. In early studies of how students read a passage of text, Marton and Säljö (1976a,b, 1984) found two characteristic approaches that students adopted. One group focused on the words used, and attempted to remember particular words or phrases of the author. The other focused on the author's meaning and tried to make sense of the passage, relating it to their own understanding. The former they described as using a *surface* approach to learning, the latter as using a *deep* approach. In many studies since, and in parallel research by other groups, similar findings have arisen and a dichotomy between a surface or atomistic and a deep or holistic approach has been noted. A third *achieving* approach has also been recognized in which students adopt an expedient stance and use either deep or surface approaches according to how they think best to cope with the pressure of time or assessment expectations (Biggs and Telfer, 1987).

33

The idea of *approaches to learning*, though apparently simple, is very useful in understanding why students react differently to what are ostensibly the same circumstances. It is not a learning style inherent in students which they manifest in all situations, but a characteristic of the interaction between an individual and a learning task. As Ramsden (1987) puts it, it is the

> description of an *intention and an action*. It is neither something inhering solely in the individual nor in the task ... It only has meaning with reference to a situation and certain types of content. (p 142)

Research on student autonomy has not progressed until relatively recently as new ways of conceptualizing research on student learning were needed to make the issue susceptible to empirical investigation. Student autonomy is not a characteristic of a student which resides in a student, but a relational quality of student and task. The same students act differently when confronted with different kinds of task; the same task is treated differently by different students.

The distinction between surface and deep approaches to learning tasks is closely related to the notion of autonomy. Deep approaches are the ones in which students are taking responsibility for their learning and are making decisions about what they are learning, and surface approaches are ones in which students are dependent on the relatively superficial features of a text or lesson. Deep approaches are not necessarily highly autonomous ones, but surface approaches are clearly not.

Importance of context

The recognition of the importance of the situations in which learning occurs has led researchers to examine factors which are conducive to the encouragement of deep learning approaches. Work of this kind suggests strongly that changing the learning environment, in particular the tasks students are required to engage in, can have a major influence on how and what students learn. This might not sound particularly surprising it itself, but it has led to the identification of barriers to learning for understanding and the development of autonomy.

One of the largest studies of student learning which examined perceptions of learning by 2208 students across six different disciplines and institutions was that undertaken by Entwistle and Ramsden from the University of Lancaster. In one part of this study Ramsden (1979) and Ramsden and Entwistle (1981) considered student perceptions of the academic environment, that is, how students responded to the context of learning defined by the teaching and assessment methods of academic departments. In follow-up interviews students clearly perceived lecturers as affecting their approaches to studying: 'surface approaches were strongly associated with perceived deficiencies in the assessment system and with a lack of freedom in learning' (Entwistle and Ramsden, 1983, p 186).

One of the measures which Entwistle and Ramsden constructed from their data was what they called *meaning orientation*. Students who exhibited a high meaning orientation were those who reported having a deep approach to learning, relating ideas in one subject to another, examining evidence carefully in what they read, and being interested in learning for its own sake. They found that meaning orientation was related to the perceived presence of freedom in learning combined with good teaching in the department in which they were enrolled. Freedom in learning included opportunities for choice in what they worked upon, and the ability to study in the way that best suited the individual student, that is, the amount of discretion possessed by students in choosing and organizing the academic work. Good teaching indicates that staff are well prepared and responsive, understand student difficulties and are ready to help.

Entwistle and Ramsden (1983) go on to point out that

> It seems that departments without good teaching and freedom in learning effectively act to *prevent* the development of meaning orientation in their students; departments which are positively evaluated encourage meaning orientation by providing the right conditions for it to grow – but it is not a necessary consequence ... Meaning orientation is perceived to be related to academic progress most strongly in conditions of freedom in learning with a light workload. (pp 189, 190)

Newble and Clarke (1986) conducted research following the Lancaster studies on learning in a problem-based learning context in medicine courses. They used the Lancaster inventory to compare traditional and innovatory courses in terms of their impact on approaches to learning. They found that the innovative problem-based course was perceived to be higher on meaning orientation than the traditional. Coles (1985) undertook the same analysis in a European study and found similar results. These results suggest that at least some autonomous learning approaches are effective in promoting learning for understanding rather than learning for reproduction.

Opportunities for students to exercise discretion over what and how they learn should not be confused with ambiguity and uncertainty about what are the requirements of learning tasks or assessments. Percy and Ramsden (1980), in their evaluation of two schools at North East London Polytechnic and the University of Lancaster in which students learned through independent study, found that lack of clarity was not helpful in promoting autonomy.

Assessment of students

Researchers investigating student learning have taken a great interest in the effects of assessment on learning. There have been a number of notable studies over the years which have demonstrated that assessment methods and requirements probably have a greater influence on how and what students learn than any other single factor. This influence may well be of greater importance than the impact of teachers or teaching materials. Becker *et al*'s (1968) intensive study of medical students in an American university clearly shows a group of students whose view of the curriculum and their academic work is mediated entirely by their perceptions of assessment requirements. Miller and Parlett (1974) showed that many students in a variety of subjects at the University of Edinburgh took an instrumental approach to studying, and picked up cues from staff about what was to be examined in order to indicate where they should devote their energies. Elton and Laurillard (1979) report that assessment tasks which are seen to require deep approaches to learning discourage students from using reproducing strategies.

Ramsden (1984) stresses that it is student perceptions of assessment which influence their behaviour. It is not simply a matter of teachers designing an assessment scheme which they believe will help promote an independent approach to learning: students must believe this to be so and find that a deep or autonomous strategy on their part is rewarded. Assessment practices can be seen as a threat by students. Marton and Säljö (1984), discussing the study by Fransson (1979), report that when students perceive themselves to be under threat this encourages surface approaches to learning.

Many teachers, concerned about the inhibiting effects of assessment on the development of autonomy, have moved away from traditional teacher-controlled forms of student assessment towards forms that place greater responsibility in the hands of students. They argue that the whole notion of autonomous learning is undermined if assessment is determined unilaterally by staff. As Rogers describes it:

> The evaluation of one's own learning is one of the major means by which self-initiated learning becomes also responsible learning. It is when the individual has to take responsibility for deciding what criteria are important to him, what goals must be achieved, and the extent to which he has achieved those goals, that he truly learns to take responsibility for himself and his directions. (Rogers, 1983, p 158)

There has been an increase in the past five years in the number of reports on the adoption of self-and collaborative assessment methods, not just in courses using autonomous learning approaches, but also in more traditional settings (Boud, 1983). Although research on these has been fairly limited to date, there has grown a range of methods which involve students as individuals or in learning groups in the assessment of their own work. Studies of these methods have identified issues which should be addressed by those attempting to implement them such as the importance of a clear rationale for self-assessment, how to address apparent resistance by students, and at what stage in courses it can profitably be introduced (Boud, 1986). Heron discusses the whole area of student assessment and autonomy in greater depth in Chapter 4, and Cowan gives an example of the use of self-assessment in an undergraduate engineering course in Chapter 12.

Student development

The final area of research which has important ramifications for student autonomy is that concerning how students change and develop over time, in particular how their views of the world influence the ways in which they conceive of learning.

The major study in this area is that undertaken by Perry (1970) and his colleagues, *Forms of Intellectual and Ethical Development in the College Years*. (See also Perry, 1981, for a summary and further discussion.) From a series of intensive interviews with undergraduate students at Harvard he identified a sequence of what he termed 'positions', which represent ways in which students view themselves and their learning. The richness and variety of response which he describes in his book cannot be portrayed briefly, but the following extract gives an indication of his findings. The main line of development of his students was as follows:

Position 1: The student sees the world in polar terms of we-right-good vs. other-wrong-bad. Right answers for everything exist in the absolute, known to authority whose role is to mediate (teach) them. Knowledge and goodness are perceived as quantitative accretions of discrete rightnesses to be collected by hard work and obedience (paradigm: a spelling test).

Position 2: The student perceives diversity of opinion and uncertainty, and accounts for them as unwarranted confusion in poorly qualified authorities or as mere exercises set by authority 'so we can learn to find the answer for ourselves'.

Position 3: The student accepts diversity and uncertainty as legitimate, but still *temporary* in areas where authority 'hasn't found the answer yet'. He supposes authority grades him in these areas on 'good expression' but remains puzzled as to standards.

Position 4: (a) The student perceives legitimate uncertainty (and therefore diversity of opinion) to be extensive and raises it to the status of an unstructured epistemological realm of its own in which 'anyone has a right to his own opinion', a realm which he sets over against authority's realm where right-wrong still prevails; or (b) the student discovers qualitative contextual relativistic reasoning as a special case of 'what they want' within authority's realm.

Position 5: The student perceives all knowledge and values (including authority's) as contextual and relativistic and subordinates dualistic right-wrong functions to the status of a special case, in context.

Position 6: The student apprehends the necessity of orienting himself in a relativistic world through some form of personal commitment (as distinct from unquestioned or unconsidered commitment to simple belief).

Position 7: The student makes an initial commitment in some area.

Position 8: The student experiences the implications of commitment, and explores the subjective and stylistic issues of responsibility.

Position 9: The student experiences the affirmation of identity among multiple responsibilities and realizes commitment as a constant, unfolding activity through which he expresses his lifestyle. (Perry, 1970, pp 9-10)

These positions do not reflect a smooth, uninterrupted path from simplicity to sophistication. Students may delay in one position for a year, exploring its implications or explicitly hesitating to take the next step. They may deflect from this path and exploit the opportunity for detachment offered by the structures of positions 4 and 5 to deny responsibility through passive or opportunistic alienation. Or they may become entrenched in the dualistic, absolutistic structures of positions 2 or 3.

Perry does not argue that these positions are manifest in the students' approach to individual subjects or topics, but rather that they reflect a general approach to knowledge and the world. These positions cannot be simply transferred to a particular course, although, of course, they do describe a broad framework through which students see their programme, and it is therefore helpful for the teacher to have in mind that within the same class there will probably be students with radically different outlooks on what is taking place, who will be reacting in very different ways.

While Perry's is the best known in higher education, there are other developmental models which can provide insights into student learning. Of particular note are the stages of moral development identified by Kohlberg (1972) and discussed by Gilligan (1981) and those of ego-development identified by Loevinger (Loevinger, 1976; Weathersby, 1981). Loevinger in particular focuses on a stage she labels as 'autonomous' which follows the 'individualistic'. Many of these are discussed in the context of higher education by the various authors in Chickering and Associates (1981).

Implications of research

On the basis of what is presently known from research and practice the following appear to enhance the promotion of autonomy:

1. Commitment to the development of autonomy by *teachers* and the confidence and ability to introduce approaches which assist in the development of autonomy. There needs to be at least tolerance by most staff in a department to the changes which are needed when autonomous approaches are introduced and to the diversity of student response.
2. Within the department or institution there needs to be a *context* which at least minimally accepts the introduction of approaches which may involve changes to course structure, teaching methods, relationships between staff and students, and, perhaps most importantly of all, to assessment methods.
3. Within the structure of *courses* there needs to be consistency between goals, approaches and assessments in the support of learning for understanding. Inappropriate requirements which undermine self-determination and discourage self-assessment seem particularly harmful. Student workload should not be excessive; in particular, class contact hours should leave sufficient time for students to work independently, and assignments that require little initiative should be kept to the minimum consistent with achieving other goals. Students need the experience of dealing with all facets of a learning task, and not just of repeating specific well-defined tasks.
4. Acceptance by *students* of more responsibility for their own learning than is usually the case in traditional settings. Students' views will be influenced by

their prior educational experience, their stage of intellectual development, the context of other courses, the attitudes of their teachers and assessment procedures. They may exhibit some initial resistance to methods which place more responsibility in their hands if they have had little experience of such methods. However, unless students at least accept the principle of taking greater responsibility for learning, then there will be major barriers to be overcome.

These propositions which have emerged from research and practice should be taken as providing directions for development rather than acting as checklists against which to assess any given situation. There are examples of the effective introduction of autonomous approaches in situations which seem far from ideal.

Conclusion

This chapter has taken as its theme moving towards autonomy both as a goal and as an educational practice. What can I say in conclusion at this stage of the book? First, I now have a clearer view of the ideal of autonomy as a goal for individual learners: they are to become their own persons in a context of working with others helping all to achieve their learning objectives, singly and collectively. This goal need not necessarily be pursued through the group of approaches which I have labelled as autonomous approaches, though commonly these will be suitable methods to adopt.

Secondly, there exists a repertoire of approaches which are well developed and which can be deployed in the process of developing student autonomy. Some of these approaches require teachers to learn new skills and substantially reorganize their programmes; others can fit more easily into present course structures and need relatively modest adjustments by teachers. What is important in my view, though, is the attitude of teachers towards their students. It is not any technique or teaching methodology which is primarily needed, but an attitude of acceptance and appreciation of the views, desires and frames of reference of learners. Perhaps the single central quality which fosters autonomy is the quality of the relationship between teachers and learners which develops through this acceptance.

Chapter 2

Planning Learning Experiences to Promote Autonomous Learning

Joy Higgs,
Cumberland College of Health Sciences, Sydney

How can teachers encourage students to learn independently and to develop their abilities as self-directed learners?

In this chapter I will discuss some of my experiences in this area as a teacher and as a learner and the work of several authors in this field. In particular, I would like to describe some of the issues and questions I have explored in order to improve my understanding and abilities as a teacher trying to promote learner independence.

There have been two major learning experiences which have contributed to my understanding of the teacher's role in this process. The first of these has been my involvement as a student and teacher in a course on self-directed learning for masters-level students studying in the School of Medical Education at the University of New South Wales. This course is run on a contract-learning basis. The students design learning contracts which specify their proposed learning goals (relating to the topic area of self-directed learning), learning activities and timetable, and evidence of the accomplishment of their goals. These contracts are negotiated with the teacher early in the course, and may be renegotiated during the course when the students have gained a clearer idea of how feasible the contracts are and what their real interests are (based on their reading and learning about the topic area).

My second avenue for exploring autonomous learning has been through research studies as a PhD student. These studies have primarily been looking at characteristics of learning programmes (such as the clarity of the learning task) which encourage learners to be self-directed.

What does autonomous learning mean to me?

The main problem I faced in both of the endeavours described above was to develop an understanding of what it means to be an autonomous learner and to gain an image of how autonomous learning differs from the traditional picture of teacher-directed learning.

To me, autonomous learning (within the context of a learning institution) is a process in which the learner works on a learning task or activity and is largely independent of the teacher who acts as manager of the learning programme and as resource person. Under these circumstances the behaviour of the learner is characterized by responsibility for his or her own learning, a high level of independence in performing learning activities and solving problems which are associated with the learning task, active input to decision-making regarding the learning task, and use of the teacher as a resource person.

The biggest distinction I have discovered between traditional learning and what I am calling autonomous or self-directed learning (1) in this chapter is in the level of dependence of the learner on the teacher. Traditionally the student was highly dependent on the teacher, and the learning/teaching picture was one of teacher-direction. At the other end of the spectrum we can envisage 'learners' who are independent of teachers or authority figures in their learning, for instance a scholar independently exploring a topic of interest. Somewhere between these two positions is the subject of this chapter, ie autonomous learning within an institutional setting.

In this case the student's autonomy is not absolute and is limited by such factors as time or curricular constraints. Therefore autonomous learning is used here to refer to relative rather than complete learner autonomy. We can see that the limitations provided by the setting are also balanced by several potential advantages which the setting provides. These include the facilitation provided by the teacher, the resources of the institution and the stimulus and resources provided by other learners. In this case the picture is potentially one of *interdependence* with all parties being able to benefit from the contributions of the others, both in terms of the outcome of the learning endeavour which may be greater than that which any one individual could have achieved alone, and in terms of the development of each individual through this interaction. That is, the learning process has the scope to bring about: completion of the task, the development of learning and interpersonal abilities (eg through reflection of the learner on his or her contribution as an individual to the interactive/interdependent process) and development of the learner as a person (eg in terms of increasing self-reliance and confidence in one's own abilities). As this development takes place, the learner gains abilities and confidence which will in turn enhance his or her performance in future learning activities.

Within this learning process I see the teacher playing the role of a manager who creates a supportive and stimulating learning environment, who is available as a resource person, who challenges learners to achieve their potential and who helps learners to become aware of institutional requirements and expectations associated with the discipline in which they are studying (eg standards associated with empirical research). This last role is an especially important one, since students bring to the learning task their own standards for their work, but they need to learn what others expect of them.

(1) In this chapter I am using the terms 'autonomous learning' and 'self-directed learning' interchangeably, while acknowledging that some authors use them more distinctly.

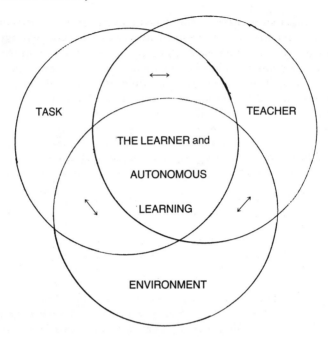

Figure 1 *Autonomous learning*

The four principal elements in this picture of autonomous learning are: the learner, the teacher, the task and the environment. Since all of these elements interact together, the successful outcome of an autonomous learning experience depends on the extent to which each element is consistent with the others. This is illustrated in figure 1. I will now go on to discuss key aspects of this view of autonomous learning in order to address the question of how to plan successful autonomous learning experiences.

How do the characteristics of learners influence their independent learning behaviour?

Probably the most important feature of autonomous learning is the relationship between the teacher and the learner. This relationship is likely to be strongly influenced by the past learning experiences of both teacher and learner since these experiences affect the extent to which both players are prepared for the challenges autonomous learning brings.

While studying the nature of autonomous learning I have come to agree with the idea that some learners are more ready for independent learning than others. The past experience of students, in particular their contact with traditional teaching/learning methods (which generally do not encourage them to act independently) is likely to result in difficulties for the students if they are suddenly asked to act as autonomous learners.

The variability of students' readiness to learn independently became very evident to me recently when I was studying a group of third-year undergraduate occupational therapy and physiotherapy students who were completing substantial independent study projects following years of primarily teacher-directed learning. The following quotes indicate a range of students' responses to these projects:

Student 1

I find the project rather daunting and I am worried a lot – I don't know if I'm on the right track. I've had very little previous experience in independent work.

Student 2

It is unrealistic to have to choose the project topic – I didn't know how to go about it. I need a lot of guidance. But it's good to do this type of project with help.

Student 3

I am enjoying my project and learning a lot – I'm doing my project in depth. I'm working largely by myself – my supervisor is a guide and a resource person – she doesn't spoonfeed me.

Three particular points emerged from this study. First, the students' attitude towards performing this type of learning project influenced their behaviour considerably. For instance, students approaching the task with a positive attitude were more prepared to learn how to cope with the new task whereas students who resented having to do the task simply 'went through the motions'. One student, for example, said 'I'm doing the project because I have to. I'm only going to do enough [work] to pass.'

Secondly, the learners' attitudes and performance were strongly influenced by their experience of past independent learning activities (in particular the enjoyment and success they experienced in these activities), and the abilities they developed from these past learning experiences. (See Student 1's remark.) This observation emphasized for me the value of assessing students' readiness for independent learning, planning curricula and learning activities which progressively develop students' autonomous learning activities and endeavouring to ensure that such learning abilities are positive experiences which the learner wishes to repeat. It was interesting to note in interviews with the students' supervisors that some supervisors gave high priority to the goal of ensuring that these projects were enjoyable and stimulating experiences, whereas others apparently focused mainly on ensuring that the learning task (project) was completed satisfactorily.

Thirdly, the students' responses supported the idea that encouraging students to develop a positive attitude towards this mode of learning is preferable to having to overcome their resistance to a new and possibly threatening learning experience. (See Student 3's remark.)

Two authors whose work I have found very helpful in dealing with the question of learner readiness for autonomous learning are Knowles (1975) and Guglielmino (1977).

Knowles' (1975) book, *Self-directed Learning*, is a good starting point for both teachers and learners who wish to learn more about this mode of learning. Knowles provides a self-rating instrument to assess 'competencies of self-directed learning'. In this one-page rating tool, learners are asked to identify the extent to which they possess the nine competencies listed. (See Table 1.)

1. An understanding of the differences in assumptions about learners and the skills required for learning under teacher-directed learning and self-directed learning, and the ability to explain these differences to others.
2. A concept of myself as being a non-dependent and a self-directing person.
3. The ability to relate to peers collaboratively, to see them as resources for diagnosing needs, planning my learning, and learning; and to give help to them and receive help from them.
4. The ability to diagnose my own learning needs realistically, with help from teachers and peers.
5. The ability to translate learning needs into learning objectives in a form that makes it possible for their accomplishment to be assessed.
6. The ability to relate to teachers as facilitators, helpers or consultants, and to take the initiative in making use of their resources.
7. The ability to identify human and material resources appropriate to different kinds of learning objective.
8. The ability to select effective strategies for making use of learning resources and to perform these strategies skilfully and with initiative.
9. The ability to collect and validate evidence of the accomplishment of various kinds of learning objectives.

Table 1 *Competencies of self-directed learning* (Knowles, 1975)

I have found this to be a simple and satisfactory means for introducing self-directed learning to students in the contract-learning course described earlier. These students are asked to complete the rating scale and to reflect on their results in order to explore the nature of this type of learning and the implications it has for themselves as learners. At the end of the course, the students are asked to complete the instrument again and consider areas in which they have developed as learners, and areas which require further attention.

Another rating tool I have found to be particularly valuable is the 'Self-directed Learner Readiness Scale' developed by Guglielmino (1977). Table 2 lists the eight factors covered in this scale. These are described as being prerequisite capabilities for learners engaging in autonomous learning experiences. I have used this scale as a 'post test' for the students in my self-directed learning course to promote individual reflection on each student's self-directed learning abilities, and group discussion on ways in which teachers can assess student readiness for independent learning. One of the most interesting outcomes of this discussion was the conclusion of the students (who are themselves teachers in a variety of health personnel education settings) that it was possible to build into self-directed learning courses 'testing' of student's 'self-directed learning readiness' and activities aimed at developing independent learning abilities.

1. Openness to learning opportunities
2. Self-concept as an effective learner
3. Initiative and independence in learning
4. Love of learning
5. Creativity
6. Future orientation
7. Ability to use basic study skills
8. Ability to use problem-solving skills

Table 2 *Self-directed Learner Readiness factors* (Guglielmino, 1977)

Another point of discussion was the need to monitor the learner's ability and progress as a self-directed learner *during* the course (as well as before and after) in order to provide feedback, encouragement and guidance as needed.

Clearly implicit in the above discussion is the recognition that readiness for autonomous learning is both a starting point for autonomous learning activities and a consequence of past learning experiences. As a corollary we may assume that learners can learn how to learn independently and that we as teachers can think in terms of learning how to learn as being a developmental process which we can promote.

The picture of autonomous learning as a developmental or growth process is illustrated in a recent research project conducted by Marilyn Taylor (1986, 1987). The students in this project were enrolled in a graduate university course entitled 'Basic processes in facilitating adult learning', in which they were expected to learn from their experience in the course. The purpose of the study was 'to identify from the learner's perspective, common patterns in the [students'] experience of learning'.

The results of this study indicated that the learners 'underwent a major reorientation of their perspective on learning, knowledge, authority and themselves' as they progressed through four phases and phase transition points in the process of developing their skills and understanding of self-directed learning (see Figure 2).

This cycle of the growth of self-directed learning consists of the following stages:

(a) Disconfirmation (phase transition). At this point some aspect of the learner's existing expectations and assumptions become challenged by the learner's current experiences and the learner becomes disoriented.
(b) Disorientation (phase). During this period of confusion the learner becomes anxious and withdraws from sources of confusion.
(c) Naming the problem (phase transition). This is the stage when the learner is able to identify the problem without blaming self and others.
(d) Exploration (phase). This is a more relaxed phase in which the learner can

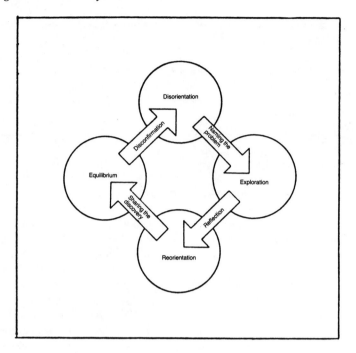

Figure 2 *Learning process sequence in self-directed learning.*

explore the problem area in an open-ended and collaborative way, gaining insights, confidence and satisfaction.

(e) Reflection (phase transition). At this point the learners engage in a private reflective review of where they are up to.

(f) Reorientation (phase). Through private reflection the learner gains a major insight or synthesis of ideas and develops a new approach to the learning task.

(g) Sharing the discovery (phase transition). Having developed new ideas, the learner then tests these out with others.

(h) Equilibrium (phase). During this phase the learner elaborates, refines and applies his or her new perspective and approach.

I found Taylor's work very meaningful since it seemed to reflect and consolidate many of my experiences as a self-directed learner and as a teacher of students working in self-directed learning programmes. For instance, I can relate well to the confusion of trying to find some direction in a complex mass of ideas and seemingly conflicting points of view at the start of a major learning project and to the enthusiasm (and relief!) which greeted a significant insight or breakthrough after a period of exploration. As a teacher I have witnessed extended periods of exploration by students as they acquire more and more information on a topic and pursue many different avenues (sidetracks?), and have faced the dilemma of deciding whether to intervene in this self-directed learning activity – or whether to wait for them to reach the transition phase of reflection and decide for themselves that they have gone far enough.

Taylor's focus on the learner's perspective provides an important message in relation to this dilemma. She says that there are 'dimensions and complexities which are not evident from the standpoint of the observer'. This is the complete opposite to the traditional picture of the teacher knowing what is best for the student. It challenges us as teachers to think about how to balance our task-facilitator role with our goal of promoting the development and use of autonomous learning behaviour in our students.

Another very interesting aspect of Taylor's model is that it points to the importance of other people within the learning process of an individual learner. This is particularly evident in the 'exploration phase' where the learner can engage in collabortive learning activities to explore the topic area and in 'sharing the discovery phase transition' where other people help the learner to test out his or her ideas. On the other hand the importance of the individual learner's personal experiences is emphasized in the following stages: 'disconfirmation', 'disorientation', 'naming the problem', 'reflection', 'reorientation' and 'equilibrium'. These 'sharing' and 'individual' aspects of self-directed learning have been very evident in my own learning. For instance, my exploration of the area of self-directed learning has been stimulated by the numerous authors whose work is discussed in this chapter, and the value of reflection to gain insights and deepen my understanding of this most challenging area has become evident to me as I have gone through the process of writing, rereading and rewriting numerous drafts of my work. This learning through writing and reflection has been an important part of clarifying my thoughts.

There are two ways to view Taylor's model of the growth process of self-directed learning. It can be seen as being the learner's overall reorientation to learning and as the phases the learner goes through during each self-directed learning activity. We could expect that some of the abilities and understanding developed during each of these activities would carry over into subsequent learning tasks. This could mean, for instance, that students can learn to identify discrepancies, to name problems without assigning blame, to gain insights through reflection and so on. Each of these abilities should help to improve the learner's approach to learning by decreasing the difficulties he or she faces and by facilitating the transition between the phases.

How does the teacher help the student learn how to learn?

Having assessed the students' autonomous learning abilities, the next step was to consider ways of helping them to acquire new skills or develop their weaker learning areas. An interesting insight into these two aspects of autonomous learning is provided by the work of Abercrombie (1981) who used a small group discussion approach to enable students to explore topic areas and 'to help each participant to understand his own behaviour and acquire better control over it'.

Abercrombie describes the learning programme as follows:

> The nature of the discussion was 'free' or 'associative', ie members were free to participate as they wished and to follow up their own and others' associations with the topic. Each participant could see how his past experience and habitual ways of reacting to the context influenced his own processes of perception and interpretation of current events. He could analyse his own reactions in comparison and contrast to the variety displayed by other members, and change if he wished to. (p 42)

This approach emphasizes the value of learners reflecting on, and verbalizing about, their own learning behaviour and 'thinking out loud' about their ideas as they deepened their understanding of the topic area.

I believe that the teacher has a major role to play (when introducing students to self-directed learning in particular) in helping students to learn about the processes involved in learning and about the effectiveness of different learning strategies. An associated factor, which I feel is an essential component of autonomous learning, is for students to learn to be conscious of the learning processes they are utilizing (Griffin, 1987).

In recent years there has been a large body of research conducted in the field of student learning. One particular research project was conducted at Lancaster University in England (Entwistle and Ramsden, 1983) and was discussed in Chapter 1. This study examined the 'approaches to studying' of tertiary students in a wide range of disciplines.

When reading about this work I was faced with two major questions. First, to what extent does autonomous learning involve a high level of independent activity? Secondly, to what extent does autonomous learning focus on a search for meaning as well as self-direction in the learning process?

In the process of answering the first question I began by presuming that self-directed learning was a very active process on the part of the learner. Yet it became evident to me that self-directed learners could well choose to learn in what we generally regard as being the more passive modes (eg listening to a lecture). Thus the 'activity' of autonomous learners, I concluded, is best thought of as the pursuit of whatever learning activities the learners consider would best help them to achieve their learning goals. Singers .

An accomplished autonomous learner, then, is one who has the capabilities for learning in an independent manner, but who can also recognize the advantages of choosing alternative modes of learning where these are considered to be more appropriate to the learning goals in question. For instance the autonomous learner may choose to adopt one of the following learning strategies:

(a) to seek and utilize relevant existing learning opportunities (eg lectures, seminars).
(b) to seek available resource personnel and to interact with them, eg as 'sounding boards' and sources of ideas, feedback, stimulation and skilled/expert information.

(c) to seek and utilize available learning resources (eg learning modules, computer literature searches).

(d) to reflect on observations of his or her own learning experiences or the ideas and findings of others.

(e) to actively experiment with an issue or conduct an investigation of a topic of interest.   *trills in singing . ornamatchion in singing*

(f) to conceptualize about acquired knowledge.

(g) to seek concrete experiences which help to further his or her understanding of the topic area.

Some of these approaches are illustrated by the following quotes which were obtained from interviews I conducted with college teachers who had completed postgraduate research degrees. Each of these reflects a high level of autonomy.

> I like to take the initiative and define a topic for myself to research. I read [the literature] and combine this with independent thinking. Sometimes I discuss my ideas with a resource person and listen to his opinions.
>
> I like to feel stimulated to solve a problem, to explore a theory and take it further than the writer did.
>
> My preference is to investigate a topic by using my previous knowledge, by doing a literature search and by seeking first-hand information from experts in the area.

The conclusion I drew from these interviews was that learners placed in autonomous learning situations should be allowed to choose their own learning method (on the assumption that they are competent autonomous learners and that it is possible for them to choose the learning goals). Where neither of these assumptions is met, the teacher needs to take a more active role in guiding the learners or providing feedback to their proposed activities. This could serve to help the learners to complete the learning task *and* to gain competence in managing their own learning. Too much freedom for an unprepared student could result in the student failing to proceed beyond Taylor's (1986) disorientation or exploration phases (as described earlier).

With regard to the second question dealing with the focus of autonomous learners on a search for meaning, this posed a more difficult problem. I was particularly interested in determining whether:

(a) a distinction should be made between learning as solving a problem or completing a task, and learning as gaining understanding and searching for meaning, and

(b) the student can solve a problem or complete a task and not gain knowledge or understanding.

49

Part of my understanding of these two concerns came from the research project I conducted (Higgs, 1987) to which I referred earlier. In this project I developed seven 'dimensions of self-directed learning behaviour', ie 'active pursuit of goals', 'search for meaning', 'self-reliance', 'pursuit of excellence', 'adventurousness', 'commitment (to task)' and 'enthusiasm (for the task)'. Two of the findings of this study are particularly relevant here. The first was that none of the students scored themselves highly on all of these dimensions (at the point of time in the students' independent study project at which the study was conducted). In addition, the students' mean scores for 'search for meaning' and 'adventurousness' were negatively correlated with their scores for 'active pursuit of goals' and 'commitment to task'. This led me to the conclusion that the actions involved in searching for meaning were more compatible with risk-taking and being adventurous than in working actively to complete the learning task. Within the context of the study, part of this observation can be related to the time constraints and external pressures of the learning environment. However, there is also the implication that the nature of the task can restrict the students' search for meaning.

Regarding the task completion versus learning concern, I have reached the conclusion that an autonomous learner who successfully solves a learning problem or completes a learning task using a deep approach (1) to learning (involving an active search for meaning) must surely gain understanding of the problem or task investigated. However, if restricting pressures occur within the learning environment, or if the learner lacks the ability to use deep learning strategies, then they may well complete the task using a surface-learning approach (which simply focuses on reproducing the information acquired) with little or no real understanding of the topic area studied.

How does the learning environment influence autonomy in learning?

As well as helping the student learn how to learn independently and effectively, the teacher is also responsible for creating and managing the learning environment. The importance of the learning context is emphasized by Paul Ramsden (1985) in a recent review paper on student learning research. He concluded that 'it is now clear that both styles of learning and approaches to learning are intimately related to the assessment and teaching context' (p 59). According to Ramsden the effects of learning environments can be best understood if they are thought of as operating at several levels:

(a) at the level of the learning task. Here relevance of the task to the student promotes intrinsic motivation and a deep (or meaning-oriented) approach to learning. Alternatively extrinsic motivation increases the likelihood of surface learning.
(b) at the teacher level. Here, teacher attitude, enthusiasm, concern for

(1) Deep and surface learning are discussed in Chapter 1.

helping students understand and ability to appreciate students' learning difficulties all influence students' approaches and attitudes to studying.

(c) at the department or course level. In particular the forms of assessment used at this level have a strong influence on approaches to studying, with many courses encouraging a surface approach to learning through the use of assessment methods which reward reproductive answers.

(d) at the institution level. Differences in institutional values and purposes can also influence students' learning.

Ramsden discusses the work of Biggs (1982) which found that Australian College of Advanced Education students relied more on surface approaches than their university counterparts.

There are many implications which could be drawn from consideration of the effects of the learning environment on students' learning. Two of the important ones for me are, first, that there is the message to teachers to be aware of the possible effects on the students of many aspects of the learning context, and to create learning environments which are likely to produce desirable effects. The second point is the importance of students' perceptions of the learning environment in affecting students' behaviours.

This is illustrated by the following statement by Ramsden (1985): 'It is not so much the techniques of assessment or anxiety-provoking situations in themselves that lead to surface approaches, but rather students' *perceptions* of what the assessment requires' (p 59).

Although it seems logical to assume that students' perceptions of the learning environment and the nature of the learning task influence the students' behaviour, this poses a number of problems:

(a) If the teacher's perception of the learning task or environment can differ from the students' perceptions, how do teachers plan learning programmes, not knowing how they will be interpreted?

(b) Compounding the above problem is the likelihood that individual students will perceive the learning programme in different ways from each other. How can the teacher cope with this?

(c) How does the teacher really know how the student is perceiving the learning task and environmental conditions?

(d) How conscious are learners of the effects their perceptions of the learning environment have on their learning behaviour?

The answer to the first two questions I feel lies in recent research on student learning. This research provides insights into the relationship between teachers' actions and students' perceptions and responses, and suggests how these might be utilized in programme planning. For instance, a project conducted by Watkins (1984) at the Australian National University reported that deep-level processing by students was encouraged when students were allowed time to think through a topic, when assessment involved essays rather than

51

examinations (especially multiple-choice tests which tended to encourage surface learning), when students perceived the department as encouraging independent thinking, when students were allowed to choose the way they learned, and when the students' interest was aroused.

The answer to the third question has been partly considered earlier in the discussion of the work of Abercrombie (1981), who presented the advantages of involving students in talking about their learning strategies and perceptions of their own learning. Her approach could be extended by having students talk about their perceptions of the learning task and environment. Such a practice is particularly suited to autonomous learning situations involving a teacher and one student when part of the interaction between the two could involve discussion about the student's interpretation of the task and their successes and difficulties in dealing with it. A second method could be for the teacher to discuss with the student the teacher's observations of the student's learning behaviour and to ask for the student's comments.

The final question deals with the extent to which students are conscious of their perceptions of the learning environment and of its effects on their behaviour. Watkins' (1984) study provides some answers to this question. He found that student consciousness of factors affecting their learning and changes in their learning approaches was a variable phenomenon which was affected by faculty and depth of processing (ie deep or surface learning). In general, students adopting a deep learning approach were more conscious of factors affecting their learning, and arts students were more aware of such factors than economics or science students.

This again highlights the importance of raising students' consciousness of their learning behaviour and of the factors that influence their learning through metalearning (learning about learning) activities. This awareness about learning is emphasized in the book *Teaching Students to Learn* by Graham Gibbs (1981) who says 'above everything else, it is the encouragement of students' active reflection about their studying which is the cornerstone to their development' (as learners). In autonomous-learning activities and particularly in sessions aimed at developing autonomous learning, such consciousness-raising must surely be even more important.

How can the teacher design and manage independent learning activities for students?

Up to this point I have been exploring the nature of autonomous learning, the characteristics and role of the learner, and the teacher's role in helping the learner to learn and to create an appropriate learning environment. This leads to consideration of the actual planning of independent learning activities.

In formulating a plan for such learning activities, there are two approaches to learning-programme design which I feel are particularly relevant. These are problem-based learning and learning programmes which emphasize adult learning principles.

The problem-based learning approach forms the basis of a number of innovative curricula today. One of these is used at the Hawkesbury Agricultural College in Australia. Richard Bawden (1985) states that 'at the heart of ... [the] problem-based educational movement is the maxim that the most effective learning occurs through our individual explorations of the ever-changing environments we experience through our lives' (p 44). Problem-based courses are designed around specific real-world problems. The problem-based curriculum aims to develop student competencies in the areas of problem-solving, communicating and learning (Macadam, 1985). These competencies are developed by the students engaging in 'reality-based problem-solving and situation-improving projects'. Key features of the programme are faculty commitment to the learning approach, replacement of the traditional system of faculty operation by a team-management approach based on functions, and student awareness of, and responsibility for, the learning process. (Some aspects of this are discussed by Richard Bawden in Chapter 14.)

This approach to learning provides a fascinating array of ideas and opportunities for teachers. In particular we can think of planning learning experiences which involve the learners in problem identification and solution. In this way we can enable them to develop skills in learning (ie problem-solving) and to prepare for their role as autonomous lifelong learners in the rapidly changing environment in which we live.

There is a strong degree of overlap between the principles and practices of experiential and problem-based learning and adult learning. Of the vast wealth of educational literature devoted to learning theory, it is adult learning theory which has the most compatibility and relevance to autonomous learning. In his book *The Adult Learner: a Neglected Species* Knowles (1978) developed a set of principles of teaching which relate to conditions suitable for adult learning. (See Table 3.) These principles are also very applicable to the facilitation of autonomous learning.

Another valuable contribution to providing guidelines for designing autonomous learning experiences is made by William Torbert (1978) who draws from his work in traditional universities to support and illustrate his notion of 'liberating structures'. Within the educational setting, he says, structure is provided by the pattern of leadership and organization that occurs. Liberating structure is a paradoxical concept and practice. That is, the very nature and presence of the *constraints* of the structure provided act to *free* the learner to pursue learning in a manner and to an end that is beyond what the learner could have achieved otherwise.

In Torbert's approach we can see an exciting possibility for self-directed learning in teacher-managed situations. The teacher is given ideas on how to create a 'deliberately ironic' type of learning environment or framework within which the learners engage in experiential learning tasks and develop skills in learning independently. The key elements of Torbert's liberating type of learning programme structure are:

(a) recognition that the learners will need to learn a new way of learning
(b) integration of the products and purposes of the learning experience
(c) planned changes to the programme structure over time to encourage

search for meaning and increasing student responsibility

(d) ongoing monitoring and feedback on the learning process

(e) use of power by the teacher to encourage learner inquiry and collaboration/responsibility in the learning process

(f) emphasis on ongoing critical inspection of the programme by learners and teacher

(g) public accountability of the teacher and commitment to correcting any incongruities that arise in the course.

Conditions of learning	Principles of teaching
	The teacher:
Learners feel a need to learn	• helps the students recognize the need to learn
	• helps students set personal learning goals
The learning environment is physically and interpersonally comfortable	• ensures physical comfort
	• accepts and respects students
	• builds mutual trust and helpfulness among students
	• acts as a co-learner
The goals of the learning experience are compatible with the learners' goals	• involves students in goal formulation
Learners share the responsibility for planning and operating the learning experience	• involves students in joint decisions regarding designing and operating the learning experience
Learners participate actively in the learning process	• involves students in the inquiry process
The learners' past experience is utilized	• helps students utilize their past experience
	• relates learning activities and content to the students' past experience
Learners have a sense of progress towards their goals.	• helps students measure progress (including self-evaluation)

Table 3 *Conditions for adult learning and principles of teaching* (after Knowles, 1978)

According to Boud (1981) 'Torbert's prescription is not for the novice. It is a high risk approach which depends on a highly skilled practitioner.' However, he says, this approach does suggest that 'it is possible to apply autonomous learning principles to courses (eg large classes of undergraduate students) whose circumstances suggest that they would not be amenable to this approach' (p 36).

In my research project with students engaged in independent study programmes, a number of students commented upon the fact that the structure provided by the learning programme, the guidance provided by the teachers and even the fact of 'having to do the project' resulted in these students gaining skills and confidence in being self-directed learners:

> Having experienced the process (under supervision) I know what's involved. I've learned skills and guidelines for future research projects.
>
> It's very important to do this project – it is a chance to learn research skills in a structured environment.
>
> Independence in learning is good – it helps you to test your abilities – and the supervisor is there to help with problems.

What is the teacher's role as manager of independent learning programmes?

The previous section looked at aspects of the design of programmes aiming to promote learner autonomy. I would like to turn now to the role of the teacher as a manager.

In 1981 Abercrombie argued that there is a need to challenge and change our basic assumptions about learning since many of these 'were developed in earlier times in response to needs now outgrown ... [and] form a barrier to change of behaviour in response to current needs' (p 38). She contends that teachers should become aware of their basic assumptions and the effects of these on their behaviour, and should adopt alternative guiding principles and behaviour if necessary.

It has become apparent to me that autonomous learning is inconsistent with the teacher being the principal/sole source of power and control. That is, there is a need to allow the student to make a large number of the decisions (eg goal setting) in the learning experience. The teacher therefore becomes a manager who delegates some or most of the power, responsibility and choice in learning to the student.

There also needs to be a considerable emphasis on the teacher's role in creating and managing a learning environment which is consistent with such delegation. In conjunction with the increased student freedom there would need to be safety, trust, acceptance and supportiveness.

It also follows that delegation can only work if learners play their part by taking responsibility for many aspects of the process and outcome of the learning experience, by being active participants in the learning process, by bringing to the learning activity their own desire to learn and their past experience and values, and by endeavouring to discover their own meaning through the learning process.

When thinking about the teaching/learning situation as being analogous to a management situation, teachers can learn a great deal from the theories and practices of personnel management. Some aspects of this field which I have found to be particularly enlightening are:

- □ the skills of an effective manager
- □ the ideas associated with 'situational leadership' (including leadership styles, and maturity level of 'followers').

Both of these areas are discussed by Hersey and Blanchard (1982).

The teacher's role as the manager of a student's independent learning project could be described as working with the student in order to help the student accomplish his or her learning goals. Hersey and Blanchard contend that there are at least three skill areas necessary for successful management:

- ☐ Technical skill (ie 'Ability to use knowledge, methods, techniques, and equipment necessary for the performance of specific tasks acquired from experience, education, and training.')
- ☐ Human skill (ie 'Ability and judgment in working with and through people, including an understanding of motivation and an application of effective leadership.')
- ☐ Conceptual skill (ie 'Ability to understand the complexities of the overall organization and where one's own operation fits into the organization. This knowledge permits one to act according to the objectives of the total organization rather than only on the basis of the goals and needs of one's own immediate group.') (p 5)

This appears to me to be a useful breakdown for comparison with the teacher's role in managing a student's learning project. I agree with these authors that the crucial skill is the human skill since many such actions of the teacher are critical to the success of the learning project both in terms of the task completion and the goals of developing the learner's autonomous learning abilities. For instance the teacher needs: to be able to judge the learner's capabilities for independent learning, to have the ability of working with people (ie the learners) and to be able to exercise leadership skills such as motivation. The extent of the student's experience in the task area and the nature of the learning task determine the relative importance of the teacher's technical skills (eg in the use of library literature searches, or in the use of research apparatus). The teacher may play the role of resource person or teacher of new techniques. Similarly the nature of the task, the learner's response to the task and the characteristics of the learning environment can influence the demands upon the teacher's conceptual skill. For instance the teacher may 'oversee' a learning project, intervening only when there is a need for the student to complete specific tasks (eg submission of a research proposal) to meet institutional or course requirements, or when the student's progress or discussion indicates that they cannot understand an important aspect (eg the global perspective) of their work.

A very interesting aspect of management theory is the concept of situational leadership (Hersey and Blanchard, 1982). The basis of situational leadership is that there is no one 'best' way to provide leadership (ie to influence people). The appropriate leadership style to use depends upon the situation, in particular upon the extent to which the people the leader is attempting to influence are able and willing to take responsibility for directing their own behaviour in relation to the task they are engaged upon. This is analogous to the level of readiness of the learner for self-directed learning, as discussed earlier.

There are four leadership styles in this model: 'telling', 'selling', 'participating' and 'delegating'. Each style is characterized by task behaviour (ie the extent to which the leader provides direction for the task, eg setting goals, defining roles) and relationship behaviour (ie the extent to which the leader attempts to establish a working relationship *with* the follower through two-way communication, active listening and providing support). The 'telling' style comprises high-task and low-relationship leadership, the 'selling' style high-task and high-relationship leadership, the 'participating' style high-relationship and low-task leadership, and the 'delegating' style low-relationship and low-task leadership.

In this model, followers (in our case, students) with a given level of 'task maturity' (ie ability/willingness to complete the task in question) are best managed by a leader who adopts a matching leadership style. That is:

☐ low task maturity followers are best managed by a 'telling' style of leader
☐ low to moderate task maturity followers by a 'selling' style leader
☐ moderate to high task maturity followers by a 'participating' style leader
☐ high task maturity followers by a 'delegating' style leader.

I believe this model can provide useful guidelines to teachers wanting to provide effective leadership for autonomous learning programmes. Consider, for instance, a group of students engaged in teacher-managed research projects. If one student needs to learn a complex new task and has little aptitude for such tasks, the teacher could tell or show him how to do it. Another student may be new to autonomous learning and may be experiencing difficulty in getting started on a literature search. The teacher could adopt a 'selling' style and provide some direction and much encouragement for the student to follow the example given. A third student could be experienced in solving problems but at times need some guidance from the teacher. Here a 'participating' style of leadership could be adopted. Finally there could be a very capable autonomous learner who needs little direction and infrequent support from her teacher, who can therefore adopt a 'delegating' style.

Conclusion

In conclusion, this chapter has presented some of the ideas I have developed in relation to the design and implementation of learning experiences which aim to promote student autonomy. I see autonomous learning as a management process in which the role of the teacher/manager is a complex one with the teacher needing to develop a good working knowledge of the nature of autonomous learning and to develop the ability to plan learning programmes (with the student) which best suit the demands of the learning task and environment and the abilities of the student. There is also a great demand on the autonomous learner to develop an understanding of their own learning abilities, to extend their learning abilities and to be active, responsible learners. With teachers and learners working effectively together, the results of autonomous learning will hopefully go beyond task accomplishment to include development of the student as a learner and as a person. In this way autonomous learning becomes a liberating experience for the learner.

Chapter 3

On the Attainment of
Subject-matter Autonomy

Philip Candy,
Centre for Administrative and Higher Education Studies, The University of New England, Armidale, New South Wales

Introduction

When people speak or write about developing student autonomy, they may mean any one of several things. First, they might be referring to the development of autonomous individuals; that is, graduates who exhibit the qualities of moral, emotional and intellectual independence. This is the long-term goal of most, if not all, educational endeavours, and as such it has a long and distinguished history in the philosophy of education (Bagnall, in press; Crittenden, 1978; Dearden, 1972, 1975; Gibbs, 1979; Lewis, 1978; Strike, 1982; White, 1982).

Secondly, in a narrower and more restricted sense, developing student autonomy may be taken to refer to developing autonomous students; that is, people who accept more and more responsibility for their own learning, for setting goals and objectives, for finding resources, and for evaluating the outcomes of their learning activities. Such an approach is predicated on the notion that these are the competencies which are called for in advanced graduate study. It is assumed that the student who is an accomplished autonomous learner will be best equipped to deal with the rigors of independent scholarly inquiry. Both of these aspects of autonomy are discussed in detail in Chapter 1.

A third approach to developing student autonomy might refer to inculcating habits of curiosity and disciplined inquiry. Often teachers and lecturers recognize that, especially in times of rapid social and technological change, the truly successful graduate is the one who leaves a programme with an orientation toward lifelong learning. Accordingly, the aim is to produce graduates who, once they complete their formal studies, are continuing self-directed learners or, as I will call them here, autodidacts (Candy, 1987; Jankovic *et al*, 1979).

Despite the apparent importance of personal autonomy or of self-determination (Bagnall, in press) as a goal of education, it is not the purpose of this chapter to examine the relationships between education and the development of personal autonomy in the wider context. Instead, I will be limiting myself in this chapter to educational interventions which focus on developing autonomous students rather than autonomous people in the broad sense.

Frequently, autonomy in learning is equated with situational independence or 'self-management' (Wang, 1983); that is, the ability to operate as a learner with minimal supervision or institutional support and affiliation. Although this is clearly an important aspect of student autonomy, it is only part of the story. All learning efforts concern some substantive content or other. Many researchers have classified learning projects according to the subject matter being learned, but few seem to have considered the processes whereby a learner actually becomes autonomous with respect to the material itself.

When a person confronts an entirely new area of knowledge or skill, one with which she or he has no familiarity, there is the problem of where to begin in attempting to learn it. In his paper on 'The authority of ideas and the student's right to autonomy', Strike (1982) puts it this way:

> The ignorance of the person just beginning the study of a subject has a special character. It is not just that the novice is ignorant of the facts and theories of the subject matter; the student is also ignorant of the principles that govern thought about the subject matter. He [or she] does not know what the problems of the field are, ... what approaches to take to solve a field's problems; and ... how to identify a reasonable solution to a problem. (p 41)

Gradually, however, through a process of inquiry and personal experimentation, the learner comes to recognize the boundaries of the subject or skill, and to internalize the 'rules' or 'codes' that inhere within it. This involves acquiring the basic 'vocabulary' of concepts in the subject being learned and, since each subject has its own rules of discourse, a person cannot properly be said to have learned a subject until he or she is familiar, at least at some minimal level, with the rules of that domain.

In short, nearly always, when we speak or write about student autonomy, a degree of expertise or subject-matter competence is also implied. We do not simply want people who can find resources for themselves, manage their time appropriately or set learning goals, but rather we want learners who know and understand enough to be able to distinguish plausible from implausible knowledge claims or convincing from unconvincing evidence. Thus it seems that autonomy has, in addition to its situational component, an epistemological or knowledge-based component as well.

In this chapter, three major notions with respect to the attainment of such subject-matter autonomy will be advanced. First, the attainment of independence with respect to a particular subject is a developmental phenomenon. As people move through various phases in a learning endeavour, their ability to function independently (as Brookfield (1984) puts it, 'to call into question the pronouncements of experts') increases.

Secondly, at the heart of growing independence as a learner is the development of personal 'frames of reference' or 'anticipatory schemes' (D. Kuhn, 1981). It is asserted that each learner builds up, for himself or herself, a 'mental map' of the subject matter being learned, and that one indication of autonomy is when a learner is able to offer, on the basis of such anticipatory schemes, coherent, plausible and internally consistent explanations concerning the subject which is being learned.

Thirdly, epistemological independence is highly content-specific. A learner who is very competent, experienced and knowledgeable in one domain may be a complete novice in another area, and must accordingly function dependently, at least at first. Contrary to the assertions of some, the attainment of autonomy in learning is not a universal, content-free accomplishment.

In this chapter, I will draw on two distinct bodies of literature: that which concerns the experience of 'self-directed learners' or autodidacts, and that which bears on learning in more formally structured educational contexts.

Knowledge and learning

Before I go on, it is necessary to make some preliminary observations about two factors: the nature of knowledge and the processes of learning. The study of the origin, nature, methods and limits of human knowledge (epistemology) is a complex branch of philosophy, and clearly it is beyond the limits of this chapter to deal adequately with such a broad subject. Accordingly, what follows is necessarily much abbreviated and somewhat oversimplified.

Until relatively recently, 'knowledge, not only in common usage, but also in most of the current psychological and philosophical literature, has always tacitly been assumed to be knowledge of an existing world. That is to say, what we know is assumed to be an aspect of an independent reality, a reality that exists by itself and in itself ...' (von Glasersfeld and Smock, 1974, p xiv). This 'objectivist' or 'naive realist' view of knowledge has been very influential in shaping conceptions of teaching and learning, because it implies that there is one objective reality to which learners should be introduced. It has also influenced many approaches to research, where it has been considered the purpose of the researcher to discover and represent this objective reality as faithfully as possible (Koetting, 1984; Merriam and Simpson, 1984; Soltis, 1984).

An alternative perspective – constructivism – differs significantly from this view of knowledge as deriving from a process of copying or replicating (von Glasersfeld, 1974, p 7). While not denying the existence of a reality that exists outside the actors involved:

cognitive structures

of learning of

the learning

> it is fundamental to the constructivists' view that the environment can never be directly known, but that conception determines perception. We know reality only by acting on it. This means that knowledge is neither a copy nor a mirror of reality, but the forms and content of knowledge are constructed by the one who experiences it. The active interaction between the individual and the environment is mediated by the cognitive structures of the individual. What we learn in interaction with the environment is dependent upon our own structuring of those experiences. Thus, according to this view, people do not merely respond to the environment, they construe it ... (Nystedt and Magnusson, 1982, p 34)

Within this constructivist point of view, and for the purpose of this chapter, I will distinguish between 'private knowledge' and 'public knowledge'. It has been argued that, in the final analysis, all knowledge is private – all understandings are wrought on the anvil of personal experience – and thus the transmission of knowledge in the conventional sense is impossible: 'Cognitive structures are never passed ready-made from a teacher to a pupil ... because cognitive structures (ie knowledge) must under all circumstances be built up by the learner' (von Glasersfeld and Smock, 1974, p xvi).

Not surprisingly, this extreme or 'radical subjectivist' position has been extensively criticized as failing to account for the socially constructed nature of knowledge and the mediating influence of social artifacts such as language and culture. Nevertheless, there are certainly many learning outcomes – some deliberate and others incidental and unanticipated – which are purely personal. Such learning outcomes include the insights which people gain into themselves as learners; how they prefer to learn new material; their motives; their level of tolerance for ambiguity; and how they interact with other people. They also include a whole range of insights and understandings which are tacit and highly situation-specific, and which accordingly are not as accessible to public scrutiny and review as learning of conventional discipline-based knowledge (Elbaz, 1983; Erickson, 1987; Kelly, 1955; Polanyi, 1967; Schön, 1983, 1987).

In this chapter, however, I do not intend to deal with such private knowledge, either in the form of self-learning or of 'personal practical' knowledge, because (at least in this regard) learners can already be assumed to be autonomous. Instead, I intend to examine how learners gain autonomy when dealing with propositional knowledge, which is often codified and 'discipline-based', where the rules are public, and where the autodidact's learning can be publicly tested and acknowledged.

More often than not, the autodidact must accept and acknowledge the existence of norms or standards against which to judge, and on which to base his or her learning. Chené (1983) has observed:

> Whether the learners are currently in relation to a teacher or not, the mediation of another person is necessary for them to assert the value of what they are aware of or of what they know ...
>
> Similarly, skill performance is evaluated according to a standard which, at least at the beginning of the learning process, is outside the self. Embroidering, using a

computer, meditating or jogging, to be recognized as such, have to conform to a set of criteria which have been communicated by somebody else, or taken from somebody else ...

Epistemologically, the relation to others is fundamental to knowledge and the psychological independence from the teacher conceals the problem of the norm in learning. In fact, the teacher cannot disappear without reappearing in another form, since learners have to test their knowledge against somebody else. (p 43, emphasis added)

Thus, as Chené points out, it is not possible for a learner ever to be fully autonomous with respect to propositional knowledge. However, given this general proviso, it still makes sense to speak and write of people becoming sufficiently familiar with the subject of their study that they can judge between expert opinions and perhaps, in some situations, even contribute to boundary- or standard-setting for the field (Brookfield, 1981; Gross and Gross, 1983; T.S. Kuhn, 1970). As Quinton (1971, p 214) writes, 'Cognitive autonomy is achieved when the capacity for the criticism of authorities and of personally-formed beliefs ... has become an operative skill ...'.

This leads me to the second of my preliminary concerns, namely the learner's approach to learning tasks, and the influence that this has on learning outcomes.

If asked, most teachers (and especially university teachers) would state that their aim is to develop in their learners an analytical disposition along with certain skills of critical thinking: 'A questioning critical attitude is one of the hallmarks of higher education' (Furedy and Furedy, 1985, p 51). Lamentably, however, research has shown, more often than not, that university studies result in 'conformity' rather than critical thinking (Entwistle and Percy, 1974), that students seek out 'cues' as to what is required of them (Miller and Parlett, 1974), and that they make 'situational adjustments' accordingly (Becker *et al*, 1968; Ramsden *et al*, 1987).

Central to the task of developing a critical stance with respect to the subject-matter being learned is the approach adopted by the learner. Research undertaken at the University of Gothenburg in the 1970s gave rise to the now-famous distinction between surface- and deep-level learning which was discussed in Chapter 1. In the original research, university students were asked to read lengthy passages from academic texts, and were then asked two sets of questions: about the content of what they had read, and about their approach or how they read it. Ramsden (1985) explains:

In the surface approach ..., the focus of the student's attention is on the words of the text itself. The student is concerned with reproducing the signs of learning. In the deep approach, the student focuses on the meaning of the text – what is signified by it. Perhaps the simplest way to think of what an approach to learning consists of is to see it in two parts – the student's intention (to understand or to reproduce) and the student's learning process (organising and integrating, or simply memorising, the content of what is being studied). (p 54)

Since this original work (Marton and Säljö, 1976a; Svensson, 1976), it has been found that the surface/deep distinction applies to all sorts of learning situations and not simply to learning from text (Biggs, 1979, 1987, Entwistle and Ramsden, 1983; Häyrynen, 1980; Marton *et al*, 1984; Ramsden, 1985). The distinction is particularly vital here, because a learner could not be considered to be truly autonomous if his or her learning were restricted to surface-level approaches but only if she or he had engaged in deep-level learning.

In addition to highlighting the distinction between surface-and deep-level (or transformational) learning, the work of the Gothenburg group also served to emphasize the fact that different learners represent their understandings in different ways, and that, accordingly, learning outcomes cannot be judged solely in terms of *quantity*, but rather in terms of their *quality* (Säljö, 1982). Traditionally in research into learning, there has been an emphasis on *how much* is learned; tests have been set up to measure, in differing situations, the sum value that a subject or group of subjects obtains on a criterion test of knowledge. 'There is thus, basically, a definition of learning which is founded on a quantitative or atomistic conception of knowledge and learning' (Säljö, 1975, p 14). However, 'non-verbatim' (Säljö, 1975) or 'meaningful' (Novak and Gowin, 1984) learning refers to *what is learned*, rather than *how much*. There are assumed to be qualitative differences in the interpretation which each learner places on any item of information or experience, whether presented in a text, a lecture, a laboratory or some other learning encounter. New learning is incorporated into the learner's total 'web of belief' (Quine and Ullian, 1978).

The result of this is, ironically, that a person who has really 'learnt' some substantive content may have internalized it and integrated it to such an extent and in such a way that he or she is totally unable to identify and display it as a discrete unit of learning. Clearly this has important implications for evaluation. More vital for the present purpose, however, is that the ability to specify whether or not a person has achieved autonomy in some subject area presupposes the ability to identify the 'level' of their learning accomplishment. This, however, is not always easy:

> In some discipline-based domains such as chess or aviation, the different levels of mastery and the criteria for their attainment are clearly and explicitly established (eg Expert or Master level play in chess). For other domains (such as medicine, carpentry or political leadership) the levels of achievement are less clearly defined (Feldman, 1980, p 10).

The development of subject-matter autonomy

Although it might be difficult to judge the 'level' of a person's learning, because of the idiosyncratic ways in which people represent their understandings, one feature does appear clear. Attaining autonomy with respect to some particular subject is not an instantaneous process, but one that involves some cumulative, or indeed developmental, aspects.

Many researchers into autonomous learning have identified the phenomenon of learners' growing independence with respect to the subject of their study. For instance, Brown (1983) in her 'Confessions of an autodidact' gives a glimpse of how feelings of inadequacy, lack of confidence, or even shame, can be turned into pride, enthusiasm and determination as the autodidact encounters success in his or her project. Brookfield (1984) writes of the learning experience of self-taught experts who develop what he calls 'critical confidence'; that is, 'the growing belief that one's knowledge was such that one could call into question the pronouncements of experts in the learner's field of interest' (p 56). In the report of his study, Brookfield (1981) gives a number of illustrative quotes which reveal the feelings and attitudes of learners who know their subject:

> The world's top ichthyologist is H.A. I don't keep his books any more, because I disagree with a lot of his theories on tropical fish keeping. I didn't at first. I don't suppose I read anything else but A., and another American, W. But after a few years, you start to realise that their idea of fish-keeping clashes with your own. Anybody who's a thinking person, anyway. (Self-taught expert on tropical fish)
>
> I think I've developed my own philosophy. I'm able to assess other people's philosophy from a definite standpoint. I've read a few people's philosophies and so assessed them. (Self-taught expert on Philosophy)
>
> I think I know enough about my subject to be able to spot a lot of mistakes in the books I read. When I buy a new book, I find I'm making alterations all the time, while I'm reading it. Things I know to be wrong are printed in there. If you look at any new books of mine, you'll find the margins are full of comments I've made about it. (Self-taught expert on railway management and modelling) (p 23)

How is that these people, who at one time knew little or nothing about the field which they now claim as their own, manage not only to acquire the subject matter, but to go beyond conventional wisdom, to achieve expertise themselves? What are the steps or stages which a learner goes through in attaining proficiency in a new subject area? One person who has addressed this issue is Feldman who, in his book *Beyond Universals in Cognitive Development* (1980), advances the notion that all learners – even prodigies – must go through certain steps or stages on their way to autonomy.

Feldman studied a number of child prodigies who demonstrated superior talent and capability, and as a result he identified what he terms 'developmental levels and transitions within the variety of discipline-based domains'. In order to test the generalizability of these 'non-universal developmental phenomena', Feldman asked students at university 'to begin a hobby that they have always wanted to learn, but had not had time to try' (p 18).

He goes on to describe the process and its outcome:

> Their learning assignment for the semester is to spend a reasonable amount of time learning how to do something challenging with which they have had little experience. The only constraint is that the hobby they choose has to be sufficiently

difficult that they are unlikely to master it fully in a semester's time. They are instructed to reflect upon the experience in a journal and try to relate their experience to developmental theory ...

Amazingly, almost all of the students thus far have been able to conceptualize their 'metahobby' projects in terms of developmental levels and developmental transitions which seem plausible and natural. The metahobbies have ranged widely – belly-dancing, ethnic cooking, sculpture, skiing, autobody work, calligraphy, radio broadcasting, to name only a few. The range is remarkable, but the common threads are, from our point of view, even more impressive. (p 18)

Through these independent learning endeavours, Feldman has attempted to study the processes whereby an independent learner 'gets on top of' or masters a subject. There is reason to suppose, on the basis of these findings, that the learner's attainment of autonomy with respect to any particular subject matter or content is likely to pass through distinct stages – slower or faster for each individual. Feldman calls this a 'non-universal' development because, although it happens in an invariant sequence and involves the hierarchical integration of ideas, it is not universal (ie not everyone learns it) and it does not happen spontaneously.

This is a valuable insight for two reasons. First, the fact of its cumulative nature implies that instruction (or even lack of instruction) cannot materially alter the necessity to go through certain stages of understanding (or perhaps even misunderstanding). The most it can hope to achieve is to 'speed up' the progression through what appears to be an invariant sequence. Secondly, the fact that its accomplishment is not universal, and hence requires at least some special conditions for its attainment, emphasizes the 'complementarity between a field of endeavor and a set of individual predispositions or talents' (Feldman, 1980, p 19).

A second important finding emerges from Feldman's work, for in discussing the students' responses to their learning projects he goes on to add:

There is a real sense that the students' analyses are not simply a relabeling of experience. The notion of developmental levels and transitions within the variety of discipline-based domains selected seems to make a profound difference to these students *as they reflect on their experiences* ... (p 18)

The notion that epistemological autonomy depends, at least in part, on reflecting on one's individual structures of meaning, as well as on the underlying structure of knowledge, is an intriguing one. It has been discussed elsewhere in relation to reflection in learning (Candy *et al* 1985), and is also foundational to aspects of deep-level learning discussed earlier in this chapter.

Thus far, I have talked about the likely existence of steps or stages in the development of autonomy, but what exactly are they? Several researchers have explored adult learning of a second or subsequent language in an attempt to understand this process (Abe *et al*, 1975; Curran, 1976; Henner-Stanchina, 1976; Nolan, 1981). Curran (1976), for instance, postulates that in all learning situations – formal and non-formal – adult learners struggle to maintain a sense of autonomy, even when the subject matter is unfamiliar, or the teaching method is a dependent one. On the basis of extended observations of second-language learners in various settings, he hypothesized that learners move through a five-stage process with respect to any particular content (see Figure 1).

I	II	III	IV	V
Total dependency	Learner attempts to move ahead independently	Learner functions independently in the language	Learner becomes open to correction	Positive self-concept; fully autonomous learning
Embryonic Stage	*Self-assertion Stage*	*Separation or Birth Stage*	*Reversal Stage*	*'Adult' Stage*

Figure 1 *The development of autonomy in adult second-language learning* (Curran, 1976, p 105)

Nolan (1981) set out to test the generalizability of Curran's scheme. Distinguishing learners in the beginning phase of their language learning project from those in an advanced stage, he asked learners to describe their perceptions and feelings about themselves as second-language learners at each phase. In the beginning:

> they described themselves as learners in both positive and negative terms. They described themselves as frustrated, childish, insecure, foolish, embarrassed, belittled, humiliated. They also described themselves as enthusiastic, confident, comfortable ...
> ...the first stage or period was described in cognitive terms as one of intense work – sheer drudgery as one subject put it – in which the learner, although highly motivated, frequently felt frustrated and foolish in the learning situation ... (1981, p 144)

In terms of the distinction made earlier in this chapter, these learners would be described as situationally autonomous (ie free of direction by others), but not yet epistemologically autonomous. It is interesting that those with higher levels of formal education, far from being at an advantage, reported themselves as experiencing the most frustration and loss of self-esteem at this stage:

> A subject who holds a Ph.D. degree described the early stages of his second-language learning experience as 'an assault on his self-esteem'. A Roman Catholic clergyman reported his early learning period as a torturous time when he felt like 'a child or an idiot'. (Nolan, 1981, p 145)

Thus, it appears that previous educational attainment may not necessarily be an advantage, and may even become an impediment, in terms of emotional adjustment to the learning situation. Fortunately, however, these feelings of helplessness and despair did not persist, as Nolan (1981) again explains:

> There then seemed to occur a breakthrough period reported most often by those whose learning had occurred in an intense, monolingual setting. This breakthrough experience accompanied the adult learner's arrival at a threshold level of linguistic competency, where the learner found it relatively easy to communicate. As one ex-Peace Corps Volunteer put it, 'It is the sudden realization that you are keeping up with the conversation without trying.' Others described it as a liberating moment ... Not all subjects interviewed reported this experience. Those who did, [however], described it as a very dramatic event which they had no trouble remembering ... (p 144)

This quote serves to emphasize the fact that attainment of subject-matter autonomy is, Feldman states, 'non-universal'. At the same time, it raises the question of whether there is any generic or trans-situational component which would allow some people to develop autonomy while others do not. It may be argued that the ability to become autonomous with respect to one domain or area occurs within a broader developmental framework, and that it is only possible for learners to achieve full independence when they come to view knowledge in relative rather than absolute terms. Accordingly, one direction for research into autonomy in learning would be to ascertain learners' views of knowledge.

As early as 1970, Perry and his associates at Harvard identified a developmental continuum, with respect to the relativity of knowledge, along which university students were found to be arrayed (see also Chapter 1). In introducing his full nine-stage model of intellectual development in the college years, he paints the following vignettes about three different types of students:

> Student A has always taken it for granted that knowledge consists of correct answers, that there is one right answer per problem, and that teachers explain these answers for students to learn. He therefore listens for the lecturer to state which theory to learn.
>
> Student B makes the same general assumptions, but with an elaboration to the effect that teachers sometimes present problems and procedures, rather than answers, 'so that we can learn to find the right answer on our own'. He therefore perceives the lecture as a kind of guessing game in which he is to 'figure out' which theory is correct, a game that is fair enough if the lecturer does not carry it so far as to hide things too obscurely.
>
> Student C assumes that an answer can be called 'right' only in the light of its context, and that contexts or 'frames of reference' differ ... Although he feels a little uneasy in such a kaleidoscopic world, he nonetheless supposes that the lecturer may be about to present three legitimate theories which can be examined for their internal coherence, their scope, their fit with various data, their predictive power, etc. (pp 1-2)

These three hypothetical students represent different positions in Perry's scheme of intellectual development. Clearly, if they were each engaged in autonomous learning, they would bring to bear different criteria to judge the adequacy of their own learning accomplishments. But educators commonly do set learners independent tasks, with little conscious thought for the developmental stage each has reached. Even at advanced graduate level, there is no guarantee that learners will have attained the ninth and ultimate stage of commitment to a personal view, alongside a tolerance for alternative perspectives (Perry, 1970; Phillips, 1981).

Although Perry's developmental continuum was derived from a study of 'students' (and a rarefied and privileged group of students at that), he points to its wider applicability:

> Can this scheme be considered a relatively enduring outline of major vicissitudes in human experience from adolescence into adulthood in a pluralistic culture? Does it help us to understand the way that 'modern man' [or woman] finds to address his [her] predicament in a relativistic world? (Perry, 1970, p x)

Cameron (1983), for her part, argues that adults generally are spread out along such a developmental spectrum and, since self-direction in learning is a widespread phenomenon, it is also reasonable to suppose that autodidacts would exhibit the same range of development with respect to their beliefs about knowledge. Thus, some self-teachers would be seeking the one 'right' or 'true' answer, and others would be seeking a better understanding of the issues involved, and possible alternative explanations or perspectives. Overall, it is difficult to conceive of learners becoming autonomous with respect to subject matter, if they had not progressed far along some general continuum of epistemological sophistication such as that offered by Perry.

Anticipatory schemes and autonomy in learning

What exactly is developed as people move through these various stages with respect to their subject? Clearly, it is more than a collection of fragmentary 'facts', such as those acquired through rote learning. Instead, it is some sort of understanding of the underlying principles, or the structure of knowledge in the domain concerned. It is this which allows people, in Bruner's (1957) evocative phrase, to 'go beyond the information given', and thereby to assert their autonomy. Although there has been relatively little research into the mechanism whereby people attain autonomy with respect to learning tasks, a promising direction is suggested by several reports which, despite the fact that they approach the question from different points of view, do tend to corroborate each other.

In conventional teaching/learning situations, whether face to face or at a distance, learners are customarily presented with pre-packaged ideas. More often than not, the ideas are presented in a sequence which seems logical to the trainer or instructor, and the learner has to accommodate to the conventions of the field of study in order to master it. The learner usually does not have to 'grapple' with the essence of the subject, and accordingly is often pushed in the direction of reproductive rather than deep level or transformational learning (Ramsden, 1985, pp 58-59).

However, if grappling with the complexities of a subject is an important part of deep-level or transformational learning, then it may be that one advantage which the independent has over the more dependent learner is the experience of 'sorting out' relevant from extraneous concepts and ideas. Eraut *et al* (1975), reporting on a course at Sussex University, comment on their initial disappointment when students failed to grasp the significance of certain basic economic concepts in a teaching package over which they had laboured. They write:

> Whilst students appeared to get very little out of the Demand Theory Package, the members of faculty who prepared it felt that they had learnt a lot from having to sort out their ideas: and it occurred to them that the 'sorting out' process might be more important than the subsequent learning. Perhaps the students could also be involved in formulating the problems, clarifying the assumptions about the situation to be studied, choosing the analytic techniques, and disentangling value judgements and empirical judgements. (p 24)

Interestingly, Farnes (1975) makes almost the same comment about the experience of course teams at the Open University:

> In the Open University, it seems paradoxical to me that the people who experience exciting and immensely demanding learning tasks are the course teams; they are acquiring and organizing knowledge, evaluating and selecting materials, designing and presenting programmes and activities. The student receives what appears to be a polished product from this process; he has to learn from material that has been agonised over by authors, course team members and many others ...
>
> If it is in the course teams that there are genuine learning experiences, should we not allow the student to participate in these learning experiences by delegating more of the job to him? ... A major effort is necessary to get students to change their passive approach to learning and to encourage them to take responsibility. (p 3)

As far as I have been able to determine, only one study of autodidacts has identified this dimension as important to the attainment of autonomy. In their study of major recurrent tasks in self-teaching, Danis and Tremblay (1985) identified 26 tasks which they found to be common to the experience of many adult self-teachers. These were grouped into five major dimensions, namely:

> *Management of the learning process*: tasks related to the planning, conducting and evaluating of the learning activities;
> *Acquisition of knowledge or skills*: tasks related to the learning of specific contents;
> *Acquisition of resources*: tasks related to the locating of the various human resources

(peers, experts, friends, parents, etc.) and material resources (books, official documents, films, pamphlets, etc.);

Use of didactic abilities: tasks related to self- instruction; and

Use of support: tasks related to getting and maintaining a satisfying emotional support with regard to the learning behaviour (Danis and Tremblay, 1985, p 286).

One function within the cluster labelled 'Use of didactic abilities' is 'Sorting out contradictory information or differing ways of proceeding' (p 291). This was rated, by learners, as one of the most frequently recurring as well as one of the most difficult tasks they have to perform (p 297). What is needed to accomplish this task of 'sorting out'?

Presumably, active involvement would be one component: it seems unlikely that 'sorting out' would be compatible with a passive, dependent mode of learning. In addition, there would need to be the application of some generic intellectual skills such as critical thinking or assumption finding. However, for the most part, the skills of learning any particular knowledge are not independent of that knowledge and cannot be mastered in a content-free course on 'study skills'. Central to the process of 'sorting out' must be the development of some categories or criteria with respect to that body of knowledge itself. In a paper entitled 'The role of self-directed activity in cognitive development', D. Kuhn (1981) reports on an experiment designed to focus on the role of 'sorting out' in the development of reasoning strategies:

> Our intent was to examine critically this alleged role by designing two identical intervention situations with the exception that in one, subjects selected the particular information-seeking activities they would engage in, while in the other, they did not. This was accomplished by pairing each experimental subject with a yoked control subject, who engaged in exactly the same activities as had been chosen by his or her experimental partner. Thus, each subject of the pair was 'active', each carried out an identical set of activities and hence was exposed to identical information stemming from those activities, but only the experimental subject selected the activities to engage in. (p 354)

Subjects were exposed to a series of problem-solving tasks of increasing complexity, and the experimenters were interested in: '(1) a comparison of the highest problem in the intervention sequence mastered by subjects in the two conditions; and (2) a comparison of the post-test performance of the subjects in the two conditions, as well as the simple control condition' (p 355).

All the subjects improved their problem-solving capacities, which substantiated earlier findings that people generally make 'significant progress in the construction of new thinking strategies when they are simply exposed to a rich problem-solving environment over a period of months' (p 356). However, the experimental subjects made noticeably greater progress than their yoked controls, and Kuhn (1981) offers the following explanation:

> The experience of the experimental subjects in the present study differed from that of their yoked controls in that [they] were required to 'direct' their own activity in the sense of planning the specific activities they would carry out. Both groups were physically active (in manipulating the materials) to an equal extent, ... [but] the critical difference, in our view, is rather that the experimental subjects were encouraged to develop an anticipatory scheme with respect to possible experimental outcomes, simply because of the fact that they had to design the set of experiments that would yield one of these outcomes ... It is our hypothesis that experimental subjects, because of these anticipatory schemes, were better able to 'make use of' in the cognitive sense – in other words assimilate into a theoretical framework – the data yielded by the experiments, and thus they gained more from the experience. (p 357)

Although the term 'anticipatory scheme' itself may be novel, the notion that learners develop cognitive schemes with respect to subjects they are learning is not new. Its antecedents, at least in the field of cognitive psychology, stretch back as far as Spearman's (1923) treatise on *The Nature of Intelligence and Principles of Cognition*. In more recent years, a similar notion may be found in sources as diverse as Ausubel (1968), Bruner (1957), Crockett (1965), Erickson (1987), Kelly (1955), Lindsay and Norman (1977), Piaget (1972), Quine and Ullian (1978), Rumelhart (1977), Thomas and Harri-Augstein (1985), and von Glasersfeld (1984).

In each case, it is envisaged that learners portray their understandings in the form of a mental representation (or 'cognitive map') of the subject of their inquiries. It is generally held that, within the overall context of a person's cognitive map, they will have various schemas to represent various domains of knowledge. According to von Glasersfeld (1984), the mental activity of bringing two or more of these schemes into relation with one another for the purpose of searching for similarities and differences (Erickson, 1987; Kelly, 1955) lies at the very heart of constructivist accounts of learning. Thus, the development and refinement of the learner's cognitive map occurs through a constant process of interaction between hierarchic integration (Crockett, 1965) or subsumption (Ausubel, 1968) on the one hand, and cognitive differentiation (Crockett, 1965) or discrimination (Ausubel, 1968) on the other, and, as Crockett observes:

> This increase in differentiation and hierarchic integration is found not only in development from childhood to adulthood, but also in the development of new knowledge in a mature individual; thus, *an adult being exposed to a content area that was initially foreign to him would proceed through the same stages in development as the maturing child*, though the process would probably be completed more rapidly than in the child. (pp 49-50, emphasis added)

What Kuhn's concept of 'anticipatory schemes' adds to this picture is the notion of anticipation. Learners are not mere passive observers in the learning situation, but active construers, and their constructions lead them to expect certain outcomes. In elaborating the relevance and significance of Kelly's

Psychology of Personal Constructs (1955) for learning, Beck (1979) emphasizes that people's understandings about the world (or some specific aspect of it) lead them to have certain expectations. They then 'invest themselves' or commit themselves to these expectations. The way in which things actually turn out may, Beck argues, either confirm or disconfirm the expectation, but in either case, it offers the opportunity to elaborate or modify the learner's existing set of constucts about that domain.

This notion of anticipation is vital to an understanding of what it means to be autonomous with regard to a subject. The true neophyte's anticipations will either be inaccurate or incomplete, whereas the person who has at least mastered the essence of his or her subject should be able to make more defensible and more complete predictions about it and, if events prove them wrong, to make better sense of the disconfirming evidence.

The content-specific nature of subject-matter autonomy

Intuitively, it seems likely that autonomy would manifest itself across a range of learning situations. This is certainly implicit in many formulations of independent learning which assert that autonomy is a 'developable capacity'. However, although a person may have an overall predisposition towards acting autonomously in the sense of managing time, setting goals, finding resources and critically evaluating ideas and events, it is clear that, with respect to any given domain of learning, he or she may not have mastered 'the logic with which bodies of beliefs are criticized and developed; and the methodology which specifies the degree of support given to theory by observation' (Quinton, 1971, p 208). In other words, he or she may not be autonomous with respect to the subject being learned. Strong (1977) states:

> It is dangerous to assume that, because someone has exhibited an ability to learn autonomously, the same situation will apply with regard to an area completely different to all previous learning. It was noted of several people in this study that whilst their basic ability to plan and to organise their learning, was well established, having been involved in, say, pure science, that when tackling a practical DIY project, there was a considerable need for assistance ... (p 139)

This 'need for assistance' does not necessarily represent some pathological inadequacy on the part of the learner. On the contrary, it may even be evidence of a higher-order form of autonomy which allows him or her 'to choose between dependence and independence as he [or she] perceives the need' (Nuffield Foundation, 1975).

In addition to such conscious and deliberate surrendering of independence in pursuit of learning, there are many other factors at work which might conspire to limit a learner's autonomy. These include: the learner's pre-existing concepts and beliefs concerning the domain being studied; past educational experiences which might, as Häyrynen (1980) comments, have effectively denied the learner access to deeper levels of meaning about what counts as knowledge in that culture (Bernard and Papagiannis, 1983; Bernstein, 1977; Stalker-Costin, 1986); individual beliefs or 'personal learning myths' (Thomas and Harri-Augstein, 1985) which the learner may have internalized concerning his or her ability to learn certain subjects; the learner's intentions and purposes in the learning situation; how the learner construes salient environmental and contextual factors which influence the decision about learning strategies; as well as other factors already alluded to such as the learner's conceptions of 'learning' and of 'knowledge'.

All of these dimensions interact with one another in complex ways and, since this combination will vary from situation to situation, a learner's autonomy might be expected, likewise, to vary from one context to another. Combined with this is the point already made that the internal structures of various domains of knowledge differ markedly from one another. Overall, although there may well exist a generic or trans-situational sort of autonomy in learning, it seems to me that, for all practical purposes, each situation should be treated on its own merits, and it comes as no surprise to find that a learner may be judged or thought of as 'independent' or autonomous by his or her peers or instructors in one domain, yet as lacking in autonomy with respect to some other field of study.

Conclusion

The move towards developing student autonomy has gathered momentum in recent years. Ignited by the increasingly rapid pace of social and technological change, and fuelled by a range of ideological convictions about self-responsibility in learning, the fire of increased learner autonomy has spread to all sectors of education – primary, secondary, higher and adult – formal and non-formal alike. This development has been accompanied by a veritable explosion in the literature; wherever we look there are books, journal articles, research reports and conference papers reporting on experimental programmes or exhorting practitioners to assist, somehow, in the development of self-directing learners.

Despite the many success stories reported in the literature, however, I cannot help feeling that many people have overlooked the central importance of knowledge, and of how our conceptions of knowledge affect educational interventions. In this chapter, I have based my argument on two basic premisses. The first is that knowledge – even public, discipline-based knowledge – is socially constructed and that accordingly learning is a social process. Autonomy in the sense of totally independent thought and action is fundamentally irreconcilable with the notion of mastering a recognized body of knowledge: in a sense, autonomous learning is a contradition in terms!

The second basic premiss is that learners are active makers of meaning: not simpy that they are, or should be, active in the learning situation, but that learning itself is an active process of constructing and transforming personal meanings. The outcomes of any learning endeavour should be gauged in qualitative rather than quantitative terms, and learners should, in Schön's (1983) memorable phrase, be 'given reason'.

74

Following from these basic convictions, I have argued three main things. The first is that the truly autonomous learner, at least in the sense which most educators would endorse, is the one who engages in deep-level learning of a subject, seeking to go beyond the overt or surface message to the underlying meaning of the topic or domain. Not everyone will be able to function at this level, or would want to do so. The achievement of subject-matter autonomy is developmental and cumulative, and learners need to have the right combination of personal interests and environmental circumstances for such deep-level understandings to emerge.

Secondly, I have stressed the importance of 'sorting out' as critical to the attainment of subject-matter autonomy. By this, I mean the development of 'anticipatory schemes' which subsume what the learner already knows about the subject, and which allow him or her to make 'intelligent guesses' about the items of information which are missing. In my view, an autonomous learner is one who knows enough to be able to distinguish defensible from indefensible knowledge claims in the area of his or her expertise.

Thirdly, I have emphasized the highly situation-specific, or content-dependent nature of subject-matter autonomy. The positivist fallacy, as I see it, assumes that behaviour and competence can be 'hacked off' from their environment without doing violence to their integrity. I believe, on the contrary, that understandings are contextual and relative, and that the ability to function independently in one domain cannot necessarily be transplanted to another subject area.

In conclusion, I would like to offer some observations about the justifications for autonomy in learning. As Boud points out in Chapter 1, autonomy is a complex and multifaceted concept. In education (particularly of adults), learner autonomy is advocated for two reasons: moral and pedagogical. The moral dimension to autonomy assumes that teachers and learners (or experts and novices) 'are equally moral agents, and owe one another the rights and respect due [to] moral agents' (Strike, 1982, p 49). Certainly learners have the right to participate or not, as they see fit. They have, as Strike (1982, p. 49) points out, the right to be listened to and to be taken seriously, to enquire freely, to ask questions, to have open access to information, to question and debate the conclusions reached by experts, and generally 'to make what they have been told their own by agreeing or disagreeing with it' (Phillips, 1973, p 140).

The pedagogical justification for learner autonomy is that adults demonstrably learn more, and more effectively, when they are consulted about dimensions such as the pace, sequence, mode of instruction and even the content of what they are studying. But when it comes to learning discipline-based knowledge, 'there is a significant inequality between the student (as novice) and the teacher (as expert) in terms of their current capacity to understand and assess the ideas and arguments of a field' (Strike, 1982, p 49). This inequality between experts and novices – between those who are autonomous with respect to their subject and those who are not – has nothing to do with moral agency, and everything to do with mastery of 'critical standards inherent in the subject itself'. As Phillips

(1973) so eloquently puts it: 'where matters of the intellect are concerned, it is fatal to confuse the statement "I can say something" with "I have something to say" ' (p 139).

Although such an assertion may seem reactionary, until we have dismantled what Lawson (1982) calls the 'apparatus of public forms of knowledge with its associated experts in the various fields', and have created instead a world in which the production, dissemination and evaluation of knowledge are seen as 'a social process involving everyone (Lawson, 1982, p 37), it seems that autonomy of the learner will always have both a different meaning and a different purpose, from the autonomy of the expert.

Acknowledgement

I am indebted to my colleague R.J.S. 'Mac' Macpherson, who cast a critical eye over an earlier version of this chapter. Much of the clarity in the argument is due to his helpful comments; any remaining obscurity is my fault.

Chapter 4

Assessment Revisited

John Heron,
Formerly British Postgraduate Medical Federation, University of London

Rationality and power

The prevailing model for assessing student work in higher education is an authoritarian one. Staff exercise unilateral intellectual authority: they decide what students shall learn, they design the programme of learning, they determine criteria of assessment and make the assessment of the student. The student does not participate in decision-making at all about his learning objectives or his learning programme, nor in setting criteria and applying them in assessment procedures. He is subject to the intellectual authority of an academic elite who have the power to exercise a very high degree of social control on the exercise of his intelligence and on his future social destiny by intellectual grading.

The issue here is a political one; that is, it is to do with the exercise of power. And power is simply to do with who makes decisions about whom. I have power *over* people if I make unilateral decisions to which they are subject. I share power *with* people if I make decisions on a bilateral basis in consultation with them. The idea of having a rational power over another's rationality seems to me to be internally contradictory. Exercise of rationality involves dialogue, discussion, and reciprocity of exchange, in which each party to the dialogue gives reasons for a point of view and has the inalienable right rationally to assent or dissent from the view put forward by the other party. As a rational being I can only consult with others about decisions that affect the exercise and assessment of their own rationality. Their rationality is impugned if I do not honour it as a party to the decision-making process.

Does the student entering higher education have a fully-fledged rational capacity? If he does not, if he is in some sort of pre-rational developmental stage, then of course I can offer the argument *in loco parentis*: it is my job as staff member to make rational decisions on his behalf that will enable him to emerge from a pre-rational to a fully rational stage of development. I cannot consult him because he is not present with a sufficiently developed intelligence to make an adequate contribution to the consultation. But does anyone seriously hold that the average 19-year-old human being entering higher education does not have fully fledged rational capacity? Surely not, since it is the general presupposition of higher education that the student has the intellectual competence to acquire a fully rational grasp of a particular discipline or subject area.

How is it, then, that he is not entitled by the prevailing system to acquire and actively exercise a fully rational grasp of his own learning objectives, of the programme that is relevant to achieve them, of criteria of assessment and the actual process of assessment of his own work? He is seen as rationally competent to grasp the discipline taught by his academic superiors and to respond appropriately to their assessment. Yet, paradoxically, he is not seen as rationally competent to *participate* in determining his own academic destiny, nor in assessing his own competence.

The traditional arguments advanced to justify this state of affairs are something like the following. (i) Academic staff are the culture carriers of our civilization: they sustain and develop the values and intellectual standards of our central bodies of knowledge. (ii) Adequately to grasp and learn to perpetuate these values and standards requires a process of student apprenticeship and initiation in which staff unilaterally model, exemplify and apply to students the values and standards. (iii) Only when thus unilaterally initiated can the student himself eventually become a culture carrier and initiator of future generations of students (Peters, 1966).

This initiation model is hierarchical and authoritarian. It does not deal with the argument that if a student is rationally competent to grasp a major discipline at the adult level, then he is competent *ipso facto* to participate in decisions about the educational process whereby he can grasp it, and in decisions about whether he has grasped it; and that if he is not invited to do these things together, his rationality is thereby impugned – and offered a distorted development. The initiation model is a rationalization of the invalid exercise of intellectual power over other rational beings.

I am *not* arguing that if a student is deemed competent to grasp an adult discipline he should also be deemed competent to decide all on his own the best way of going about grasping it or to decide all on his own that he has adequately grasped it. I am not declaring the redundancy of teachers, of academic guides and mentors. I am arguing that for the young adult, three things go together: the capacity to get to know the content of a discipline, the capacity to know how to get to know it, and the capacity to know that he has got to know it. Or put in other words: the capacity to learn, the capacity to know how to learn, the capacity to know that he has learned. For a well-rounded education, these three facts of intellectual capacity need to be developed together. And they can be developed by a significant amount of self-directed practice, facilitated and guided by, and in collaboration with, teachers. The initiation of students therefore needs to be more reciprocal and consultative, with students not simply learning their subjects but also participating in decisions about how they learn them and in the assessment of their learning.

And as we shall see in a later section, I do not advocate that everything about the educational process is to be a matter of negotiation and consultation between staff and students. If absolutely everything is negotiable, then the negotiator stands for nothing, is not committed to any principles or values, in short, is not really educated. For the mark of an educated person, I believe, is that through study, reflection, dialogue and experience he or she has at any given time a considered commitment to certain values which provide the stable ground from which free discussion and negotiation proceed.

What, then, are further arguments against the current system of unilateral intellectual authority exercised by staff over students? In the following section I will present a radical critique in a somewhat extreme form, and will redress the balance toward the end of the section, while retaining much of the force of the critique.

A radical critique of unilateral control and assessment

Staff unilaterally assess students, some of whom then become staff and unilaterally assess more students, and so on. Where did it all start? However much it may be obscured by a variety of other cultural factors, for any domain of human inquiry there is a source point when its originators flourished through self-directed learning and inquiry and through self and peer assessment. These or their successors at some point become the original unilateral academic assessors and commence their role with a significant threefold act of assessment. They assess and continue to assess themselves and each other as competent in having mastered their branch of knowledge through self-directed inquiry. They assess themselves as competent to assess others. And they assess others as relatively incompetent to be self- and peer-assessing and self-directing in learning and discovery. They thus set up a unilateral assessment and education system from which they necessarily exempted themselves, and in the absence of which one may assume their own vigorous discovery, excitement in learning and originality flourished. This is a phenomenon within the politics of knowledge. Knowledge is always potential power. If I am among the first to establish knowledge in some field, I can use that knowledge to establish a power base in the social order, by discriminating unilaterally for or against others on the grounds of my judgements about their relative competence or incompetence. If I can make others, through their hunger for power, collude with my unjust discrimination toward them (even though it may be exercised in their favour), then I have established a new profession, a body of experts, who sustain their power and perpetuate the injustice through the myth of maintaining excellence. The founding treason is that founders through this professional dominion betray their own origins in self-directed learning, self and peer assessment.

Unilateral control and assessment of students by staff mean that the process of education is at odds with the objective of that process. I believe the objective of the process is the emergence of an educated person: that is, a person who is self-determining – who can set his own learning objectives, devise a rational programme to attain them, set criteria of excellence by which to assess the work he produces, and assess his own work in the light of those criteria – indeed all that we *attribute* to and *hope* for from the ideal academic himself. But the

79

traditional educational process does not prepare the student to acquire any of these self-determining competencies. In each respect, the staff do it for or to the students. An educational process that is so determined by others cannot seriously intend to have as its outcome a person who is truly self-determining.

Authoritarian control and assessment of students breed intellectual and vocational conformity in students. Given a pre-determined syllabus, learning in a way dictated by others, taught by those who make the continuous and final assessment often according to hidden and undisclosed criteria, the average student has an understandable tendency to play safe, to conform his thinking and performance to what he divines to be the expectations of his intellectual masters, to get through his final exams by reproducing what he believes to be staff-approved knowledge and critical judgement.

But there is not only conformity in terms of the intellectual content of the students' work. There is a subtler, more insidious, more intellectually distorting and durable conformity. For the student absorbs the whole authoritarian educational process, and those students who go on to become future staff reproduce the unilateral model with remarkable lack of critical acumen and awareness. It is notorious that academics, who normally would pride themselves on their ability critically to evaluate the assumptions on which a body of theory and practice is based, are so uncritical and unthinking about the educational process which they mediate.

The authoritarian educational model is thus an agent of social control at the higher education end of the spectrum of conditioning procedures to which the person is subjected in our society. It precipitates into the adult world a person whose intellect is developed somewhat in relation to the content of knowledge, but truncated, distorted and oppressed in relation to the politics of knowledge, the process of truly acquiring it. A general social and political attitude of conformity and a relative sense of powerlessness is reinforced by a partial sort of intellectual competence: 'To survive I must go along with the system and divine what is expected of me. I must accept the fact that I am here so that other people can do it for me and to me and tell me whether I have made it or not. And if I subscribe to all this with sufficient intellectual application I may if I am lucky arrive at a point where I can dictate the system that other people have to conform to.'

Unilateral control and assessment of students by staff generates the wrong sort of motivation in students. They tend to become extrinsically motivated to learn and work. The degree is a ticket to status, career, and opportunity in the adult social world; it is designed by others, awarded by others and withheld by others, according to criteria of others. The student's intellectual masters manipulate his motivation without ever involving him as a self-determining being. External rewards and punishments tend to motivate learning rather than intrinsic factors such as authentic interest and involvement in the subject matter, the excitement of inquiry and discovery, the internal commitment to personally considered standards of excellence, self- and peer-determined debate, dialogue and discussion.

80

Such extrinsic motivation to learn can breed intellectual alienation: the student becomes habituated to exercise his intellect in a way that is divorced from his real interests, curiosities and learning needs. The acquisition of knowledge loses the excitement of discovery and becomes the onerous assimilation of a mass of alien and oppressive information. Such alienation during the learning process while acquiring knowledge and skills, can extend after qualification and graduation, into vocational alienation: the person exercises his vocational role in a way that is cut off from his real needs, interests, concerns and feelings, and hence uses the role in his human relations with his clients somewhat defensively and rigidly. There are two extreme variants of this: the professionalization of misfits and the misfit of professionalism. The former occurs when the extrinsic attractions of a profession's power and status seduce into it those whose real interest and abilities lie elsewhere. The latter occurs when the professional blindly and unawarely tries to close the gap between self and role by compulsively and inappropriately 'helping' his clients.

An authoritarian educational system is only able to focus on intellectual and technical competence, on the cultivation of theoretical and applied intellect. Personal development, interpersonal skills, ability to be aware of and work with feelings – all these are excluded from the formal curricular educational process, since an authoritarian system represses – in staff member, in student, and in the relation between them – the kinds of autonomy, reciprocity and mutuality required for the building of such development, skills and ability.

The roots of this situation lie deep in the philosophical past, but a past that is still present with us in a very pervasive way. Our educational system rests on an ancient, hierarchical view of the person. In Aristotelian terms, intellect is that which supremely differentiates man from animals, and the cultivation of this prime differentium, in its purely theoretical form, is that which constitutes the highest virtue. In Platonic terms, intellect rules over the nobler emotions, which under the guidance of intellect rule over the baser passions. This authoritarian, hierarchical role anciently ascribed to intellect is with us still today.

The prevailing norm about feelings, in our educational culture and indeed in our culture at large, is that they are to be controlled. The message is unmistakable, coming over in all kinds of tacit and explicit ways: the intelligent, educated adult is one who knows how to control feelings. But if control is the *only* guiding norm, it can rapidly degenerate into suppression, repression, denial and then blind displacement of feelings. The authoritarian academic projects unawarely his denied feelings on to the students: hence academic intransigence about reform, for if academic control of students is a way of acting out denied feelings within, it will not lightly be given up. Only significant personal development among staff can liberate them from this particular compulsion.

The unilateral model of control and assessment in education is a form of political exploitation, of oppression by professionalism. The academic maintains the myth of superior excellence and educational expertise from which the student is necessarily debarred and which it would be irresponsible and dangerous for the student in any degree to practise. Thus the academics, by the

WELSH COLLEGE OF MUSIC & DRAMA LIBRARY

control and assessment system they run, condition students to see themselves as inadequate and dependent with respect to all major decisions about the educational process (learning objectives, programme design, assessment). So staff maintain their power as a privileged elite to determine unilaterally the future social destinies of their dependent students. Psychodynamically, the academics deal unawarely with their own distressed dependency needs by conditioning students to be dependent on them. The result is that students are oppressed and manipulated by educationally extrinsic factors, by being assessed and graded – all in the name of 'higher' education.

Finally, of course, unilateral assessment methods are notoriously unreliable. Different examiners marking the same scripts show significant variability; the same examiner may vary considerably the stringency with which he marks on one occasion compared to another. All this adds up to a very palpable injustice – so long as the assessment is unilateral. The only way to avoid such injustice is to make the student party to the assessment procedure, and hence party to the general unreliability. I cannot cry injustice when I have been a free negotiating participant in the assessment of my work

The whole of this radical critique as presented above is something of a caricature. It overstates the case. So I will briefly mention some of the main considerations which countermand it and present a more balanced view.

Academics do continually engage in a variety of informal and more formal equivalents of self and peer assessment, if not with students, then at any rate amongst themselves: in offering their written work for comment and judgement from their peers, both before and after its presentation or publication. And this at least provides a model for students in their professional work after graduation.

The traditional educational system has produced and continues to produce persons who may be to a greater or lesser degree self-determining. This is not least because, whatever its defects of method, central to its teaching is the importance of rational critical thinking, of assessment of views and of evidence. So the central precepts which it teaches may survive, more or less impaired, the methods by which they are taught.

And the corollary, of course, is that some academic tutors do genuinely seek to elicit in their students sound reasoning, judgement and critical appraisal, and do genuinely rejoice in students who exhibit originality, intellectual competence and independence of judgement.

An increasing though still relatively small number of academics are becoming critical of the assumptions underlying the traditional educational process which they are mediating to students. Staff development and innovation is a growing movement in higher education.

Despite the rigidity of the educational system, both staff and, to a lesser extent, students can become intrinsically motivated and committed to pursue standards of excellence in pursuing their disciplines. And some tutors do exhibit great sensitivity, skill and humanity in dialogue, both intellectual and personal, with their students. Not all academics or professionals use their roles defensively.

The positive account is therefore not inconsiderable. But in my view the general thrust of the radical critique prevails and requires an alternative model of the person, a redistribution of educational power, and a new approach to assessment.

An alternative model of the person

The hierarchical, authoritarian model of intellect-in-charge referred to above has served its historical and cultural purpose. The time is ripe for an alternative, democratic model: that of equal human capacities which mutually support and enhance each other – intellectual capacities for understanding our world and ourselves, affective capacities for caring for and delighting in other persons and ourselves, conative capacities for making real choices about how we want to live, relate to others and shape our world. On this model, intellectual competence, emotional and interpersonal competence and self-determining competence go hand in hand. You cannot properly cultivate any one without at the same time cultivating the other two. Single-stranded development necessarily involves distortion of that strand.

Staff-student collaboration and consultation about the educational process – that is, with respect to objectives, programme design and assessment – require, for all concerned, the exercise of discriminating choice, the cultivation of intellectual grasp, awareness of and skill in managing feelings, and other interpersonal skills. Thus it honours the alternative, democratic model of the person.

The democratic model also generates a more sophisticated set of guiding norms for the management of feeling. It proposes not only conscious control of feelings of all kinds when appropriate, but also spontaneous expression of positive feelings when appropriate; conscious, intentional discharge or abreaction of distress feelings at appropriate times and places and with apppropriate skills; the transmutation of tense emotion through art, meditation, symbolic imagination and related methods.

The ability to work with feelings in this comprehensive and flexible manner is a precondition of political liberation. The interlocking compulsions to oppress and wield power, and to be powerless, dependent and helpless, are rigidities of character structure which each person needs to dissolve in himself by uncovering and dispersing the hidden affect that holds them in place. To exercise power *with* others in collaborative ways requires the ability to be aware of and take charge of feelings – to dismantle tendencies to act out denied feelings through politically oppressive or submissive behaviour. Skills in control, expression, catharsis, and transmutation are the intra-psychic pillars of political release.

The redistribution of educational power

The redistribution of power in educational decision-making is what is at stake: who decides what about whom, with respect to all the many and varied aspects of the educational process. The main parts of the process are well-known to all of us. I enumerate them here as a reminder that there is a very wide canvas on which to experiment with different decision models. (1) Objectives: (i) outcome objectives relating to what knowledge, skills and attitudes students and staff are to acquire from a course; (ii) process objectives relating to what sorts of behaviours and experience are to go on during the course to achieve intended outcomes. (2) The programme: which puts together (i) topics; (ii) teaching and learning methods; (iii) time available; (iv) human resources; (v) physical resources. (3) Assessment: of student performance, continuous, periodically through the course, final at its end. (4) Evaluation: of teaching and of the course as a whole, again both continuous and final. Ancillary to the educational process as such are: the selection of staff and of students; the administrative structures that support it; and the underlying philosophy and principles which it exemplifies.

Elaborating a point already made in the opening section, it is absurd to suppose that everything on this list must be a matter of staff-student negotiation and consultation. It is absurd for two reasons, a strong and a weak one. The strong one stems from the fact that staff are permanent members of the educational institution; students are transient members. If staff have really thought through the matter, there will be some parts of the educational process which will be non-negotiable because they exemplify principles to which staff are committed. These parts define the sort of educational institution that staff are dedicated to realize. It may be that students are to be significantly self-assessing, or self-pacing or whatever else. These parts, stated in the course prospectus, constitute the non-negotiated educational contract to which prospective students are invited to subscribe, and which defines the lesser, negotiable contracts – the way in which decision-making about the educational process is to be shared by staff and students. Of course, any such initial contract need not be totally rigid, but sooner or later the full-time educationalist, *qua* moral being, will stand for principles, values and their concomitant procedures which are *necessary conditions for entering into* collaboration and negotiation with other staff and students. They may change and develop as a function of interaction with past students, but for the prospective student they are a given, which define the culture into which he is entering.

The weak reason is that the transition from authoritarian control to collaborative control needs to be gradual. Conditioning induced by the traditional model is not undone in one term, one course or even one decade. And there is scope for a great deal of variety and experiment in effecting the transition. Thus if we consider the main parts of the educational process – objectives, the programme, assessment, evaluation – then within each of these with their many components, and as between each of these, decision-making can occur according to one of seven basic models

1. Staff decide all (educational process issues)
2. Staff decide some   Staff with students decide some
3. Staff decide some   Staff with students decide some   Students decide some
4. Staff decide some   Students decide some

Contact with past students to evaluate the course.

5.	Staff with students decide some	Students decide some
6.	Staff with students decide all	
7.		Students decide all

On the left are unilateral decisions by staff, on the right unilateral decisions by students, in the middle collaborative decisions. Model 1 is the traditional unilateral control model. Model 7 would make staff redundant or at most resource persons waiting to be called on by students on terms unilaterally determined by students. Model 6, I have already suggested, is the absurd one: if everything is negotiable, then staff do not stand for anything, have nothing on offer. The most comprehensive model is model 3; and within itself it can encompass the widest range of alternatives along a spectrum from staff control to student control (Heron, 1979a).

All this, I am sure, is a necessary precursor to looking at issues of assessment. Assessment is the most political of all the educational processes: it is the area where issues of power are most at stake. If there is no staff-student collaboration on assessment, then staff exert a stranglehold that inhibits the development of collaboration with respect to all other processes. Once varying mixtures of self, peer and collaborative assessment replace unilateral assessment by staff, a completely new educational climate can be created. Self-determination with respect to setting learning objectives and to programme design is not likely to make much headway, in my view, without some measure of self-assessment.

Self and peer assessment

What, then, is assessment for? Traditionally it has had a two-fold purpose. First, to provide the student with knowledge of results about his performance with regard to the content of the course; this is an aid to revising past learning, and to preparing future learning. This purpose is fulfilled by assessment of student work during the course. Secondly, it awards the student a certificate of intellectual competence, theoretical and/or applied, which accredits him in the eyes of the wider community to fulfil this or that social or occupational role. This purpose is fulfilled typically by the final exam. Nowadays continuous assessment often contributes a significant percentage to the final assessment, as well as the final exam – in which case the second purpose pervades the whole course. But the traditional focus in both purposes is entirely on what the student does with the content of the course.

If the student is seen as a self-determining person, and thereby significantly self-assessing, then assessment will include the process of learning as well as work done on the content of learning. Thus if – to whatever degree – I set my own learning objectives, devise my learning programme, set myself and perform appropriate tasks – then I can assess my objectives, the way I have put the programme together, how I have worked, as well as the work I have done. We are therefore immediately presented with the importance of process assessment, as well as content assessment. Assessing *how* I learn and *how* I provide evidence

85

of what I have learned is really more fundamental than assessing *what* I have learned. The shift to self-direction and self-assessment starts to make process more important than content. Procedural competence is more basic than product competence, since the former is a precondition of providing many good products, while the latter is one off – each good product is strictly a witness only to itself.

Next, a self-determining person can only be so in appropriate relations with other self-determining persons. Persons are necessarily persons in relation and in dialogue, where each enhances the identity and self-discovery of the other. On this view, self-assessment is necessarily interwoven with peer assessment. I refine my assessment of myself in the light of feedback from my peers. My judgement of myself is not subordinate to that of my peers. Rather, I use what my peers say to acquire the art of balance between self-denigration and self-inflation. A just self-appraisal requires the wisdom of my peer group.

In a self and peer assessment group each person assesses himself before the group (using common or autonomous criteria – see below), then receives some feedback from members of the group on whatever it is that is being assessed, and also on the self-assessment itself. The process can also occur reciprocally in pairs, but a group of six or eight gives more scope for peer impact. The person receiving peer feedback is invited to use it discriminatingly to refine his original self-assessment. On one model there is no negotiation with peers about a final agreed assessment: the primacy of self-assessment is affirmed, together with the assumption, elegantly borne out in practice, that a rational person has no interest in deluding himself about his own competence and will use the insights of his peers to attain a just self-appraisal. On another model self and peers negotiate until agreement is reached about a final assessment.

Of course to participate effectively in this process requires a measure of affective and interpersonal competence. I must be willing to take risks, to disclose the full range of my self-perceptions both positive and negative, to confront others supportively with negative feedback, to discriminate between authentic peer insights and unaware peer projections, to trust others, and so on. Hence the importance in practice of the alternative, democratic model of the person mentioned earlier, in which intellectual competence, emotional and interpersonal competence, and self-determining competence go hand in hand.

The student *qua* self-determining person, then, engages in a combined self and peer assessment procedure that looks at both the process and the content of learning, but gives more weight to process than content. The purpose is threefold: (i) to raise awareness of, and improve mastery of, the process of learning in all its many aspects; (ii) to raise awareness about the range of, and to improve mastery of, content; and (iii) at some appropriate point along the road to accredit himself or herself in association with the wisdom of his or her peers as competent to offer this or the other service to the wider community.

I have used this self and peer assessment model for one or other of the three purposes mentioned in a variety of continuing education settings, such as co-counselling teacher training courses, and in-service courses for a variety of different professional groups. These courses are run as peer learning communities (Heron, 1974) in which I function as facilitator and participant, but in neither case do I have any special role as staff assessor. My function as facilitator includes, *inter alia*, enabling the group to work through an acceptable self and peer assessment procedure. These courses are obviously not within the aegis of the traditional undergraduate and postgraduate educational bureaucracies: they are not awarded degrees and are not subject to unilateral assessment by staff and external assessors. Hence they have provided a very useful crucible for important innovation and experiment, using an experiential research model (Heron, 1979a, 1981; Rowan, 1981; Rowan and Reason, 1981), in which everyone involved is both student and subject on the one hand, and tutor and educational researcher on the other, thus combining within his own person a fundamental dialogue and a collaborative inquiry, as well as engaging in a collaborative inquiry with his peers.

A fundamental extension of the model takes it into the heart of professional life. Self and peer assessment is in my judgement the central way of maintaining and developing standards of professional practice. A group of professional peers meet to pick out the central procedures of their daily practice, to determine criteria for performing those procedures well, and to devise some form of self-assessment whereby they can sample their own daily work and assess it in the light of the criteria. They then go off and apply the self-assessment format to their daily work; and meet together at a later date to take turns to disclose their self-assessment findings to their peers and receive systematic feedback on the disclosure. Such peer review audit of professional practice has a strong if not exclusive emphasis on process assessment – hence the very great importance of building up skills in such process assessment from the very beginning of professional education and training. I have introduced peer review of this sort to doctors and dentists (Heron, 1979b) and to teachers, researchers, managers and others.

Sometimes I use a truncated version in which the self-assessment is done mentally and retrospectively on past practice, then shared with peers: in this way the whole procedure can be done at one session. The full-blown model can run through many cycles of individual work and self-assessment, peer review, individual work and self-assessment, peer review – and so on. As such it is an educational model, a professional development model and an action or experiential research model in which the procedures of professional practice are developed through action and review and the criteria for assessing them are likewise developed. There is clearly an important future for this approach.

I wish now to mention briefly the four parts of the assessment process itself. First, there is a decision about *what to assess*: whether process or product and then which bit of process or which product. Secondly, there is the all-important phase of deciding *which criteria to use* in the assessment. Thirdly, there is a decision about *how to apply the criteria*, whether individually and serially, whether collectively and simultaneously; whether to weigh the criteria equally or differentially; whether to have pass/fail results only or whether to have a range

87

of qualitative or numerical grades. Fourthly, there is *doing the assessment itself*: applying the criteria and coming out with the result. If what is being assessed is the assessment process itself, then we have a fifth part.

The most critical part other than doing the assessment itself, is deciding which criteria to use. Because of the prevailing authoritarian system, people are not used to criterial thinking. Some staff in traditional insitutions have difficulty: they do not make the criteria which they unilaterally use explicit to themselves and each other, let alone to their students. So an important part of facilitating self and peer assessment groups is consciousness raising about criteria and criterial thinking. I have explored two alternative strategies about criteria with these groups. One is to start with each person generating criteria and then, through sharing and discussion, move on until there is an agreed set of criteria to which everyone subscribes, and which each person subsequently applies in his self-assessment and which all use in the peer feedback. The other strategy is for each person to generate, say, three primary criteria; these are then shared, and each person in his self-assessment uses any three from the total list – he may retain his own and others', or use others' criteria entirely; peer feedback is given in terms of whatever criteria he has used on himself.

The first strategy emphasizes common standards, the second strategy emphasizes autonomous standards, which also have the benefit of the pool of peer wisdom. Which emphasis is appropriate depends on the sort of group, on what is being assessed, and on the purposes of assessment in relation to the wider community. In my judgement, common standards are more appropriate when technical issues are the focus of assessment; whereas autonomous standards are more appropriate when personal and interpersonal issues are the focus. Again, common standards are more appropriate when there is a high level of accountability to the wider community for the provision of technical, expert services; autonomous standards apply more when accountability is primarily to oneself and one's intimates for personal values being realized.

Collaborative assessment

Collaborative assessment I see as an important intermediary stage between traditional unilateral assessment of students by staff, and the sort of self and peer assessment model I have used in continuing education. In collaborative assessment, the student assesses himself in the light of criteria agreed with his tutor, the tutor assesses the student in the light of the same criteria and they then negotiate a final grade, rating or judgement. This model can be introduced and applied quite quickly to students' course work by staff working in the authoritarian system – although it then stands in somewhat glaring contradiction to the model applied in final examination assessment. Still, if course work counts for some percentage of final marks, then the student has had some small say in his own degree award.

Typically, in the current educational climate, collaborative assessment is made on students' work. It could, however, even within the traditional system, be about process issues: thus the assessment could be about how the student plans his time, paces himself over time, uses available resources (library, lectures, seminars, his academic tutor, other students), takes notes, reads books, writes essays, and so on. Indeed it is typical of the restricted educational awareness that widely prevails in higher education that so little attention is paid, relatively, to how students manage their end of the learning process. But it is probably best to start practising collaborative assessment on students' work handed in. There is a weak model and a strong model.

The weak model applies where criteria of assessment are already laid down, made explicit to staff and written out, and where the system does not allow for any current modification of them either by staff or students. In this case the tutor can make the following moves. (1) Inform the students of the criteria and explain that they are non-negotiable and why. Share your own views on both these matters. Agree with students on the most acceptable interpretation of criteria that you and they find problematic or objectionable. (2) If a rating or grading method is laid down for how to apply the criteria, then discuss this with students and seek to reach agreement on the most appropriate way of using this. (3) Invite the student to assess his or her work using the criteria and the agreed method of applying them. He can do this first mentally and then verbally. (4) You then assess the student's work using the criteria and the agreed method. Compare, contrast and discuss the two assessments. (5) Negotiate and agree a final assessment.

The strong model applies where there are no criteria of assessment laid down, and what they are and how they are used is left to staff discretion. There is usually some sort of grading system, so whatever the criteria are, their application has to be fitted into this. But there is space here to launch students into criterial thinking, to encourage them to start thinking about setting themselves standards of excellence by which to assess their own work. In this model stage (1) is different, but stages (2) through (5) are the same as in the previous model. There are also at least two alternative versions of stage (1): (1a) Where students have great difficulty in thinking in terms of criteria, present them with your own list, ask them to discuss each item, to seek clarification on it, to raise arguments for and against it, to propose modifications, deletions or amendments to it, to raise issues about the list as a whole – any items not included that should be included – and so on. Continue until there is general assent. (1b) Where students are better able to think in terms of criteria, invite each one to work out his own list, have the students share their lists and then share yours with them. Collate all the lists, continue discussion and debate until there is general assent to a final composite list.

What are you to do if students insist on criteria that you find totally unacceptable? There are three basic solutions (1) You can set the thing up so that you have final powers of veto. It is important to tell students in advance about this. (2) You can reason with them until they grasp and are persuaded by your arguments about the irrationality of their criteria. (3) You can invite them to use the irrational criteria in assessing their own work and so discover by experience whether they really believe in them and want to use them. In my judgement this is the best strategy. It means of course that you and the student will not be using identical sets of criteria in assessing the student's work. But this can be interesting too.

In my experience of using collaborative assessment in one-to-one tutorials on undergraduates' essays, there is a definite tendency – not large, but noticeable – for students to mark themselves down. This is not surprising, given that years spent at the receiving end of unilateral assessment make for a somewhat negative self-image. But once the process is under way, students show an authentic conscientiousness and thoroughness in the way they handle it.

For the future, I see collaborative assessment as the next step forward, first with respect to students' course work, then with respect to final essays and examinations. As more contract learning comes in and students start to determine their own learning objectives and learning programmes to a greater or lesser degree, then collaborative assessment will tend to have as its primary focus *how* the student is handling the whole learning process as distinct from *what* it is that he has learned, although assessment of products will presumably always be relevant and important.

Collaborative assessment between staff and student can also be interwoven with a variety of self and peer assessment procedures on the student side. Thus a student can first go through a self and peer assessment exercise with his fellow students, then take the assessment that emerges from the exercise into a collaborative assessment session with his tutor. A more adventurous model involving greater staff-student parity is one in which the tutor participates directly in the self and peer assessment session between the student and his fellow students, and the tutor, the student concerned, and his peers negotiate together until an agreed assessment is reached.

Chapter 5

Technology and Lifelong Learning

Christopher Knapper,
Director, Teaching Resources and Continuing Education, University of Waterloo

Technology as a magic bullet

In thinking through some ideas for this chapter during a recent long-distance automobile trip, I turned on the car radio and found myself listening to a discussion on technology and work. Panellists (they included a writer, a university professor, and a couple of senior managers from large corporations) agreed that we are in the middle of an 'information age', that the nature of society and work is rapidly changing, and that virtually every employee in the medium-term future will have to possess computing skills if they are to succeed in all but the most menial jobs. The speakers made some good points (and indulged in a little foolishness about just what computers do and what computing skills will be necessary in the future), but on the whole they provided a remarkable confirmation of how quickly people in Western industrialized societies have come to accept computers as an essential component of day-to-day life and work. Though the transformation to what Daniel Bell (1967) has termed the 'information society' is not yet complete, its inevitability appears to have been accepted not just by technologists and academics, but also by a significant proportion of the general public.

This is partly a result of the proliferation of information technology (especially cheap microcomputers) and the fact that increasing numbers of people encounter technology in their day-to-day lives – for example at work, in banks and stores, at places of entertainment, and so on. The process of familiarization is reinforced by the mass media and by the educational system, where 'computer literacy' (a term unheard of less than a decade ago) is becoming an essential component in curriculum planning.

While educational institutions have played an important role in disseminating information about technology, education itself has been affected by technological change, and has been seen as a means to transform and enhance the activities of schools and universities, in particular to improve the quality of teaching and learning. The purpose of this chapter is to examine these claims, and to address the issue of whether (or how) technology might foster desirable educational goals.

Education and technology: some definitions

Before proceeding further it is necessary to clarify what is meant here by technology and by 'desirable educational goals'. Writers on technology in education have adopted two general approaches to the meaning of the term. The most straightforward position is to regard educational technology as any non-human instructional medium or aid that can enhance learning. The other, more complex definition (favoured by educationists rather than technologists) refers to a 'system' or process for applying certain educational strategies in teaching – including specification of instructional objectives, selection of appropriate delivery mechanisms, evaluation of outcomes, etc. – whether or not the instructional medium is technology-based or relies primarily on a human teacher. (For a fuller discussion of this distinction see Knapper, 1980.) Both types of definition have points in their favour, but it is the former, simpler approach that is employed here – largely because the view of educational technology as primarily 'hardware' is the notion adopted by most recent commentators, especially those who have looked to technology to provide a radical transformation in educational practice. In fact, most of the following discussion is predicated on an even more limited definition that focuses primarily on the dominant and powerful 'new information technologies' or 'informatics' – computers linked to electronic communication systems. At the same time, other technologies are not entirely ignored here, especially when (like satellites or videodiscs) they can be combined with computer-based delivery systems to produce especially sophisticated instructional approaches.

My concept of appropriate educational goals is reflected in the theme and title of this book: *Developing Student Autonomy in Learning*. Fostering independent, self-directed learning can be viewed as part of a broader philosophical rationale for education, summarized by the term 'lifelong learning' that is used in the title of the present chapter. The concept of lifelong learning was first introduced by Edgar Faure and his associates (Faure Report, 1972), and subsequently adopted by Unesco as a blueprint for educational reform. It is based on the self-evident notion that individuals continue to learn throughout their lives and in a variety of situations: learning is not confined to certain years or indeed to educational institutions. The ability to learn from and throughout life has always been important, but it is especially so in a world experiencing rapid and profound change – change that affects not only the workplace, but also such basic social institutions as the family. Hence the notion that the school system can in effect 'inoculate' an individual with sufficient education to last for the next 50 or so years is no longer appropriate. Rather, individuals must develop skills that enable them to learn throughout their lives and from a variety of sources – not simply those provided by formal educational institutions or through traditional courses of instruction. These generic learning skills are very similar to the concepts of self-directed autonomous learning discussed by many other contributors to this volume. Indeed, Knapper and Cropley (1985), in extending the work of Faure, have argued that a major purpose of the educational system (and higher education in particular) should be to teach not traditional 'content' but rather the process of 'learning how to learn'.

Faure and his associates advance a number of arguments for adopting educational systems and methods that might foster lifelong learning. They include the need to enhance equality of opportunity, to provide links between education and real life, especially the world of work (or what Knapper and Cropley refer to as 'life-wide' learning), the importance of encouraging democracy and general participation in decision-making, and the desirability of encouraging self-development and self-actualization. Clearly these are not the only possible goals for an educational system. They do, however, reflect the position adopted in this chapter.

Knapper and Cropley (1985), in their critique of higher education, argue that much traditional teaching practice (eg great reliance on teacher-centred didactic instruction, student assessment methods that stress acquisition of knowledge rather than mastery of higher-order skills) do little to encourage independent lifelong learning. If this is true, then what alternative methods are available? In particular, can information technology, which has had remarkable success in other spheres, succeed in transforming education in ways that are consistent with the goal of fostering lifelong learning skills?

Technology and education: a brief history and overview

Education has always made use of technological aids, and many educators over the years have been fascinated by the possibility that a particular innovation could transform educational practice. For example, in the 1950s it was widely believed that educational television would radically change the organization of schools and the role of the teacher: entire colleges were designed and built to exploit the concept that instruction would be delivered by television instead of live teachers. Less then a decade later, teaching machines and programmed learning (the forerunners of computer-assisted learning) were seen as having the potential to displace human teachers. And in the last century extravagant claims were made for the blackboard!

As already anticipated, in the past 20 years attention has turned to the instructional implications of computers – initially (in the 1960s and 1970s) large mainframe machines and, more recently, the ubiquitous microcomputer. The distinguished British educator, Eric Ashby (Carnegie Foundation, 1972) described the potential of computer-based educational technology as heralding a 'fourth revolution' in education – the other three revolutions being no less than establishment of the formal school, the invention of writing, and the development of the printing press. This is no small claim, especially in view of the fact that most of the recent innovations I listed earlier have had little permanent impact on educational practice (although television, to cite just one innovation, has had profound effects outside the school in changing attitudes and lifestyles, and undoubtedly stimulates a great deal of non-formal learning).

Despite the widespread availability of teaching aids, and the gradual diffusion of non-technological teaching innovations described elsewhere in this book, the most accurate generalization that could be made about teaching in universities worldwide is how traditional it remains. Lecturing is the predominant method of teaching, generally with little opportunity for interaction and with student activity confined to taking notes. Practical 'hands-on' experience is frequently restricted to formal laboratories, which may often be predictable and ritualistic. A good deal of assessment is by essays or multiple-choice examinations that test content mastery and can bear little relationship to skills that are useful in the real world. This prevailing academic culture is so dominant that such approaches are not only favoured by most university teachers: they have also come to be expected by students.

Knapper and Cropley (1985), after reviewing prevailing teaching methods, discuss the extent to which they might foster lifelong learning. Their conclusions are largely pessimistic, and these authors go on to consider a variety of alternative approaches that might better help to fulfil the educational goals they espouse. The focus of the present chapter is on one set of alternatives – educational technology, and especially instructional approaches based upon the new information technologies.

Before discussing these technologies at greater length it is necessary to examine in a little more detail what types of skills are subsumed in the concept of lifelong learning. I have already made the point that, if learning is to take place throughout life, such learning cannot be confined to formal educational institutions. Hence the most important task of the school or university is to teach generic problem-solving or 'learning to learn' skills that might serve students long after they have left to enter the outside world. But what might characterize a learning experience in which students 'learn how to learn'? An examination of the writings of Faure, Knapper and Cropley, and others suggests the following attributes.

In the first place *active* student involvement in the learning process is seen as highly important, so that they are not simply passive receivers of 'conventional wisdom' passed on by 'teachers-as-experts'. It therefore follows that the context for learning should be *democratic* (as opposed to authoritarian), with students being involved in decisions about what and how they learn. A third aspect of the learning situation is that it be as *flexible* as possible, especially in regard to the times and places in which learning can take place. Teaching should also make allowances for *individual differences* among learners – not just with respect to different abilities and speeds of learning, but also in terms of different learning styles. Fifthly (a characteristic that is certainly not unique to the promotion of lifelong learning), the learning environment should *motivate* students and have some *relevance* to their real-life goals. Sixthly, although learning situations should foster independent problem-solving and decision-making, this does not mean that the only worthwhile learning is by individuals working in isolation from others: an important aspect of successful lifelong learning is the ability to learn and work *collaboratively*, which in turn assumes appropriate interpersonal communication skills. Seventh, learning should allow students to *integrate* knowledge from different fields, and should not be confined by disciplinary boundaries. Lastly (and linked to the notions of democratic and collaborative learning mentioned above), students should be able to pursue their learning tasks *without fear of embarrassment or loss of status*. (Whereas this may in some ways seem a redundant criterion in the regular classroom setting, it assumes considerable importance for adults returning to education – for example in job retraining.)

To what extent does educational technology allow the foregoing criteria to be met? This is the central question of the present chapter. It is of course possible to apply the list to any or all of the educational technologies of the past. For example, in some ways educational television admirably fulfils certain criteria (eg by its ability to bring 'real-life' examples into the home or classroom), but fails quite badly in terms of others (it is not generally an interactive medium, and hence learning via television usually entails a good deal of student passivity). The focus here, however, will be upon what might be termed the 'current' educational technologies, which in practice means computer-mediated approaches. This is not to imply that other technologies (ranging from the blackboard to programmed instruction) have been entirely abandoned by education. For the most part, however, they either occupy a fairly limited role in contemporary learning – often as teaching aids rather than primary delivery systems (the overhead projector would be a good example), or have been incorporated into more modern computer-assisted technologies (such as the marrying of videodiscs with computer-assisted learning or the use of slow-scan television in some modern satellite-based distance education systems).

The fact that a good many much-praised earlier educational technologies were quickly abandoned does not mean that they failed to meet the criteria for lifelong learning spelled out above. Indeed, educational innovations are often rejected for bad reasons (eg instructor laziness) as well as good. Despite the fairly idealistic list presented here, it is important to take into account other criteria that are not necessarily related to lifelong education, but frequently crucial in facilitating educational change. The most important are *cost* and the *amount of time* investment required on the part of the teacher.

The new information technologies: some current and future applications

Before considering our list of criteria in relation to educational technology it will be necessary to have a brief state-of-the art review of the more recent technological applications in education, taking up the brief history where it was left off at the advent of the microcomputer.

The new information technologies, which so excited Ashby, Bell and many other commentators, involve combining the immense power of the computer to store and manipulate information with the capacity of various electronic communications media (ranging from satellites to fibre optic cable) to transmit information rapidly and cheaply over vast physical distances. This formidable combination has already revolutionized a number of societal institutions ranging from the stock exchange to the daily press. The potential for more dramatic effects on education (whose stock-in-trade after all is communicating information) would appear to be considerable.

Educators have been exploring applications of computers in the classroom ever since the days of the early mainframe machines, and the effort has been vastly expanded since the advent of widely available, cheap microcomputers which, in the Western world at least, are now found in virtually every classroom and in many homes. There have been three principal applications of computers in education: to deliver or manage instruction (as in computer-assisted or computer-managed learning), as a learning tool for students (eg in such areas as word processing or statistical calculation), or to teach something about computers themselves. (Computer programming, which until recently was the most common classroom activity for students who had access to a terminal, could be said to fall into both of the last two categories.) Though it is undoubtedly true that citizens of the future will need to know something about the way computers work and what they can do, the third application will be largely ignored in the remaining discussion.

The idea of a mechanical system that can take over from the human teacher (with the consequent saving of money and resources) has been a type of holy grail, sought after by many educational innovators for many years. Presumably the invention of writing must have been seen by some as a marvellous chance to free education from the previous oral tradition (and the inevitable presence of a human teacher). Printed documents, especially in the compact and portable format represented by books, constitute an impressive self-contained 'instructional system'. More recently, programmed learning and teaching machines were seen by their advocates as having the potential to replace the classroom teacher – or at least to change their role from the primary deliverers of instruction to that of managers and of writers of learning material. There is no question that educational television attracted the enthusiasm it did largely because it was thought it could produce great economies of scale by 'piping in' to classrooms a few of the existing (and presumably most effective) teachers, leaving the rest to undertake other tasks. As mentioned above, however, the role of the traditional classroom teacher, both in schools and universities, has remained largely impervious to such educational innovations.

Computers as instructional delivery and management systems

The ways in which the computer can be used to deliver instruction can all be traced back to principles employed by the teaching machine of the 1950s. The underlining idea is quite simple: the instructional material or task is presented to students in manageable chunks, and test questions are provided at appropriate intervals to ensure student comprehension or mastery. Depending on whether the presentation and testing sequences are short (as, for example, in teaching French vocabulary) or long (describing the five main causes of the French

Revolution), this type of CAL is known as 'drill-and-practice' or 'tutorial'. Based upon the answers students give, they can be 'branched' to remedial teaching sequences or directed to more advanced material. Quite detailed records of student performance can be kept, and – at least in theory – the teaching program can be modified to take account of student difficulties.

All this could be done (and was) by the old mechanical teaching machines. The latter, however, were severely limited in the attractiveness of their display format. In contrast, modern microcomputers can enhance the material presented with graphics, still photographs, moving video sequences, or even audio, controlled by the computer but sometimes generated by ancillary devices. Such devices allow much more complicated learning sequences, in which the computer goes beyond the didactic presentation of fairly straightforward textual material and takes the student through a simulation of some outside situation that it might otherwise be awkward or impossible to bring into the classroom. Examples range from simulations of laboratory experiments to such complex tasks as flying a plane or operating an industrial plant. In these more complicated instances the computer generally serves as a control device for a number of components, and student input and output is not confined to the monitor or keyboard. Ability to link microcomputers with videodisc players offers the possibility to incorporate large amounts of still or moving sequences into an instructional program, which appears to have great potential for simulations – although the technology as yet is quite costly and somewhat inflexible (ie once the videodisc is manufactured it is impossible to change it).

A somewhat different application (and one not possible in the case of the old teaching machines) is to have the computer 'manage' learning. Based upon the results of an initial diagnosis of student abilities and learning needs, students are directed to appropriate instructional modules (which may be computer-based or in some other format). Learners are tested on the computer at frequent intervals to ensure satisfactory progress, and class records are maintained for the teacher. Perhaps surprisingly, computer-managed learning (CML) has had only limited use, despite what would appear to be its considerable potential.

Some mention should also be made of the so-called 'expert systems' or 'adaptive' CAL, which has been widely discussed as potentially the most sophisticated use of computers as an instructional delivery system. The idea here is that the machine adapts its teaching strategy to the particular style, knowledge and idiosyncrasies of the student, and in this sense it is truly 'individualized' – in the way that a private tutor might tailor teaching based upon the way that her student copes with various tasks set during the course of a lesson. Although there were adaptive teaching machines some 25 years ago (see Lewis, 1963), the application of expert systems and artificial intelligence to computer-based learning is presently in its infancy, and there are no commercial applications in widespread use.

Computers as a learning tool

The use of computers to deliver instruction in some of the ways described above has made some inroads in traditional educational settings. But outside industrial training programs and the armed forces, computer-assisted learning has generally been used as a supplement to regular classroom teaching, not as a replacement. Even with this qualification, its application in most schools and in higher education is extremely limited. If this is so, then just what are the tasks that engage those students who can be seen by the hundreds sitting in front of terminals or microcomputers in so many colleges and universities? Ten years ago these learners would have been almost entirely from mathematics or engineering, and they would have been involved in programming – or, more precisely, learning a formal programming language, such as FORTRAN or PASCAL. Nowadays, however, the students will be drawn from all sectors of the university, and are probably engaged in a variety of activities, only one of which is learning a programming language. Most likely they will be learning to use one of the many application 'packages' that help accomplish a variety of tasks that in themselves have nothing to do with computing.

Among the earliest implementations of this type was the use of computers for statistical calculation. More recently there has been a recognition that computers are just as adept at handling verbal information as they are at manipulating numbers, and word processing developed into the major application for microcomputers. (There is still considerable prejudice against it in academia, and some universities, including Harvard, have refused to allow students access to university computing facilities for word processing.)

Other uses of the computer as a tool include access (via an external communications device linked to the computer) to large databases which can be used for research purposes and provide an effective substitute for long hours spent in the library. More specialized applications depend upon the needs of the discipline concerned. For example, packages are available to facilitate many different tasks, from landscape surveying to producing concordances for literary works. In most cases little knowledge of the computer is required, although some familiarity with the operating system is desirable in order to use the package as efficiently as possible. In this sense, then, the computer can be regarded as a personal learning aid in much the same sense as a pocket calculator – except that the number of possible applications is much wider and constantly growing as commercial vendors compete to develop new applications.

It might be added that the roles computers in the delivery of instruction and as learning tools are not mutually exclusive. Some innovative CAL programs not only present information but also incorporate opportunities for students to work with the material in various other ways. For example, a history program prepared for use in Canadian schools offers tutorial-type instruction about a settler family in the early eighteenth century. But learners can also divert from the principal lessons to explore on their own at the terminal. Options include games and simulations related to the central theme (one involves preparing a meal using ingredients available during the historical period being studied), use of an on-line calculator (eg to work out acreage of crops to be planted on the farm), a simple database in which unfamiliar terms can be checked for their meaning, a 'notebook' in which students can record their observations by means of a word processor, etc. Evidence suggests that this type of approach is highly engaging for students.

Educational technology and lifelong learning criteria

It is now possible to consider some of the common applications of information technology in education in the light of the criteria for lifelong learning listed earlier. Table 1 presents a matrix showing eight lifelong learning criteria plus the two additional general educational criteria mentioned above (cost and instructor time) in relation to five major applications of computers in education. It is clear from a cursory inspection of the table that the picture is not black and white. In some ways the technological applications appear to be conducive to the promotion of lifelong learning; in other cases they do not. In further instances the matrix shows a question mark, indicating that the situation depends upon the way the application is implemented. It is not my intention here to embark upon a cell-by-cell examination of the matrix. Rather, some general comments will be made about the pedagogical implications of each criterion in relation to the different types of educational technology.

Most forms of computer-based instruction do entail *active learning* in the sense that the student is actively engaged with the task at hand (as opposed to sitting in a lecture, for example). In some cases the level of engagement can be very high: this is especially true for simulations, the best of which provide a moment-by-moment challenge to students in much the same way as the popular computer games. In fact some of the most successful CAL software for primary and secondary schools comprises what might best be termed educational games that involve a large component of simulation. Of course it is also quite possible to design CAL material where the level of engagement is low: for example, tutorial courseware with long didactic sequences and trivial test questions. On the whole, though, most young people (and many older students) enjoy working with computers, in large part because the intensive level of interaction between student and machine is a stimulating and active form of learning.

Instructional technology may or may not lead to *shared decision-making* or a more *democratic approach* to education, depending on how it is implemented. For instance, most drill-and-practice and tutorial CAL, as well as computer-managed learning, retains the teacher-centred model of education that is essentially 'authoritarian'. Here, because the nature of the educational experience is more or less 'fixed', there is little opportunity to involve students in decisions about what they are learning as might be possible in the live classroom. On the other hand, the use of computers as a general tool could be seen as giving students more responsibility for their own learning, and perhaps this is why student

	Drill and practice/ tutorial CAL	Computer simulation	CML	Computers as a tool	Computer conferencing
Encourages active learning	Yes	Yes	?	Yes	Yes
Democratic – broadens access and shares responsibility for decision-making	No	?	?	Yes	Yes
Responds to individual differences among learners	Partly	Partly	Yes	?	?
Flexible (eg in terms of time and place of learning)	Yes	Yes	?	Yes	Yes
Motivating, and relevant	?	Yes	?	Yes	Yes
Integrates knowledge from different fields	No	?	?	?	?
Collaborative (vs competitive)	No	?	No	?	Yes
Avoids embarrassment to students	Yes	Yes	Yes	Yes	Yes
Reasonable instructor workload/ time investment	No	No	Yes	Yes	Yes
Reasonable cost	?	?	Yes	Yes	?

Table 1 *Characteristics of educational technology in terms of criteria for lifelong learning*

access to all-purpose software packages like word processors has been staunchly resisted by some institutions.

Another component of this criterion, as developed by Faure and his colleagues, was the idea of broadening access to education and providing equality of opportunity for learning. Some educators have seen technology as a major force for bringing education to the disadvantaged, especially in Third World countries. The idea here appears to be that computers could provide instruction where human teachers in schools are not available. However, this point of view overlooks the obvious problems of cost, need for logistical support (eg repair services), and technological sophistication required to operate the equipment. This dilemma was rather poignantly brought home when I attended an international conference on distance education in 1985 at which a keynote speaker argued that educational technology could be used to enhance learning opportunities around the world and redress the imbalance between rich and poorer nations. In the following question period a teacher from a developing African nation recalled that similar claims for technology had been made several years ago when her school had been provided with a number of overhead projectors. The equipment had remained unused for most of the time since it was learned that the cost of replacing one bulb was the equivalent of the school caretaker/technician's salary for a month. Under these circumstances it seems plausible that what Wilbur Schramm (1977) called the 'little' (ie cheap and flexible) media may be more effective than the glamorous and sophisticated 'big' media. At the same time there is a good deal of experimentation with computer-based educational technology in the Third World, much of it under the auspices of international development agencies.

Just as it is not yet clear what effect educational technology will have on equalizing opportunities in disadvantaged nations, so the potential for use of computers by handicapped individuals has yet to be realized. A number of experiments are underway involving the physically disabled (eg those with problems of muscular coordination or visual impairment). Many of the trials have been promising, but the impact to date on education of the handicapped is extremely limited.

A major claim for many forms of educational technology (including computer-based learning) is that they cater for *individual differences among learners* in a way that traditional education cannot. For example, with CAL students can proceed at their own pace and, through the branching arrangement described earlier, can be directed through different instructional sequences. It might be argued that many simpler media are also 'self-pacing': after all, a book may be read quickly or slowly, right through or in parts, forwards or backwards. And the branching capability of most computer-based learning is often no more sophisticated than in the early teaching machines. So while in principle computer technology permits very sophisticated branching sequences (in effect this is what the 'adaptive' instructional programs are attempting), in fact the potential of the technology has rarely been fully exploited, probably because of the considerable investment of time and expertise required to do so. Nor has CAL successfully tackled the issue of how to deal with students who have different learning styles. Theoretically, students could be given diagnostic tests that would measure not only prior knowledge and general ability in the subject matter being taught, but also their preferred mode of learning. Presentation of subsequent learning tasks could then be tailored appropriately to each student's needs. Despite the current interest in learning styles there has been very little work on exploring how they might be accommodated in computer-based learning.

Before leaving the topic of individual differences in learning it is perhaps worth calling into question the implicit assumption by most advocates of CAL that the regular classroom inevitably ignores such differences and treats students as a homogeneous mass. Whereas this may be true in many large lecture classes, the smaller classroom setting, both in school and university, affords the insightful teacher with many opportunities to respond to students as individuals, provide different levels of explanation, set different tasks, give different types of evaluative comments, and so on. This ability is based upon experience, accurate perception of student characteristics, and a certain amount of intuition – qualities that computers to date are largely lacking. This is of course a major reason why research on artificial intelligence is so difficult and so challenging.

A fourth criterion for effective lifelong learning is *flexibility*. Depending on how this term is interpreted, much computer-based learning is at an advantage over the traditional educational delivery system. From a pedagogical point of view a great amount of computer courseware is inferior to the good intuitive classroom teacher. One major advantage of microcomputers, however, is that they can overcome limitations of time, space and distance common to most live classroom teaching. It is for this reason that there has been considerable interest in the use of computer-aided learning in distance education.

Teaching at a distance involves instruction that takes place without face-to-face contact between teacher and students. It has been used for many years in countries like Australia and Canada where great physical distances limit access to schools and colleges. In recent years the British Open University has attracted worldwide attention by its success in bringing high quality post-secondary education to students in their homes, using a variety of instructional media. Unofficial estimates suggest that today there are some 4 million students worldwide in distance education programmes, 3 million of them in just four countries – the USSR, China, South Korea and Thailand. By definition, distance education relies on educational media to transmit learning material to students and to allow communication between learners and teacher. Both 'big' and 'little' media (Schramm, 1977) have been employed, particularly print (the basis of many correspondence programme), audio tapes, radio, and television.

More recently there has been a burgeoning of interest in using computers as a primary learning medium. The notion has considerable attractions, especially if microcomputers in the home or workplace can be linked electronically to the base institution. This would permit – at least in principle – a high level of student-teacher interaction, something that is largely missing from distance education. So far, however, despite a number of experiments with computer-based distance teaching, there appears to be uncertainty about how best to use the technology for promotion of effective learning. For example, there have been some attempts to use computers for the actual delivery of teaching materials – eg sent out on diskettes or transmitted electronically via a modem. But there is so far a paucity of good CAL material to be used in this way, and in any case simpler media like print appear to be cheaper and more effective ways of transmitting information.

More promising approaches involve use of computers to deliver and mark student assignments, provide feedback on student work, and answer student questions about the course. The opportunity to provide immediate interaction of this sort is a considerable advantage over existing methods of exchange, which generally rely on the mails. This type of interaction is often referred to as 'computer conferencing' in which all members of a group (or class) can interact with each other, with a teacher and even with outside experts. Participants are free from the contraints of space and time since, unlike a real conference or tutorial, they may add comments or questions at any time that is convenient: the computer will store the information indefinitely. In the sense that it provides flexibility, encourages peer learning, allows sharing of decision-making, and permits access to a wide range of learning resources (which might encompass not just outside experts, but also databases), computer conferencing can be said to fulfil a number of the lifelong learning criteria listed in Table 1.

There are, however, a number of difficulties that have prevented the widespread use of such conferencing for educational purposes. These include the costs involved (not just the cost of the computing equipment but also communication expenses to use the system), problems of equipment compatibility, and the need for mastery of the skills to use this type of unfamiliar communication system with maximum effectiveness. Hence although computer conferencing can be said to allow broadening of access to education for those wealthy enough to afford the necessary equipment, at the moment it does little for the educationally disadvantaged. Furthermore, despite some extravagant claims for 'electronic universities' relying entirely on computer-based distance education, in reality most applications to this point are experimental, and distance education continues to rely primarily upon much less sophisticated technologies.

Turning to the fifth criterion in Table 1, there are many studies showing that students like to learn from computers, and in this sense computer-based education can be quite *motivating*. It should be cautioned, however, that the studies of educational innovations that get published are usually those showing positive results, and there is little doubt that bad computer-based learning is just as boring and frustrating as bad teaching from a live teacher. Furthermore, certain types of student probably find it easier to use and learn from computers than others. For example, people with less prior exposure to technology (older people, students from Third World countries) may find it more threatening to learn with and from a machine than with the help of a human teacher.

There is nothing inherent to computer-assisted teaching that fosters the *integration of knowledge from different fields* any more than other teaching methods, and hence no particular advantage can be claimed in terms of this criterion.

In the case of encouraging *collaborative learning* versus learning that is essentially individualistic and in competition with other students, most computer-based learning rates poorly. Indeed one of the boasts of CAL is that the teaching is tailored to the needs of the individual, and although we have seen above that these claims may be exaggerated, it remains true that most computer-based instructional technology focuses on the single learner, not groups or teams. This is partly due to the physical configuration of computer terminals which do not permit ready access by more than one person, because of the size of the screen and the keyboard that is generally used for input. Indeed the image of computer-assisted learning (fostered by many advertising brochures from computer manufacturers) is one of rows of students sitting in individual carrels, each physically separate from the other. This is a very far cry from the dynamic social situation that can often be found in the live classroom, and indeed the highly individualistic and asocial nature of some CAL has disturbed many teachers. A number of educators are experimenting with more collaborative use of computers for learning, but the physical limitations of the equipment and the fact that most courseware is geared to individual study remain a problem.

In the case of the last lifelong learning criterion listed in Table 1, the highly individualistic – indeed virtually private – nature of study at a terminal can be a marked advantage over regular classroom learning. Hence the *embarrassment and loss of status* that can be fears for some students when working with peers can be largely avoided in a situation where students work on their own and proceed at their own pace, and where errors are quietly pointed out by a machine instead of noted by the teacher in front of the whole class. Whereas many schoolchildren and university students become inured to this type of classroom rough-and-tumble, the ability to work individually (and in particular to make mistakes in private) can be a major advantage for certain special groups, including minority students and older learners returning to the classroom, especially in industrial training situations where fear of revealing ignorance before workmates can be extremely threatening. Hence it is perhaps not surprising that some students who do poorly in regular classroom settings can excel with computer-based education. On the other hand, learning in relative isolation can also be frustrating, especially where problems are encountered with the instructional program that students cannot solve: in the live classroom they could often turn to peers for help, sympathy and encouragement.

The last two criteria in Table 1 have no particular relationship to lifelong learning but are simply common-sense requirements of any teaching system. If teaching provides an intolerable *workload for instructors*, then it is unlikely to be widely accepted. Similarly if the *teaching costs* are excessive, it is likely the approach will be rejected by those who must provide the institution's budget.

In the case of computer-based learning there is some tentative evidence of time savings for students (compared with the time they would spend in a conventional classroom setting). In contrast, however, it is generally accepted that the preparation time to prepare effective CAL is considerable. Furthermore the process of preparing pedagogically sound computer courseware is quite complex, and requires skills in instructional design, expertise in the particular content area, knowledge of computer programming, and perhaps some skill with illustration and graphics. This range of abilities is generally beyond the scope of 'amateurs' – despite the development of various authoring languages that aim to help prepare CAL material without specialist knowledge of programming. Hence most of the sophisticated courseware emanates either from specialist research and development groups in universities or – more commonly – from commercial software houses that can call upon a wide range of expertise. Naturally this does not come cheaply, and good educational courseware can easily cost millions of dollars to develop. There are of course many thousands of CAL lessons available for a hundred dollars or so, but the general principle is that in this field, as in most others, you get what you pay for. Since broad accessibility is an underlying assumption of lifelong learning, then clearly excessive costs to learners (both for equipment and instruction) constitute a significant barrier.

The future

In this chapter I have advocated as a key principle to guide contemporary education the promotion of lifelong learning – the ability to learn from life and throughout life. An important component of such learning is the ability to take responsibility for one's own learning – in other words the ability to study autonomously and independently. I laid out a set of possible criteria for fulfilling the goals of lifelong learning, and then went on to review developments in educational technology – especially computer-based learning – to determine how such technologies might be consistent with my criteria and how they could help promote the type of learning I have argued is so important.

In its short history information technology has had a remarkable influence on many quite fundamental aspects of our lives. The economic impact of the information age – affecting both work and lifestyle – has yet to be fully realized. Ironically, however, despite enthusiastic forecasts by advocates, educational institutions have changed only marginally in terms of a move to more computer-delivered instruction. There are signs that this may change, but the precise effects of technology on education may not be those that present-day experts expect. The history of technology is replete with examples of innovations that were discarded or which gave rise to quite unanticipated effects. The example of television has already been mentioned. Another instance of an innovation that seemed a small change to existing methods but had a marked influence on teaching and learning practice is the dry copier (Xerox machine).

One interesting feature of many types of computer-based education is that the new delivery system is based upon an older instructional model: in this case the notion of the book or human teacher that contains all the appropriate information and communicates it to students as necessary. This teacher-centred (or even 'authoritarian') model of instruction does not accord with most of the basic principles of lifelong learning, which stress more student-centred approaches. However, if we look at the way computers are in fact used in education, most implementations do not involve this type of didactic instruction. Rather, they entail students using computers as tools to solve a wide range of problems they will encounter in their academic work and subsequent careers. Ironically, most of these applications were not developed particularly for the educational market, and learning to use these tools is primarily a means to an end. (In passing it is worth noting that a good deal of unintentional independent learning takes place in mastering computer skills – much of it by informal means, as any computer user who has struggled with inadequate documentation for a software package will testify!)

Although it is still too early to say, the possibility exists that information technology will – unwittingly – help promote the goals of lifelong education by passing responsibility for learning from 'experts' (teachers, textbook writers, courseware designers) to students themselves. If this happens, it would be especially important, for the likely dominance of technology in the world of the future makes it essential that control is not left to the 'authorities' but broadly shared among the population. And for this to take place there will need to be a citizenry who are not only knowledgeable about technological matters, but can also use technology effectively for their own purposes, whether these are in the realm of education or beyond.

Part II
Case Studies

Chapter 6
Reducing Teacher Control

J P Powell,
Formerly Director, Tertiary Education Research Centre,
University of New South Wales

Introduction

When I began my career as a university teacher, I was fortunate in being required to give only one lecture a week; most of the rest of my time was devoted to reading and preparing material. As a result I learned a great deal about the subject but all that most of the students did was to listen for an hour, take a few notes, and perhaps spend a little time reading. At first I saw nothing odd in this but gradually the absurdity of teachers learning more than students became clear to me. The way in which teaching is organized in higher education ensures that the greatest beneficiaries are the teachers. A consequence of this is that students become dependent upon their teachers to such an extent that they cannot envisage learning very much without them. The evidence for the truth of this lies all around us and one illustration must suffice here. One winter evening in Manchester I watched a small stream of MEd students arrive at the university, many of them having driven perhaps 30 miles after a day's work, to be greeted by a notice which announced that Dr Smith was ill and his 7 pm lecture was cancelled. After reading it they returned to their cars and set off for home. It seemed that they were helpless without Dr Smith and unable to learn anything together except under his personal direction. The whole of their previous experience of institutional learning had been such that they had become totally dependent upon being taught.

It must also be said that most teachers are similarly dependent upon students, in that they see their job as being essentially to tell or show things to other people; which they equate with learning. They may complain about heavy teaching loads but are often remarkably reluctant to reduce them and allow students greater opportunities to learn outside the classroom.

A somewhat extreme response to this situation is to remove teachers from classrooms altogether and in 1962 I did this by beginning a series of experiments with tutorless groups. These shifted on to the students all the responsibility for learning and group organisation. They also created opportunities for learning which were simply not available in conventional lectures and tutorials. More recently I have been seeking ways in which teachers can effectively contribute to learning in small groups without always being in the centre of the stage and in control of virtually everything which takes place. In 1976 I had a chance to organize an entire course along these lines. It was part of a master's degree programme designed to increase the educational expertise of experienced teachers of the health professions. In what follows a description of the development and outcomes of that course will be offered.

Information about the progress of the course was gathered from several sources. After each class I attended a de-briefing session with two colleagues which usually lasted for about 30 minutes and was tape-recorded. During these sessions I gave an account of what had happened together with my reactions and feelings, and responded to questions and comments. At the end of each class the students reflected, in writing, on what took place during the meeting and tried to relate this to what they felt they had learned. There was also an end of course evaluation but, unfortunately, only four students completed that. All these data sources have been drawn upon here.

Aims of the course

The 'official' outline of the course was as follows:

> This course will focus primarily on theoretical and practical aspects of human learning. Recent research on skill and concept acquisition, problem-solving, memory, and motivation will be reviewed. Consideration will be given to the effects of cultural and emotional factors in learning. There will be an emphasis throughout on the skills required to identify and analyse the differences between individuals in their approach to a variety of learning tasks. A secondary focus will be the nature of the connections between learning and teaching and the development of an ability to devise teaching procedures and environments which are appropriate to specific learning tasks.

This was produced in order to satisfy university requirements for a course description and mainly comprised the 'official content' of the course. When teaching began I was far from clear about the 'real content' of the course or the form it would take. What I was clear about was a determination to keep my own contributions at a low level in an attempt to transfer responsibility to the students. There is no ready-made vocabulary with which to describe the kind of course which I had in mind for this purpose. It was to have less 'structure' than most conventional courses – the meaning of which can best be made plain by looking at conventional courses. In these the teacher prepares a syllabus detailing the content to be covered, assembles all the material to be taught, produces booklists and hand-outs, controls the process of class sessions and usually monopolizes their verbal content, specifies the number and nature of assignments to be completed, and determines assessment procedures. A course which is completely structured would be one in which the students play a passive role with respect to all these activities. A totally unstructured course would be the reverse of this, although it is doubtful if any examples could be found in institutional settings. Most university courses exhibit a very high degree of structure with perhaps some scope for choosing areas of content specialization and assignment topics. My aim was to maintain the educational values of the course with the least possible structure without producing undue anxiety in the students.

A course, however, has to be 'about' something: what was it the students could be expected to learn? As has already been said, this was not a question which I could have answered, except in the most general terms, before the course began: the details of the answer only emerged clearly as we went along. The major foci of attention would be the power and authority of the teacher and the effects of this upon learning, the role of the student and the ways in which this interacts with that of the teacher, the significance of individual differences, the influence of the milieu within which learning has its setting, and the place of the emotions in relation to learning. More important, however, was the manner in which this material was approached and handled. These topics together with the events and processes which occurred in the classroom made up the real content of the course. Some relevant information could probably be gleaned from the psychological literature although I was very sceptical about the value of what could be learned from that source and in that fashion. I therefore intended to make the immediate, and the recollected, experiences of learning of the students form the bulk of the content of the course with the 'official' content serving only as a series of starting points.

There were thus an 'official' course and a 'real' course developing in parallel week by week as we examined what we were doing and analysed the many ways in which this influenced what was learned. The official course was a necessity because without it there would be no raw material to which we could respond, and it was the analysis and exploration of those responses which the course was really concerned with. It must be stressed that the nature and significance of this distinction only became completely clear to me as we went along and I was thus unable to make use of it to give a convincing outline of the course to the students when we began.

Adopting this approach had the great advantage of allowing me to shed all responsibility for being familiar with the literature and for preparing material for classes. If anything were to be done in those areas it would have to be done by the students. My own contributions would be limited to commenting upon classroom events and encouraging discussion of their significance for learning. Prior to the first meeting, however, it would still be necessary for me to plan sufficient of the official material and activities for the real course to get off the ground.

Events prior to the first class

There were 11 students: three were full-time and came from the Pacific region and the remainder came from Australia and were part-time, returning to their own professional responsibilities after each class. Most had postgraduate qualifications in their own specialities but none had any formal qualifications in the field of education. The part-time students were also doing another course in the degree programme and were thus extremely busy and very much aware of the demands being made on their time. The overseas students had also made considerable personal and financial sacrifices in order to enrol in the programme. They were all highly motivated and anxious to gain skills and knowledge which they felt would be immediately applicable to their own professional work.

A week prior to the first class there was a meeting of all staff and students. This was primarily a social occasion but it was also an opportunity for staff to give an outline of what their courses would be about. I said that I had no very clear idea of the content of the course and that we would develop it as we went along. I also indicated that the course would have some experimental aspects. This limited amount of information accurately reflected the state of my own planning and preparation activities. It had already been determined that there would be one weekly class lasting for two hours and that performance in each course would be determined on a pass/fail basis.

Although I undertook few of the usual preparations for teaching a course, some preliminary work was unavoidable. I made a list of half a dozen books, which I felt would be useful for people to read if they wished, and I planned some activities for the first two meetings. As soon as possible I hoped that students would take over the classes by presenting material on topics which were of interest to them, but it would obviously take some time for these topics to be identified and for the material to be prepared. It proved rather more difficult than I had anticipated to avoid the preparatory work associated with conventional courses: so strong is the force of habit that at times I made some notes almost inadvertently. I also experienced a good deal of anxiety and had serious doubts about my ability to manage a course of this type successfully.

The progress of the course

During the first meeting I gave a brief sketch of the course and the way in which I proposed to conduct it, and again stressed that I did not know very much about the subject-matter and had no intention of remedying that deficiency. We then tackled some problem-solving games so that we could discuss the various ways in which solutions were sought and evaluated. The first meeting of any class is of great importance because it tends to set the tone for what is to follow and, in a small group, reveals something of each member's interests and personality. The students' written reflections at the end of the class indicated that some of my disclaimers had not been taken at face value. They also showed some anxiety about lack of direction associated with the unfamiliar role adopted by the teacher. Some of their comments included:

> ...disappointment that the teacher did not indicate what to expect from the course.
> ...intrigued by lecturer's style: a bit like the magician whose act is to appear unprepared and lacking in skill but still manages to get the rabbits out of the hat on time.

...felt frustrated that I was not going to achieve anything substantial from this course because of the vagueness of the introduction, but the penny dropped and later I felt more enthusiastic.

I felt that the teacher was inventing a lack of preparation as an example in promoting dissatisfaction.

I was wondering if you had really given the course much thought and my feelings were that you were filling in until next week when something more concrete would develop.

...characteristics of some of us: some like it structured, others do not.

...lack of structure and direction; too theoretical; discussion of semantics boring.

This final point was made fairly often and it should be mentioned that my own background is in philosophy and I am therefore naturally inclined to show a keen interest in definitions and conceptual issues. It seems clear that I sometimes took insufficient care to suppress my own predilections.

Two further points merit comment. The first is the wide range of reactions to the degree of structure which a course exhibits: one of the students remarked on this and it is a serious difficulty when there is a considerable mis-match between expectations and reality. The second is that the style of teaching which is required for a course of this type keeps the teacher very busy monitoring and managing the discussion and this can lead to the error of supposing that all the students are also very actively involved when in fact they may be feeling that the discussion is dragging itself along.

In the second and third weeks games and problem-solving activities, many of them provided by the students, continued to be used as the raw material for discussion in order to provide time for presentation topics to be identified and prepared. The written reflections of the students continued to show an extremely wide range of reactions. After a class, one remarked that it had been one of the most significant educational experiences he had ever had, while another said that it had largely been boring and a waste of time! Such dramatic differences in response to what is often taken to be a shared experience pose a great challenge to teachers, especially in universities where it is commonly assumed that individual differences can largely be accounted for by variations in degree of idleness.

Another major difficulty which became apparent at this stage was the inability of many students to shift the focus of their attention back and forth from the official content to the real content. This was a much more difficult task than I had anticipated and it became apparent that insufficient opportunities to practise shifting focus had been provided during the first couple of meetings. Many of my comments were interpreted as being either irrelevant or as resented intrusions into what was perceived as the 'real 'discussion. This came out in some of the reflections:

...satisfaction at successfully solving problem but frustration at wide-ranging discussion of irrelevant concepts: I want to get stuck into narrower field of exploration.

...sometimes frustrating because some people cannot see things which are pretty obvious to me.

...frustrated at times by what I felt was irrelevant discussion.

At this point I became increasingly concerned with the need to complete arrangements for the students to take over the running of the classes by contributing material, in pairs, on topics of interest to them. This was, admittedly, a highly unoriginal way of doing things but it was all that I could think of at the time and it had the advantage of exposing a variety of teaching styles and personalities which we could then examine in relation to our own learning experiences. I was also beginning to feel that I could not continue running the classes for very much longer without doing a good deal of preparatory work. A difficulty with the transfer of responsibility is that the 'housekeeping' tasks associated with it inevitably take up a good deal of class time and this can be resented rather than viewed as an important part of learning.

In the fourth week I began by giving a short lecture which attempted to pull together some of the earlier discussions by giving a more systematic analysis of the concept of learning. This provoked a variety of responses.

> Too much time spent discussing definitions: need more intervention and explanation by the teacher to make atmosphere of the class more orderly.
> I felt good about the whole session in that we explored people's ideas and allowed free discussion of these.
> People talk for the sake of talking, often about things which are obvious.
> I understood better some aspects of conducting group discussion. Felt impatient because I feel we are standing still because I feel I have worked through these conceptual areas already. Not as good a session as some that have gone before: not productive for me.
> I am enjoying the course very much, perhaps more than any other educational activity I have so far taken part in.
> Lectures can be really boring.

The lecture was not very well received, partly because an expectation had been created that none would be given. It was also, of course, unprepared. It may be that very well-prepared lectures block discussion in that they leave no loose ends which students can seize upon in order to unravel the whole. All one can do is applaud and go home. A tightly constructed lecture also seeks to impose upon students the teacher's ordering of the material and this may prevent the learner from making a meaningful approach to the content. You either take it or you leave it. There is no psychological space within which the individual learner can move and seek to get to grips with the material in his own way.

The remainder of that session was spent in allocating responsibility for topics and arranging the order of presentation, and for the next few weeks we listened to and discussed the contribution of each pair. The following are fairly typical comments on one of these sessions:

...challenged my previous ideas rather than taught me anything.

A very structured and frustrating session because the two leaders insisted on sticking to their prepared material and did not encourage free thought.

Felt that the presenters did not seem to understand some of the theories they were discussing.

I become confused when the presenter lectures and when he or she is also confused, ie when there is no discussion. I was angry at being lectured to and felt rejected and unfulfilled.

I felt relaxed and enjoyed it all. Pity there was no time to complete what we wanted to do. [A presenter]

I continued to make pedagogic comments as opportunity offered but felt that I was not making anywhere near enough of them and that the official course was supplanting the real one. The last of the above quotations, for example, should have been discussed in relation to some of the other comments indicating that there had not been enough time for discussion. My reluctance to intervene was partly based on a fear of diverting interest away from the students' concerns towards those of the teacher. Teachers have the power to do this and students are usually unable to resist. Instead of struggling with their own problems and ideas they are constantly forced to confront those of the teacher. In this course, however, it was essential to intervene frequently in order to focus on what the course was really about and so make it possible for the students to make interventions of the same character instead of continually returning to the official content.

A significant event occurred in the sixth week: unable to inform the students that I had influenza I failed to turn up for the class. The meeting went ahead as planned but I was unable to discover very much about what happened beyond the fact that the group had experienced a crisis of some kind revolving around discussion of the tendency of some members to monopolize the meetings and make leadership bids. Several people doubted the explanation for my absence and suspected that I had deliberately stayed away in order to see what would happen. This reinforced my view of the importance of the first meeting of any class. The impression that what I said could not always be taken at face value, which had been formed during the first meeting, had apparently remained.

At about this time I was also concerned with the issue of how the students were to be assessed. I had raised this briefly at the beginning of the course but it failed to generate any interest. In the eighth week I expressed my concerns at some length and said that I felt it was important for everyone to produce a fairly substantial piece of written work. Several students were concerned that I should be worried about this and said that they were willing to help me by writing something, although another said later that he suspected that this was yet another pedagogic move on my part. Nobody seemed to be worried about assessment and a quite clear assurance must have been given at the beginning about this, although I have no recollection of giving it. One student wrote at the end:

WELSH COLLEGE OF LIBRARY MUSIC & DRAMA

115

The freedom from worry about a summative assessment on the course and relief of anxiety about passing or failing was a major contribution to learning for me. To be able to undertake the major assignment out of concern for John Powell's needs rather than from a need to pass or fail made a difference to the sort of effort that went into it. I am sure it added to the quality of the work, because it became an assessment of me by myself – and I was not satisfied with it when completed, where I suspect an external examiner would have been.

After the completion of the presentations there were still three weeks to go to the end of the semester and I was unsure what to do with this time and the group was slow to come forward with suggestions. One week was spent considering a document which I had distributed and which set out some of my own reflections on the course, and then things ran downhill. I was in the same position as most of the students who in their presentations had shown that they should attempt to 'cover the ground' even though we could not identify anything which we wanted to go over. If this had been faced squarely then the time could have been used to examine in detail the nature of what had been learned.

What did the students learn?

It is not easy to answer this question because I unfortunately failed to require the students to provide a written account of their reactions to the course and what they felt they had learned from it. Only four evaluations were completed, one of them a year later. With hindsight, it would have been extremely useful to have spent the last two weeks in a detailed analysis of the course with special attention being given to factors and events which had helped or hindered learning. Some useful information, however, can be gathered from the weekly reflections and the four final evaluations. The latter each yielded a summative comment:

My main conclusion was that real learning is not possible without meaningful involvement in the teaching-learning process. I very largely abandoned my previous almost totally content-oriented attitudes to learning ... (what matters is that) *I* feel that *I* learned something which had significant influence on my views and attitudes to life and education.

This course has positively identified in me the urge to generate change in my teaching methods – to foster a better learning system for my students. This is the most valuable contribution to one who has taught for 15 years non-stop.

The dawning of many understandings have flowed from all the sessions ... The understandings are neither complete nor simple and I find them continually affecting all the facets of my life and knowledge as I continue to reflect on them.

The ultimate benefit of this course (for me) will only emerge in time as I cope (or try to) with the difficulties of 'teaching' my students attitudes and interpersonal skills. I am sure that there are real benefits to come.

These are all rather vague statements, although it must be admitted that it is extremely difficult to state explicitly what one has learned from a course. They tend to focus on attitudes and to look forward to possible future effects of these on professional practice. Those who felt that they had gained little from the course were probably too polite to say so.

One of the most striking features of the comments made in the weekly reflections on the course was the frequency with which feelings were mentioned, eg disappointment, frustration, enjoyment, enthusiasm, annoyance, resentment, interest, anger, rejection, anxiety, irritation, fulfillment. The emotions play an important part in all teaching and learning situations yet their role is rarely openly discussed. It seems likely that most of these students gained a greater appreciation of the role of the emotions in learning.

There was also quite frequent mention of the gaining of insights related to group processes: understanding others' viewpoints, the need to feel a sense of group coherence, the influence of the teacher's style, the uneven contributions made by members and the difficulties of involving non-contributors, and the problem of keeping discussion relevant. All this could be considered as part of the content of the real course. Surprisingly, the official course material was not often mentioned and this suggests that I may have overestimated the extent to which the students were involved in it.

There were many comments on the need for leadership, more structure, a sense of direction and points of departure. As one student put it:

> I do not feel that I am an expert and I require a start or need to start in some direction before I can operate. This would make me dependent on direction or on a need to work on a particular problem or need.

The relative lack of these was seen by many as an obstacle to learning and there is little doubt that for some this unfamiliar situation created an insuperable barrier which they never managed to overcome.

What did the teacher learn?

At the end of the course I was convinced that, despite all my efforts to the contrary, I had learned a great deal more than the students. On further reflection, however, this seemed a rather simple-minded conclusion. When a course is being taught for the first time it is quite likely that the teacher will learn more than the students: there is much truth in the saying that the best way to learn something is to teach it. But with practice this effect vanishes and everything becomes routine and familiar. This explains why teachers tend to become bored with repeatedly offering the same course. Enthusiasm and interest can then only be maintained through variations in the mode of presentation or by the introduction of new content.

In the course which has been discussed here I was learning how to teach that particular course. Naturally I learned much more about this than the students because they were concerned with quite different problems. Prominent among what was learned was the importance of distinguishing clearly between the official course and the real course, and establishing from the outset the skills and procedures required for the latter. Almost as significant was perceiving the central importance of fully exploring the interests and concerns of the students so as to ensure that any gap between these and what the course offered was not dangerously wide.

This raises a major problem. Some students do not wish to accept more responsibility for their own learning. They prefer to cast the teacher in the role of expert and are quite happy to do little more than take notes and read books as directed. The analogy with doctors and patients is quite strong: we even 'prescribe' texts. How far should one go in respecting and making provision for such preferences? If one adopts the neutral role of facilitator then the problem does not arise although there is still the difficulty of attempting to satisfy what may be a very diverse set of preferences. A teacher, however, has an obligation to try to ensure that certain things are learned and this responsibility cannot be abdicated in favour of leaving everything in the hands of the students. To do this would be to give up the very idea of teaching.

The role of the teacher is crucial in creating, from the beginning, an atmosphere of trust and confidence within which the learners are able to feel free to exercise their independent judgement and pursue their interests within a fairly loose framework of content and procedures. The teacher must give a lead by providing starting points without subsequently transporting everyone to a pre-determined destination.

The reduction of teacher control as a means of fostering independence involves the creation of a role for the teacher which lies outside the experience of most students. They are thus apt to reject it and exert pressure intended to compel the teacher to behave in a more conventional manner. This must be resisted without alienating the learners or provoking disabling anxieties. There is a very strong case for introducing some courses of this type from the beginning of the undergraduate programme. Delaying until it is believed that students are more 'mature' or 'expert' will not work because each experience of a conventional course only locks them more firmly into a passive and dependent role. Primary schools have long allowed and encouraged a high degree of independence in learners: universities should display the same confidence in their students.

Note
For an account of the subsequent development of this course and further discussion of some topics that have only been touched upon here, see Powell (1981, 1985).

Chapter 7

Independent Study:
A Matter of Confidence?

Harry Stanton,
Consultant on Higher Education, University of Tasmania

Introduction

It has long been accepted that no one 'best' way to learn exists for all students under all conditions. Traditionally, however, institutions of higher education have behaved as if this were not so, using the lecture format, supported by tutorials or laboratory sessions, to the virtual exclusion of other approaches. In this chapter, one possible alternative will be explored, which emphasizes independent work undertaken by the student on an individual basis. Under such an approach, contact with the lecturer is minimized, and it is assumed that a student is capable of assuming a considerable degree of responsibility for his or her own learning.

The theoretical basis of such a learning method is outlined, drawing on the principles of humanistic psychology. A case study involving an actual course in educational psychology conducted according to these principles is described, and is discussed in terms of students' willingness to assume responsibility for their own learning.

The latter part of the chapter is devoted to the description of a particular method for helping students develop more confidence in their own ability to work independently. Drawing heavily on a therapeutic framework, this approach involves relaxation, positive suggestion, and success imagery. A number of empirical studies attesting to the efficacy of this approach are presented, and the link between improved student self-confidence and improved capacity to undertake independent study is elaborated.

The nature of the course

Some years ago I designed a rather 'freewheeling' course. My aim was to encourage students to take more responsibility for their own learning. Entitled 'Psychology and Education', this course was taken by Diploma of Education students at the Flinders University of South Australia over a period of one semester. During the four years of its life, the course underwent certain

119

modifications but the basic elements, as set out below, remained unaltered.

The first element, *content*, centred on eight topic areas:

- □ humanistic approaches to education
- □ groups
- □ motivation
- □ behaviour modification
- □ instructional systems approach to education
- □ theories of learning and instruction
- □ factors facilitating learning
- □ programmed instruction and computer assisted instruction.

Obviously this list is only one possible sample of topics which could be included under the label 'educational psychology'. If a student, therefore, did not wish to concentrate his major effort for the semester on one or more of these topics, he could discuss alternatives with me. As an important principle upon which this course was based involved the concept of meaningfulness, I considered it essential that each student should have the opportunity to study something within the context of educational psychology which he found personally significant. If, for a particular student, my initial choice of content failed to provide such a topic, it became necessary to expand the list to meet his needs more satisfactorily.

Teaching method, the second element, was a combination of lectures and student reading for the first three weeks. Four lectures were presented. These provided an overview of the eight topics, emphasis falling upon stimulation of interest rather than upon the provision of information. These lectures, the only ones given in the course, served as an introduction to give students some idea of the material encompassed by each topic. In addition, they were to read two key books in each of the eight areas. I encouraged skim reading at this point, for my intention was to have students overview the material rather than study it in detail.

After the three-week period, students saw me, or my tutor, on an individual basis. At this interview, the student was expected to reveal his familiarity with each of the eight topics, demonstrating that he had actually completed the set readings. Discussion then centred upon which area, or areas, appeared most meaningful to the student. He was free to select any number, ranging from one to eight. A reading list comprising a minimum of 20 items was available for each topic, and the student who opted for depth study focusing on one area only was expected to read everything on the list. Those who preferred more breadth made up a composite reading list drawn from asterisk-marked items on the individual lists.

Voluntary group tutorials were provided on demand. Students who wished to clarify points which had emerged from their reading placed their names on the sheets outside my office. For each topic, there was a separate sheet. I checked these lists daily and when five or six names appeared under a particular topic a tutorial was arranged. Students could come to as many tutorials as they wished. As one would expect, considerable variation existed, with some students attending frequently, others occasionally, and some not at all.

Individual tutorials were also available. Students could arrange to see either my tutor or myself at a mutually convenient time. Approximately 75 per cent of students enrolled in the courses did make use of this opportunity for personal discussion. Time consuming it was, but it certainly helped me to establish a closer rapport with my students than had been possible under the lecture dominated method I had used previously.

The third element, *assessment*, presented something of a problem. Although I felt that self-evaluation was an essential element in helping students take more responsibility for their own learning, I was unable to resolve the essential dilemma posed by this concept. My experience (Stanton, 1978a) has been that self-evaluation is of immense educational value to students. Through consultation with their lecturers and tutors about their self-assessments, students learn how to evaluate themselves realistically. By so doing they also learn a great deal about themselves as individuals.

Yet, the university is held responsible by society for assessing its products. If it permits students to assess themselves, and they do so unrealistically, the university is seen as turning unqualified people loose on the community. Thus it is open to the criticism of shirking its task, of abdicating from its responsibility to place its stamp of approval upon the students it graduates.

I talked over this problem with the first group of students who took the course. A conventional examination, common to all, was obviously inappropriate, for no two students would necessarily be pursuing the same course of study. The alternative at which we arrived was to set 6000 words as a reasonable requirement for a half-year course. How these words were presented was up to the individual student, who could, if he or she wished, submit a single essay. Just as acceptable would be a number of shorter essays. Choice of topic was the student's responsibility. I made it clear that should he or she be unable to think of something personally meaningful I would, as a last resort, provide a specific title, but no one made use of this 'service'. A deadline date was set. If students so desired, they could submit their 6000 words before this date. This procedure carried with it the advantage of a rewrite should their first effort be deemed a failure.

Criteria for making such a judgement were again clarified in discussion with the students. First, the students had to make it clear to me that they had read the material on the reading lists and, I hoped, other books and articles followed up on their initiative. Secondly, this material, as far as possible, was to be expressed in the student's own words rather than in those of the various authors consulted. My feeling is that if a person cannot express an idea in his own words, it is unlikely that he actually understands it. Similarly, I encouraged the student to draw on personal experiences to illustrate the general theoretical points he made, for use of ready-made examples from the literature seems to suggest a lack of understanding of the concepts involved. After all, these students were writing about educational psychology, about learners and learning. They were learners so their own experience was clearly of greatest relevance.

So far I have outlined the main elements of a course which could be labelled 'independent learning' or 'individual learning'. I have not, however, outlined the reasons why I chose to set up a course in this particular way. This I shall now attempt to do.

Rationale

I see teaching as the facilitation of learning. It is warranted insofar as it makes learning easier and/or more efficient than it would otherwise be. If, through his exposure to a lecturer, a student learns something better than he would have done alone, the teaching is of value. If no such facilitation takes place, I cannot see any real justification for teaching. As I considered my own teaching in this light, I had certain doubts about my value to the students. Like the majority of my colleagues, I 'taught' by means of lectures and tutorials, giving out information by 'telling'. Underlying such a procedure is the assumption that students learn by being 'told' things. Yet my own experience as a learner and my reading of the literature relating to how people learn would suggest that such an assumption is incorrect.

I do not see learning as primarily a process of accumulating information which is then stored for use on later occasions. Something more is needed which involves the student as an active participant rather than a passive recipient. As Combs *et al* (1971) put it:

> Learning is the discovery of meaning. The problem of learning, modern psychologists tell us, always involves two aspects: one is the acquisition of new knowledge or experience; the other has to do with the individual's personal discovery of the meaning of information for him. The provision of information can be controlled by an outsider with or without the co-operation of the learner. It can even be done, when necessary, by mechanical means which do not require a person at all. The discovery of meaning, however, can only take place in people and cannot occur without the involvement of persons. (p 21)

If this definition of learning can be accepted, it would seem that in our lectures, and perhaps in our tutorials, we concentrate unduly on Combs' first aspect, that of information transmission. We tend to neglect the second aspect by failing to create an environment in which students are encouraged to find personal meaning in the avalanche of material with which they are presented.

Thus, dissatisfaction with lecturing as a method of facilitating students' search for meaning lay at the basis of my change in course design. Also, I had confidence that a viable alternative was available. In his book *Freedom to Learn*, Rogers (1969) has pointed out that the traditional approach to teaching is virtually guaranteed to reduce meaningful learning to a minimum. This it does by prescribing that all students should follow the same curriculum, write similar assignments, listen to the same lectures, and be assessed by the same examination. To change this state of affairs, Rogers has suggested creation of a learning environment involving a largley self-chosen curriculum, student-generated assignments, a relative absence of lectures, and a reduction in the importance of grades. If a teacher is able to provide such an environment he will, according to Rogers, help students find the relationship between the material they study and the personal significance it holds for them. A lecturer cannot do this learning for his students, but he can make it easier for them to do so themselves. Gibran (1926) puts it beautifully when he says of the teacher:

> If he is indeed wise he does not bid you enter the house of his wisdom but rather leads you to the threshold of your own mind.

Assessment of the course

My course, then, was an attempt to put into practice some of the principles of humanistic learning propounded by Combs and Rogers. In terms of process it was a very rewarding experience for me, and also for some of my students. They put a great deal into it, reading widely, attending group tutorials, talking with me, and writing superb essays, ranging in length from the 6000 words set to well over 12,000 words. It was not only the length of essay which was so impressive – the content was often very moving. A number of students re-evaluated their lives in terms of self-concept theory, or applied the principles of behaviour modification to their family situation, or attempted to formulate a mode of education which would be superior to one which they had experienced. From such writings it became painfully obvious that many of our best students were completely alienated by the education they had received at school and university.
Comments such as the following were not uncommon:

> I think this has been the most relevant assignment that I have done this year – it's been a piece of work in which I have really discovered and not merely regurgitated masses of material which we have had to read in order to fulfil someone's requirements. It's been a refreshing change and, I think, one of the rare instances of real learning in my whole time at this University.

In fact, a consistent thread running through many of the anonymous responses made by students on the end of course evaluation questionnaire was the contrast between the sense of personal discovery in this cousre and the complete irrelevance, in terms of relationship to important life issues, of their other university courses.
Heady stuff this, but the observant reader will have noted that I said *some* students found the course a rewarding experience. Others obviously did not. Despite initial enthusiasm for a course which actually gave them the freedom they said they wanted, many students, approximately one-third of the class, did very little work at all. They dashed off their essays as just another meaningless

academic exercise to be disposed of with as little effort as possible and with a minimum of personal involvement. This attitude disappointed me greatly, but that was my problem. Probably I was quite unrealistic in expecting all my students to respond to the type of course I had provided. In fact, I was forced to reassess a basic assumption which had guided much of my effort to provide enhanced learning experiences for my students.

Like many of my colleagues I believed, perhaps naively, that students at a university were there because they wanted to learn. Where my experience indicated that they were not learning, I attributed this to poor teaching methods or to an irrelevant, pedestrian curriculum. The evidence produced by the humanistically based course which I have described, however, made it difficult for me to continue to explain student indifference in this way. Some students obviously do want to learn; many others do not. No matter how a course is designed, it will not, I believe, encourage more than a certain percentage of students to actually learn.

Perhaps I am overstating the case here, my view being distorted by my definition of learning as a two-stage process involving both information acquisition and the discovery of personal meaning in that information. If my definition was restricted only to information acquisition, then many more students could be described as learners. Or could they? Our usual measure of learning is examination performance, and it is no great task for students to pass by feeding back the lecturer's own words. These words, though, are frequently quite meaningless to the student and have to be learned by rote, almost like nonsense syllables in a psychological experiment. Such 'learning' is likely to be of a very short-term nature.

My feeling that a sizeable proportion of our students have no real desire to learn has been confirmed by others. Many journal reports of educational initiatives bear eloquent testimony to the lack of student interest and response, even when these experimental methods directly incorporate the features students claim they want most (eg Goldman *et al*, 1974; Paskow, 1974).

Before I commenced my own experimental course, I asked several Diploma of Education classes whether they would prefer it to the more traditional course they were at present taking. Something like two-thirds of these groups expressed a preference for the unstructured, 'freewheeling' course. However, over three-quarters of these favourably inclined students doubted their ability to handle such a course. The idea appealed to them but they had little confidence they would actually complete the work without regular compulsory tutorials, or assignment deadlines. That is, they felt unable to timetable themselves, unable to take responsibility for their own learning without someone to force them to do so. One student summed up the attitude of many of his fellows when he said:

> Without constant compulsion and supervision I wouldn't do any work. Going to lectures is the easy way. The lecturer does all the work and all I have to do is sit there and copy down as much as possible of what he says. Then I give it back to him in an examination. No sweat at all.

124

Remember that these students were graduates. Already they had spent three, or sometimes four years, at a university one of whose avowed aims was to encourage students to take increased responsibility for their own learning. A very depressing situation, surely, one which certainly drained from me much of my enthusiasm for modifying learning environments. If students showed so little interest in managing their own learning why should I bother? Yet something continued to niggle at me. Was it simply that students did not want to take responsibility for their own learning, or was it that they lacked the confidence in themselves to do so? In so many of the comments made by the students, the theme of self-doubt emerged, taking the form of a negative attitude towards anything which required real effort. Alexander Dumas summed up the effect of such an atittude in these words:

> A person who doubts himself is like a man who would enlist in the ranks of his enemies and bear arms against himself. He makes failure certain by himself being the first person to be convinced of it.

I hypothesized, then, that if I could find some way of helping students to increase their self-confidence, this might effect a change in their attitude towards independent study. Instead of doubting their ability to undertake such courses, they might be able to attain an expectancy of success. As Gindes (1973) has pointed out in the context of psychotherapy, the patient who expects to get well is likely to do so. Perhaps this concept is generalizable to the educational environment.

In fact, there appear to be many similarities between teaching and therapy (Stanton, 1978b), for both involve learning. With the course I have described earlier in this chapter, I was attempting to establish an environment in which students could learn meaningfully and in a way which was significant to them. I hoped that they would be helped to discover meaning in the material encountered so that their potentialities as human beings might be more fully realized.

My work as a psychotherapist embraces the same principles. I do not think I can cure anyone, nor can I do a student's learning for him. However, what I can do is help patients to cure themselves by helping them to discover meaning in their own lives, in the hope that through this contact with me they may learn how to organize their lives more successfully (Stanton, 1979). Similarly, I hope I can help students learn more effectively than they otherwise would.

As I considered this basic concordance between therapy and teaching, I speculated that the method I had been using in the former context might apply equally well to the latter. This method, comprising a combination of three elements, relaxation, suggestion and imagery, has proved most successful in helping people lose weight (Stanton, 1975a), conquer insomnia (Stanton, 1975b) and stop smoking (Stanton, 1978c).

Three or four treatment sessions were used, the same general procedure being followed on each occasion. First, patients were helped to relax. A variety of

125

means was used to achieve this end, including deep breathing, counting, fixation of eyes on a bright object, muscle heaviness, and mental visualization of a pleasant scene. Possibly the last of these proved to be the technique most consistently successful in inducing a state of deep physical and mental relaxation.

Once the patients had allowed themselves to 'let go', I talked to them quietly, employing a series of positively worded suggestions designed to produce ego enhancement. These pertained to increased energy, improved health, ability to cope with problems, increased calmness, personal well-being, feelings of contentment, increased self-confidence and improved concentration. Details of a comprehensive script suitable for use in a wide range of therapeutic situations may be found in a previous article (Stanton, 1975c).

It would appear that when a person relaxes, the normal critical 'watchdog' faculty of his mind becomes less marked, permitting easy acceptance of suggestions which are in accordance with his wishes. People cannot, of course, be made to do things they do not wish to do, nor can they be given abilities they do not already possess. However, they can be helped to gain confidence in their own power to change themselves in ways in which they want to change and to transcend the often unreasoned limits they have tended to place upon themselves.

Particular emphasis, then, was placed upon the way in which the patient's confidence would increase as he realized the power he had to control his own life. This emphasis was achieved both through verbal suggestion and through encouraging the patient to think of himself the way he wanted to be. For example, the person wanting to lose weight would mentally visualize himself standing on a set of scales showing the weight he wanted to be. Also he would see himself looking the way he wanted to look when he was that weight.

My first attempt to generalize this relaxation-suggestion-imagery (RSI) technique to an educational context was directed towards the reduction of test-anxiety in primary school children (Stanton, 1977). Test anxiety, operationalized in terms of scores on the Test Anxiety Scale for Children (Sarason *et al*, 1960) was considerably reduced for an experimental group as compared to a control group which experienced no RSI treatment ($t = 22.57$, *df* $= 49$, p < 0.001). These gains were maintained in a subsequent test administered six months later.

When the RSI technique was used with student teachers feeling anxious about their first teaching practice, similar positive results were achieved. The measuring instrument used was a self-report confidence scale on which students were asked to rate their confidence in themselves as teachers (see Figure 1).

I have employed this type of scale in most of my studies into self-confidence enhancement. In so doing I have been greatly influenced by Allport (1960) who maintained that the most effective way of finding out what a person is like is to ask him. This view he contrasted with that propounded by the advocates of projective and disguised purpose testing who, he felt, needlessly complicated a relatively straightforward issue. Combs and Snygg (1959) have made the same point:

... it is a person's perception of his personality that would seem to be more important than some 'objective' personality, discoverable only through projective measures which deceive the respondee over the true purpose of the test. If a person thinks he is highly anxious, his behaviour is likely to reflect this personality trait.

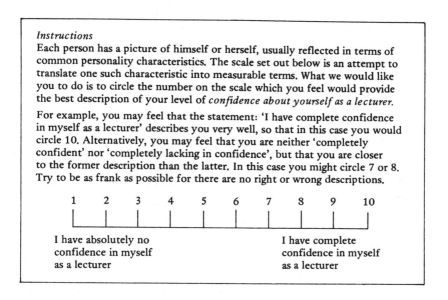

Figure 1 *Confidence scale*

Whatever the particular trait might be, if a person believes he is anxious, or lacking in self-confidence, or anything else, he is likely to behave as if that perception were true. Therefore, if he can be helped to change his perception, there is a strong possibility that his behaviour will be modified accordingly.

In the student teacher study there was no measure of behaviour change. However, of the 18 subjects who experienced four RSI treatment sessions, 13 improved their score on the confidence scale. Further studies using matched pairs of Diploma of Education students and tertiary level teachers drawn from universities and colleges of advanced education produced favourable results. In all cases, the RSI treatment enabled subjects to report themselves as feeling more self-confident.

An indirect measure of behavioural change was then added to the experimental programme. In an attempt to discover whether improved teaching performance resulted from increased self-confidence, students evaluated a group of lecturers both before and after they experienced the RSI treatment on a simple rating-of-performance scale (see Figure 2).

I reasoned that if students rated a particular lecturer at the same level on both evaluations, this would suggest the RSI treatment, though effective in helping a person feel more self-confident as a teacher, was not effective in actually modifying his or her teacher behaviour. However, if a lecturer was rated more highly after treatment than before, this would indicate behavioural change in a positive direction.

Of the 20 experimental group subjects, 11 improved their scores on the student evaluation scale. No member of this group recorded a lower score on the post-treatment measure than he did on the pre-treatment measure.

Students had no knowledge that these particular lecturers had been undergoing any special treatment, and the evaluations were carried out as part of institution wide surveys.

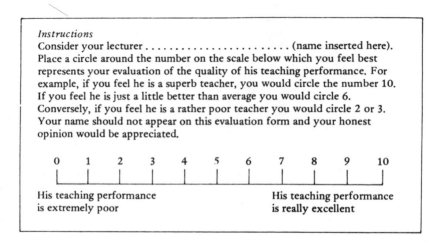

Figure 2 *Student evaluation of teaching scale*

These positive results encouraged me to investigate whether the RSI procedure could help students to feel more confident in their ability to study independently, and to take more responsibility for their own learning instead of relying on lecture-imposed structure.

From a class of 128 Diploma of Education students, 40 were selected at random. They were matched in pairs on the basis of their scores on a structure of course scale which is set out in Figure 3.

One member of each pair became a control and the other, allocated at random, experienced three RSI sessions. These sessions were spaced at weekly intervals, the first of them being of 50 minutes' duration. This time was used in the following way:

☐ Fifteen minutes spent in the establishment of rapport, the answering of questions, and the inculcation of a positive expectancy of success.

Instructions

Each of us has a preference for the way a course is structured. You may, for example, prefer the lecturer or teacher to organize it completely so that he tells you exactly what to do at all times. If this is the case, you would place a circle around 1 on the scale below. On the other hand, if you prefer to work completely independently of your lecturer or teacher, you would place a circle around 10 on the scale. Probably your preference will fall somewhere between these two extremes but whatever your choice feel free to indicate it for there are no right or wrong answers.

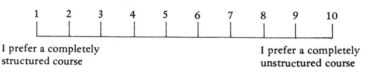

I prefer a completely structured course   I prefer a completely unstructured course

Figure 3 *Structure of course scale*

- ☐ Twenty minutes spent in the induction of a relaxed state, the delivery and reception of ego-enhancing suggestions, and the creation of success imagery. This involved subjects visualizing themselves organizing their time, reading attentively, participating informally in discussion with peers, writing essays well before due dates, and covering a lot of material effortlessly and with enjoyment.
- ☐ Five minutes of discussion with me relative to their feelings and thoughts during the 20-minute RSI treatment.
- ☐ Ten minutes of further RSI activity.

The two succeeding sessions were of 25 minutes' duration. Each involved an initial relaxation period, reception of ego-enhancing suggestions, and creation of success imagery. After the first induction, virtually all subjects achieved relaxation very quickly so they had ample time for very specific visualizations.

The attitude of the experimental group towards independent study as opposed to a tightly structured lecture course in which virtually everything was organized for them was measured by the structure of course scale. This scale was administered before and after the three RSI sessions, as was the confidence scale mentioned earlier in the chapter. This same measurement procedure was adopted with the control group which received no treatment. They did, however, discuss, for a comparable period, the advantages and disadvantages of independent study relative to highly structured lecture courses. This discussion was rather anecdotal, involving the exchange of experiences in differing types of courses. The role I adopted in the group was that of moderator, although I contributed information about my own experiences, both as student and teacher.

A comparison of experimental and control groups on the structure of course scale scores revealed a marked difference. Naturally the two means (3.7) were similar on the pre-treatment measure, for this score was the basis on which the groups were matched. However, after the three RSI sessions, the experimental group mean was 6.3. That of the control group, tested at the same time, was 3.5. This difference was highly significant ($t = 11.1$, $df = 18$, $p < 0.001$). Of the 20 subjects in the experimental group, 18 recorded an increased score of at least one point in the structure of course scale while two remained the same. Comparable figures for the control group were three improvements, four decreases, and 13 remaining the same.

A similar result was produced by the confidence scale where the post-treatment difference in means between the two groups was again highly significant ($t = 6.9$, $df = 18$, $p < 0.001$). Seventeen members of the experimental group showed an increase of at least one point while only four members of the control group showed a gain. No experimental subject recorded a lower confidence scale score, whereas four control subjects did so.

A very pleasing aspect of this investigation was the six-month follow up which involved a further administration of the two scales. At this times, the gains of the experimental group over the control group were still maintained. Earlier studies had indicated that the RSI treatment produced gains enduring beyond the actual experimental situation and the results of this investigation confirmed this finding.

One further study has been conducted with senior secondary school students who were to be offered the choice between a conventional teacher-dominated course and a more loosely structured course in which they were to receive greatly reduced guidance. In this latter option, the teacher was to act as a resource person. When requested to do so, he or she would provide assistance but basically students were to be furnished with a list of objectives, a comprehensive reading list and a sample examination paper indicating precisely how they would be assessed on the work done. They were then allowed to achieve these objectives in their own way. Working in pairs or groups was encouraged.

Of the 74 students given the choice of the two options, only 21 preferred the independent study programme. In an open discussion on what their choice revealed, students admitted to a lack of confidence in their ability to handle the freedom. They felt they would let down both themselves and their teacher, and did not wish to take the responsibility of organizing their own study. However, after these 74 students experienced the three RSI treatment sessions, 53 decided they would tackle the independent study option.

This study, and the one described previously, do seem to indicate that the RSI treatment will help students feel more confident in their ability to handle an independent study programme. However, the question remains as to whether this increased confidence will enable them to actually achieve the success they now believe is possible for them. On this issue, I have no hard data, for I have not been in a position to conduct another course on the lines of the one I described at the commencement of this chapter.

Fortunately some anecdotal evidence is available. The teacher who proposed the two-option course to his senior secondary students was delighted with the results achieved. Actually, this was his third attempt to encourage his students to take more responsibility for their own learning, the first two having produced a very disappointing outcome. This time, he felt the majority of the students taking the independent study option had worked really well. This effort was reflected in excellent examination results which compared more than favourably with the group taking the teacher-dominated option. Both these groups sat a common examination. Although one cannot discount the teacher's bias here, for he wanted the 'independents' to do well, the fact does remain that they performed far more creditably than had the students in the two previous attempts. An added bonus was the positive attitude of most of the 'independents' at the end of the course. They had demonstrated to themselves that they could organize their own learning and this contributed to a marked increase in self-esteem.

I would not claim, of course, that every one of the 53 students taking the independent option showed this improved self-concept. Despite their initial confidence that they could take more responsibility for their own learning, 17 students found performance did not match intent. With the best of intentions, they were unable to timetable themselves or to discipline themselves to work without close supervision.

Somewhat the same proportion, approximately one-third, behaved in this way when the Diploma of Education students referred to earlier undertook an independent study course. According to the lecturer in charge of the 40 members of the experimental group, 28 performed well. This compared quite favourably with the control group, of whom only 12 were considered by the lecturer to have put any real effort into their work.

These anecdotal reports suggest that the RSI treatment does not only help students to feel more confident in their ability to cope with independent study but also to perform in accordance with this belief. As attitude change is so difficult to achieve, it is more encouraging to find that a method as simple as RSI should be able to produce the effect it does. This is particularly so when it is realized that the actual time involved is only 100 minutes.

The RSI method has other advantages, too. In itself, it is an enjoyable experience. People like the feeling of relaxation, of 'letting go'. They feel good about the control they are able to take over their own lives, for the effect of the RSI treatment extends far beyond that of helping students feel more confident about their ability to study independently. It results in a general increase of confidence so that people feel more competent to transcend the limits they have been placing on themselves. Schwartz (1971) put it neatly when he said:

> You are what you think you are.
> Think more of yourself and there is more of you.

Through the RSI technique people can, it would seem, be helped to think more of themselves, to feel competent to cope with situations which had previously overawed them. More specifically, it would appear that RSI offers a reasonable prospect for helping students to handle independent study courses more confidently and, perhaps, more successfully.

Chapter 8
One-to-one Learning

David Potts,
Department of History, La Trobe University, Melbourne

Introduction and background

In 1973 I began a series of workshops in a history-sociology course at La Trobe University, Melbourne. They were 'workshops', as opposed to one-hour tutorials, in that they each ran for three hours of varied learning activities. In them I tried to integrate academic learning with a growth in self-confidence, self-knowledge and enjoyment and identity with the group. All this both implied and led to autonomy. The main method I used – and this is a central theme of this article – was what I call one-to-one discussion, something like an application of co-counselling techniques to academic work.

Some of my ideas for these workshops sprang spontaneously from a long standing interest in learning innovation, including experience as a schoolteacher and, more recently, study for a degree in tertiary education. However, the big fillip came when my department and the university allowed me to look at tertiary learning experiments overseas. In 1972, in London and New York, I experienced anything that I thought might expand my sense of how people learn in groups. I went to teachers' conferences and training programmes, kindergartens, schools, universities (especially New York experimental colleges), humanistic psychology groups, communes, and religious sect meetings; and I talked to anyone anywhere. Out of the vast flurry of experiences and ideas, and nights of restless excitement, I gradually concocted plans for my workshop programme.

The one-to-one discussion technique that was central to these plans can best be described from a set of narrative accounts of how I came by the idea. The first, and most important experience for me in this respect, was what was called an 'Enlightenment Intensive'. I attended a group run along these lines by Jeff Love, through Quaesitor, at a farmhouse in Worcestershire, England. Here, the whole experience was based on paired learning. The 20 people who attended were split up into ten pairs, scattered throughout a large room. They were instructed to sit up alertly and face each other, then one asked the other, 'Tell me who you are'. The speaker had seven minutes to work on the question, while the listener, always paying supportive attention, would not interrupt in any way. The roles would then be reversed. After 42 minutes, that is, after three talk periods for each partner, everyone got up, formed into new pairs, and repeated the process. Occasionally there were short breaks for exercise or light meals, but basically the one-to-one talk pattern was maintained over an 18-hour day, for three days.

The object was to formulate a simple answer, to convince oneself and not be dissuaded by the group leader. No one reached this point until the third day. But it was the experience of exploration, not the answer itself, that mattered most. Even those who at the beginning were self-denigratory (such as a drug addict who said he was 'fucking nothing' and spent most of his time silent or weeping) eventually battled through, with nothing but the space provided by attentive listening, to a position of huge self-affirmation.

Those who formulated answers satisfying to themselves went on to other questions, such as, 'What is another?' and 'How is life fulfilled?' Particularly from these latter questions I became inspired with ideas for adapting self-enlightenment to other forms of enlightenment. The 18-hour day of effort also fascinated me, in the fact that people could pay attention so long if given a 50-50 chance for self-expression.

Next, I discovered various forms of co-counselling, and I came to see further advantages of uninterrupted talking-through. Jerome Liss gave me a paper in which he argued as follows:

> People in their daily lives are too often interrupted and not permitted to complete their thoughts. Direct interruptions, meaning one person speaks while the other is still talking, can block one talker's mind if he does not finish his say ... Repetitive interruptions not only chop up the ongoing stream of thoughts and feelings of the moment, but the two-person pattern is internalised and repeated by the interrupted person's mind when alone. Thus, people who feel 'blocked', 'stuck', 'bogged down' or 'hemmed in' have been stopped by others from unravelling their thoughts and feelings and are plagued by self-interrupted thoughts when alone.

From this, it struck me that students' experiences of traditional tutorial discussions are more of interruption than self-expression. A dozen students at a one-hour session mostly average only a couple of minutes of talking time each. This gives some chance for a fruitful clash of competing ideas already formed, but not for careful and individual development of ideas. In my experience, students trying to work up their ideas are quickly attacked on any weaknesses, weaknesses they could have corrected themselves given more space. They become frustrated and defensive, and few I think try later to work it all out. Most give up before they start under such conditions, and simply listen to two or three leaders being herded along by the tutor. It is inadequate practice for the personal articulation of thoughts, and this shows up in poor written work.

I went on to discover more about co-counselling (from Harvey Jackins, John Heron and others), particularly about blockage in rationality through emotional tension. Any learning is about the processing of experience, and is generally inadequate if initiated and consolidated under stress. Yet students start at school and tertiary institutions with self-doubts about their worth and ability, and this may be added to by the pressures of competition with others and the judgements of authority. I came to believe that they need structured space in which to explore ideas, without criticism or other interruption, to assist them to feel values, to clear blockages, and to learn to think both freely and, from that, rationally. It was to create such a space that I decided on the three-hour workshops with extensive one-to-one talking.

When I returned to Australia I began to plan workshops in more detail for our course in Mexican history-sociology. I designed these around a few major principles. First, for a tertiary course of somewhat conscripted participants, I made the one-to-one talk periods briefer and more varied than in Jeff Love's enlightenment intensive, not to make things too tough. Secondly, even academic questions were worded on the Zen-like principle that the process of exploration is more important than the answer. For instance, I preferred 'What is the Mexican Revolution?' to 'What caused the Mexican Revolution?' It is more inexhaustibly explorative. I especially eschewed anything as potentially factual as 'How was the Mexican Constitution formed in 1917?' I believed open-ended questions would give students more chance to work from limited information and to develop more autonomy. Thirdly, I decided to include activities to build self-confidence and self-knowledge, group identity and so on, as steps towards other learning, but they were to remain steps and not become prime objectives; I decided I would always try to integrate them with coursework and make links apparent. Fourthly, I sought, and was thankfully granted the right, to have the course non-graded; anyone would pass as long as they attended and did a set quantity of written work (quality judgement was not to be a control). And lastly, and quite as important as all the other aspects of method, I decided to demand a weekly written statement or 'journal' from students on their workshop experience, to consolidate learning, to help develop writing skills, and to give me feedback.

My feeling that Australian university students would respond positively to all this was, of course, quite untested. Several colleagues condemned the programme. Some, for instance, said students should not be made to talk, and that it could not be done anyhow; others said I had no right to tamper with psychology and navel-gazing. I argued vigorously. Eventually the chairman, with many regrets, quietly gave me permission to try.

The first workshop and the course in general

At the beginning of the academic year, in the first lecture on Mexican history, a first-year course, I called for volunteers for the experimental workshops. Out of 130 students I was able to form two groups which stabilized out after a week at one of 15 students and the other of 16. We were given a professor's large room to work in, with a carpeted floor and a scattering of ordinary chairs (which allow people to sit up alertly). Altogether, I had just what I wanted.

I planned the first workshop in detail, and this is outlined below. The one-to-one partnerships are presented in shorthand form. For instance, one pattern reads: 'One-to-one: "What is fact?", A 3 min, B 3 min; A 3 min, B 3 min'. This means that each partner talks twice for uninterrupted times of three minutes. Students were always instructed to address their partner by name in asking the set question, and to thank each other by name at the end of each partnership. I regard these courtesies as very important. All timing was done with an oven-timer and I took part in the pairs where there were unequal numbers of students. The numbers in the left-hand column are the hours and minutes of the start of each section, from 0.00, at the beginning, to 3.00, the end of the third hour. Note, too, each stretch of uninterrupted talk time is short, for these first experiences. Later I expanded them to 3 to 6 minutes and set more repetitions.

1. Plan of first workshop

(As adhered to and with some additions to what actually happened.)

0.00   Loss due to delays

0.10   Introduction: Express pleasure that the group has formed. Broadly explain the one-to-one method, something of my experiences and the general philosophy behind it. Ask students to keep in mind for immediate purposes that the listeners are serving the speakers; their job is (a) to pay alert attention and (b) not to interrupt in any way. Answer questions, but suggest main discussion should come after experience.

0.30   *Getting to know each other*

One-to-one: 'Tell me something about yourself.' A 2 min, B gives résumé of what A said (purely an attention test) 1 min; B 2 min, A résumé 1 min. Change partners: A 2 min, B 2 min (ie this time no résumés).

Group (everyone in a full circle): comments, complaints, attitudes to non-interruption. Group (making sure no one is sitting next to either of his or her previous partners): Turn by turn going around the circle, each person to identify himself and each of the two people who partnered him to give one or two sentence comments on what was remembered as most interesting, everyone constantly naming each other, eg, A, 'I'm Joan'; B, 'I'm Harry. I listened to Joan, and what I found most interesting was that Joan was brought up at Apollo Bay and she has a pet magpie'; 'I'm Pat. I listened to Joan, and ... '. In this process everyone is eventually named several times, at dispersed intervals. At the end of it call on volunteers (everyone forewarned) to name the group one by one till everyone can do it.

1.20   Filling in departmental record sheets.

1.30   *History method*

Purpose: to discuss distinction between 'fact' and 'interpretation'. Brief discussion in group to set up problem.

One-to-one: 'What is fact?' A 3 min, B 3 min; A 3 min, B 3 min. Describe each other's face in factual terms (as near as you can): A 2 min, B 2 min; A and B (open discussion) 2 min.

1.55 Group: one volunteer to attempt to describe someone's face factually, followed by group critical discussion of the exercise. Students are shown a large photograph, unlabelled (it was of Zapata); each write (a) a short factual description of the face, and (b) an interpretative description. General discussion of the exercise including my reading some of the written observations and asking for comments, and my leading individuals into difficulties over justifying their interpretations.

2.15 Individual: reading of a short document (a mainly narrative description of a hacienda), 5 min.
One-to-one: 'What parts of the document are factual *v* interpretative?' A 2 min, B 2 min.
Individual: reading of a second document (an interpretation of an Indian's attitudes of mind in his response to a flogging), 5 min.
One-to-one (new partners): discuss second document. A 2 min, B 2 min; A 2 min, B 2 min.
Group: sharing of main conclusions on the two documents, 7 min.

2.45 *History content* (preparation)
One-to-one: 'What is Mexican?' (Instruction: if you are short on information, discuss it as a *type* of question.) A 2 min, B 2 min; A 2 min, B 2 min. Change partners: A 2 min, B 2 min; A 2 min, B 2 min.

2.55 Instructions for next week:
(a) We will continue with 'What is Mexican?' and introduce 'What is revolution?'
(b) Suggestions for reading.
(c) Journals: to be about 500 words, as a recollection of your main learning experiences in the workshop; any emphasis you choose but I would appreciate some comment on each of the three major sections and the general learning method. Keep carbon copies. Original copies to be handed to me as soon after the workshop as practical.

3.00 Conclusion: express pleasure that we have shared our first workshop; thank everyone for participating.

In the opening sections of this first workshop I felt awkward and anxious, while putting on a bold front. Students sat in silence while I explained the method. The whole idea began to overwhelm me as ridiculously contrived; 16 blank faces watched me as I talked. Then I had to give the orders: pair up, await further instructions. An endless five seconds followed before anyone moved; gradually they found partners, shuffling into position. I gave the instructions: face your partner, introduce each other; decide who is going to talk first; listener, address your partner by name and ask him, 'Tell me something about yourself'; remember, listen attentively and do not interrupt in any way; start now. As I actually spoke the words I felt an immense inner wave of insecurity; what if my colleagues were right, what if they wouldn't talk? Pause. Then began a faint surge of speech. The exercise staggered under way. That was the worst moment. Thereafter energy and enthusiasm picked up all round.

The other most intense emotion for me in the first workshop, and for several other workshops until I was used to it, was a strange sense of loss of role of authority as a teacher. Once people were paired up they were on their own. Sitting back to take it in (where I was not in a pair if there were even numbers of students) I watched animated faces and gestures, heard bursts of laughter, saw pained expressions and noted moments of silence. The arguments might be wrong; someone might need encouragement; someone might need prodding. But it was all beyond my influence. The oven-timer ticked away as a watchful guide over the protected space; no directing, no judging. What was happening out there? I could only find out, roughly, in a chosen set of confidences, when the journals came in a day or so later, though I learned a little along the way, from a few people in group discussion. For the great part, however, the immediate experience was, as I said, one of lost control, lost authority. Colleagues have since had similar experiences.

From here on I continued to plan each workshop to the last minute (drawing on direct experience and on criticism from journals). However, in practice I treated the plans rather flexibly. As the students in the workshops were volunteers from the main lecture and set-reading course, a formal academic structure was always there for them to use. The one-to-one questions were broad enough for them either to do the reading as set or to develop their own lines of inquiry and find their own reading.

The assessment of the workshops which follows is based mostly on students' journals, and each student comment is identified by the author's first name and a bracketed number indicating the week in which it was written (over the 13 weeks of the course).

2. The journals

In the workshop groups students were under constraint to produce a 500-word journal each week or else they would have to do a final examination. I prewarned them at the end of each workshop, and sometimes we made brief notes on the main structure of the three hours, as a memory guide. Apart from that, they were instructed to write as they wished on what they wished, as long as it bore some relation to the three-hour session. Given the large range of issues touched on in workshops, that gave a lot of scope for variety. I did not correct the journals in any way or comment on them or return them (students kept copies for themselves). I felt that any opinions would be prescriptive. As a requirement, journals were in excess of the traditional essay work and other exercises on which I did offer criticism, so they could safely be left as a learning rather than a teaching tool. All I did was comment at the next week's workshop on problems raised or on questions of general importance to the group and so on, often primarily just to assure students that the journals were always read.

As a task for me, even when I had 60 students in workshop courses in later years, I did not find reading journals a chore. It took only a couple of minutes to read each one and my incentive was always high because they were a continuous reflection on my role as a teacher, whether they were very specifically on history problems, or on the impacts of methods, or about personalities and personal problems or perspectives. Some were very moving, insightful, passionate; some were highly skilled and perceptive pieces of history; some were very funny or creative (dialogues, mock biographies, narratives, comic form, paste-ups ...); and one or two from year to year were utterly exhausting in their personal abuse (a Maoist woman, for instance, attacked me regularly as a 'bourgeois individualist shit'). Throughout it all I remained silent. If students wanted to discuss something, they had to see me personally. Journals were to be unjudged, a sort of natural extension of one-to-one.

As a task for students, attitudes to journals varied. Nearly everyone submitted them regularly without trouble, and many wrote well beyond the minimum required length. Different people had different ups and downs about the writing. Some took to it immediately. Some had periods of alienation and got over them. Many pushed me with questions about what I wanted; what 'should' they write about. I kept telling them to make their own choice, to discover their own areas of interest from their own issues raised in one-to-one. A growth of autonomy in this respect is reflected in the following pair of comments from Marylin: '[I find writing the journal] annoying ... I'm just filling up a gap of 500 words' (week 4). Then, 'I found that by writing the journals regularly I have lost the hang-up completely of writing them. It is no longer a dread to write a journal, in fact it gives me a little satisfaction' (6). Paul (13) discovered 'The best way to write journals is to write them to yourself and not to David or history department heads or to anyone else.' A couple of students regarded journal writing as a chore from beginning to end. But these were clearly exceptions. I think it was a measure of students' learning to express themselves in journals, and to value the experience, that a few began to write them in other subjects.

For my own part the journals were invaluable. They gave me a deeper sense of contact with everyone, which one-to-one did not allow. They helped me to meet problems as they arose, or even reduced problems in themselves as they seemed to give the students a cathartic sense of release from lows (as well as a consolidation of highs); they gave me insights into what was happening in group discussion that I could never judge from the dominant spokespeople; they were inspiring in showing what people could write from their own drive and interest, from prior articulation; and they gave me both tremendous confidence to judge the value of particular exercises and questions and a flood of ideas towards planning each coming workshop.

3. The one-to-one method in general

Students mostly felt very uneasy about one-to-one at first. They claimed to feel 'strange' (Robyn), 'defensive' (Betty), 'frightened ... nervous' (Gary) and 'shy' (Doris). John, a very sociable 28-year-old ex-truckdriver, said, 'I felt some unease at being drawn, nay forced, into conversation with a total stranger ... '. At the personal level, however, John found the 'barriers quickly came down'. Students were generally thrilled at getting to know each other so well within the first workshop. On the method itself for general purposes, week by week, they had most difficulty with non-interruption. I had to be strict about this, moving across the room to ask the student not to interrupt if I saw him break the rule, and spending several moments of group discussion over various weeks to look at problems with the technique. Students came to accept it. They did, however, ask for a pattern of open discussion at the end of one-to-one rounds, and this procedure I adopted more and more frequently for later workshops. Thus a likely pattern on a given question would become: A 3 min, B 3 min; A 3 min, B 3 min; AB 4 min (the 'AB' indicating that cross-questioning and argument were allowed). Another complaint was against the oven-timer. Some people objected that it cut them off at a peak moment of insight, and so on. But no one could think of a way round it if each talker's space were to be clearly delineated and if the whole group were to be working on the same time-span for changes of partners and questions.

Another problem caused by the system of partners was the formation of favourites or complaints about partners who had not prepared properly. My main response to complaints was to try to persuade the members of the group not to let the partner establish a tone, or style, for the whole partnership. I reminded them that they were not engaged in a discussion but that they were each working for himself. Too often, I argued, people were accusing their partners of sins they themselves were committing (being repetitive, off the question, or overgeneralized). If they looked to themselves they had plenty of work on. They could provide a service to their partners by self-improvement and good example; and they could use their listening time to try to think out what explicitly bored or troubled them with their partner's observations – to raise their own consciousness of how they could improve themselves. In sum, my message was: you cannot, and should not try to, assume responsibility for your partner; but you can and should assume responsibility for yourself. This message got through to some.

By and large the problems, even if not resolved, were outweighed by the successes. My main expectations of one-to-one were confirmed. First, students felt they became more articulate, both in their pairs and, from there, generally; Gary (2), 'I felt ... my ability to express my thoughts had been improved'; Paul (13), 'because the one-to-one established an open casual atmosphere, small and large group discussions became easier'; John (4), 'I am finding it easier to engage in conversation about any subject I am doing'. Secondly, they felt the method generally boosted their confidence to tackle ideas: Kevin (13), 'It was very big to know you could throw it in and kick it around and not get shouted down. Maybe it is real security blanket stuff, but it certainly encouraged some original thought.' Jeff (later in the year, from a report to the sociologists): '[In one-to-one] ... the talker can "confront" the listener with ideas of his own without fear of being knocked back or laughed at (and thus becoming defensive), reaching conclusions he may not have otherwise reached.' And thirdly, the method led people to new incentives to read. Doris (3) summed this up: 'As usual I came away from the workshop stimulated. I want to bury myself in books and read as much as possible ... There is far greater desire to read when attending the workshop when compared with other formal tutorials. I feel I gain so much more from talking to other students that it would be positively immoral for me not to be as well-informed as they are. Also, this constant interaction breeds new concepts which I feel I must follow up by more reading and further discussion.'

In relation to learning to talk more structurally, I began to receive comments on the value of non-interruption such as the following: James (5), 'I agree a person must not be interrupted ... I was interrupted very gently but I realized later that I had forgotten to say some of my main ideas as a result'; and Linda (13) who for several weeks had attacked one-to-one and had preferred group discussions: 'With regard to the one-to-one discussions I considered this approach to have been most beneficial ... [Non-interruption] did prove quite frustrating at times ... however I also discovered that if my partner interrupted my discussion it generally destroyed my train of thought or forced my pattern of conversation to change. Thus in general I consider the idea of non-interruption to be a valuable approach to analysing and articulating one's ideas.' Indeed students got so used to one-to-one space they began to resent group talk as 'drifting', or, as John (5) put it, '[in group] ... ideas that are aired are not given time to settle before we are off on a different tangent listening to someone else'.

Another major benefit of one-to-one which seemed more marked for the students than I originally expected, was that it taught them to listen to a partner. Many students raised this point, for example Jenny (13), '[One-to-one] helps the listener discipline himself to *hear*'. Some students referred to an overflow beyond university life; one, for instance, to better relations with his girlfriend, from giving and expecting more attention.

For all this, my biggest effort with one-to-one, my attempt at its most sustained use towards the greatest autonomy for students, met only with ambiguous moments of success. My central scheme was to keep the students, after a couple of introductory weeks, to two main questions, week-in and week-out, for six weeks. I intended a variety of other exercises, but the two key questions would always be tackled. These were to be 'Tell me something about yourself' and 'What is the Mexican Revolution?'. I held students to the personal question in the hope that they would explore different ways of perceiving and presenting themselves in the university environment. And from the second question, I hoped students would develop their own approach to history.

Types of reaction to both questions, and the times at which they surfaced, varied tremendously, but by the fourth week the honeymoon period seemed to be over for a significant number of students. I began to receive such complaints as the following: Lyzbeth (4), 'I am bored with what I say ... similarity in the answers ... a lot of repetition ... cannot seem to break through into new areas'.

In response to this barrage I discussed the problems with the group. I tried to persuade them that if they were bored, they were boring themselves, and that they should and could do something about it for themselves. I stressed that in answer to 'Tell me something about yourself' they could project themselves in much richer and more challenging forms than by merely presenting a superficial life history (most had talked of schooling, domestic situation and so on – safe public information). We suggested different types of personality projections. Some students took a lead in opening up, which encouraged others to follow. But still the complaints remained. Many simply would not make a choice and continued to take the question at a peculiarly unsatisfying sort of face value. It struck me that the very people most dissatisfied with their self-projection to the set question were the ones least confident to make a choice to change. Had I felt I had an open mandate to help in human relations, I might have kept on the pressure for them to solve the problem themselves. But, as I was running a history course, I decided to back down. I shifted off the ongoing self-presentation question on to varying ones, starting with 'What are your main life values?'. A general sigh of relief followed. Even students who had been prepared to battle on with the original question expressed satisfaction at having something more specific to follow. The new question invited more openness, and the less confident students found it easier to work under that sort of direction.

Meanwhile, I continued for a further couple of weeks with the broad history question, 'What is the Mexican Revolution?' – in the teeth of continuous protests from several students. It seemed to me more imporant to stick at this one, if students were to develop academic self-confidence, their sense of self-discovery of what history is about. I argued: 'If the question is monotonous, form interesting sub-questions; if you are bored with being too general, be more specific; if your approach is colourless, colour it; if you are being repetitious, read up on the subject and present new and varied content.' This was to little avail. There were students who continued to complain of being 'bogged' and so on. Linda (4) was most outspoken when she insisted she could not shape her own sub-questions, that they were 'only useful when introduced by another person', that with the current question she felt 'discontent and hostility'. She asserted flatly to me, 'so much for your theory'. For all that, the next week she came up against a new partner who impressed her with his formation of sub-questions, and she said she began to 'wonder' what her 'inability to explore different angles means'. Others like Gary (5) accepted that 'the answer lies within the group – to stimulate their own interest'. And Ronis, who had dropped out from Monash University in the previous year, was one who continuously expressed support for the open method: 'I enjoy not being told what to read but I'm still having trouble finding my resources. I'm used to being told what to read and am enjoying the confidence I feel someone (I guess David) has in me … Got really mad at everyone for wanting more direction, and didn't feel very much a part of the group. Felt that people weren't making the most of what I thought was a terrific opportunity.'

The problem for me about whether to stick to 'What is the Mexican Revolution?' was that week by week, for every couple of people complaining, there was one making some sort of breakthrough. There were people like Linda, as above, being jolted into some form of self-recognition, starting to wonder, to choose. Several went flat and then began to lift themselves, using phrases like the following from Doug (5): 'Improvement because I wanted it to be' and

WELSH COLLEGE OF MUSIC & DRAMA LIBRARY

141

'thought-provoking ... I was determined to get something out of it'. Several simply continued the whole way through using their time to their own satisfaction. For instance a few were referring through weeks 4 to 6 to reading whole major historical texts, sometimes even two or three. Such free reading, taking pleasure in historical research and follow-through is, in my experience, very rare amongst undergraduate students.

Finally, however, I decided to tighten things up. There was, in any case, a natural tightener in the set essay, in its submission and discussion. And I became concerned towards the end of term about a number of students who were doing very little work. I felt that we should drive the Revolution study through to some sort of conclusion. So for weeks seven and eight, having warned everyone beforehand (and a number bustled into a new burst of reading) I presented the students with a grinding run of specific historical questions on the Revolution. Many immediately liked this, as a big lift in purpose and direction. Some spoke of the sessions as 'exhausting' but 'exciting' or 'deeply satisfying'. But Ronis (8) solidly reminded me that I had deserted the cause of students finding self-responsibility. She wrote, 'I was angry at the heavily directed history questions. I am not able to research things my way. Also I am not motivating myself. We now have to do what teacher wants.' So, not unusual in the workshops, I had fallen between two stools, or rather, in response to majority pressure, I had deserted a minority by opting for the stool of more direction.

I still believe that the intensified approach of one-to-one has enormous potential. However, it can also be extremely difficult, even painful, especially in the extreme form I had experienced in the London group. Its benefit, even for a history question, would come from students driving themselves into corners. From there they would need to build up self-initiative and will to pull themselves out. I believe everyone would be able to do that eventually, and that all would be joyous and fulfilled in their victory, but it would only come after a lot of agony about being in a corner. Anyone aiming for the fullest potential of one-to-one should at least consider it in such an extensive form. Out there lies the chance for students to achieve true autonomy. However, it took more courage, determination, and force of personality than I was able to muster at the time. I also felt that history, in a rather standard course, should be more enjoyable than that, and the achievements not necessarily so high.

4. Variations on one-to-one for academic questions

For basic history purposes I settled in to a variety of one-to-one questions, interspersed with other learning techniques. I now wish to refer briefly to the more successful of these patterns.

One technique was to mix one-to-one with lecturettes. I would set up a question and let students discuss it one-to-one, and then I would give them a five-minute lecturette to remind them of basic content and to raise problems or suggest various perspectives, and then I would let them return to one-to-one discussion. I was a bit concerned lest I dominated students' thought patterns, but overall the responses suggested a large degree of independence from my opinions yet some interest in them. After I had overcome my hurt pride at not having my penetrating insights widely applauded, I decided to feel pleased.

The most direct teaching I did was through essays, but here too I tried to reduce the authority of my opinions. There was no grading but three sets of comments were given on each essay. Students made two photocopies of their essay; one went to each of two pre-selected partners, while I took the original. At the following workshop they received my written comments on their essay as well as discussing it with each of their partners in turn. Nongrading, I believe, helped in this exercise. All I insisted on was that an essay of a certain length be submitted by a certain time. Simon actually asked me if that meant he could turn in something copied from a telephone directory. I said yes. (It seemed worth a risk.) In fact, he wrote an essay of first class honours standard. In general, the release from formal grading did not result in any loss of incentive. As Marylin (6) put it, 'It was quite strange writing this essay. I knew it was not going to be marked, all I had to do was hand it in, yet I think I put more work into the essay than I have previously where my work has been marked.' Indeed, nearly everyone worked hard, and only a couple failed to get their essays in on the exact due date. And overall, though the quality of individual essays still varied from poor to excellent, I thought the standard higher than in the traditional tutorials. Students learned a lot, too, from criticizing each other.

Several other patterns of approach to weekly history reading proved effective. I led into some historical problems with perceptual ones. For instance, before tackling a critique of the revolutionary government, we worked on 'What is democracy?'. Students were excited by that question. I also varied the structure. For instance it could be tackled as follows (all on the question of democracy): Group: warm up, pooling of variety of initial ideas, 5-10 min. One-to-one: A 3 min, B 3 min; repeat. Threes-or-fours (no one with his original partner): each in turn, summarize your own and your previous partner's ideas, discuss generally, 15 min. Group: discuss results, 10 min. If the energy was good, I might even conclude with a one-to-one for all students to articulate their own conclusions.) Another structure I used which generated enthusiasm was this: One-to-one: 'Tell me what you would do if you were president of Mexico in the 1920s.' A 6 min, B offer criticism 4 min, AB 4 min; reverse roles. Such variations, including interspersals of source material from documents or lecturettes, are endless. And they always involve effort by and for each individual student.

The most distinctive use to which I put one-to-one for history purposes was to set patterns of questions that could lead from self-understanding to historical understanding. In some ways connections between personal and historical questions were made by some students very quickly, even where I had not clearly set up an association. For instance, Mike (2): 'The two questions "Who am I?" and "What is Mexican?" did seem relatively close. Why? Both required meticulous sifting of particulars, yet one could not discard any, rather all the particulars … established a character.' Illustrative of my deliberate mixing of the two perspectives are the following questions, one after the other for students to try in rounds of one-to-one talks: 'What are your main hopes and expectations?',

'What were the hopes and expectations of the Zapatistas?', 'What are your main hopes and expectations for the Mexican Revolution?'. Moving towards my intentions behind this chain of questions, Marylin (8) wrote: 'It made it easier to talk about the revolutionaries. I felt I had understandings of their feelings.' But she did not simply stop at attributing to others what she felt for herself. She began to contrast her own emotions and incentives with those suggested by the statements and behaviour of the Mexicans. She went on to say, 'It was not until I said what I wanted for the Mexicans that I realized what I had said was really what I wanted for myself.' By that realization she was better able to understand the Mexicans in their own context.

5. One-to-one and personality questions

My first personality question, 'Tell me something about yourself' had been loosely conceived as helping group members to enjoy each others' company and to talk more easily, to develop social incentives to attend the workshops. Gradually I came to realize I had broached much more important issues of self-confidence and self-projection and how they affect learning in general. When I tried to persuade students to be more open on their personal life (such as to include feelings), a lot of bugs crawled out of the woodwork. For instance, Jan wrote, 'I cannot discuss my personal self ... Things close to me will always remain for a few trusted people.' So I talked with the group as a whole about taking risks to share, about self-trust, and so on. Perhaps they just learned from experience, but either way, three weeks later Jan wrote, 'I now feel able to be frank in my discussion with any members and I no longer have a preference whom to talk to.' Similar shifts occurred for others. I feel sure it freed them to tackle the academic questions more confidently. And similarly I began to discover that the academic purpose of the course gave students a focus for the development and use of self-confidence (or a retreat from being personal when they needed it). The two sides of the workshop seemed to help each other more than I had expected.

As the workshops went on I began to tackle the personal aspects of learning problems more directly. For instance, I used one-to-one for students to discuss their attitudes to criticism (to try to distinguish the legitimate response of a peer from deeply antagonizing ancestral voices from afar postulating shoulds and shouldn'ts). I also used personal questions to generate incentive for our work. One set went as follows: 'How is life fulfilled?', 'How is life best fulfilled?' and 'How can I best fulfil myself in these workshops?'. Lastly, I plotted some questions in response to journals when I found that a few students were casually accusing themselves of being 'not too bright', of having 'limited intelligence' or 'poor capacity for attention', and so on. In week 5 I tried, 'Tell me how intelligent you believe you are and how you came by that belief'. That sparked off some valuable reactions. So the next week I tried a chain of questions to seek to promote a positive self-image (or at least a recognition of the arbitrariness of some of the self-denigration). We did two main one-to-ones: 'Tell me one good thing that happened to you this week' and 'What are your greatest joys and abilities?'. (For the latter I suggested they elephant-shit, not just bullshit). Then I set up a little exercise: people faced each other in pairs while I recited three phrases for each person to say to his partner, one after the other with the partner looking him straight in the face and replying 'I agree'. The phrases were 'I am a warm loving person', 'I am a very talented and intelligent person', and 'I am a very *very* magnificent person'.

With all personal questions I took care to explain what I had in mind. If anyone wished to opt out, they could do so. Everyone was encouraged to try, just to see what it felt like, without necessarily implying support for my intentions. Of course, a question like the last one generated some deep emotion. A few students were very angry that I should encourge self-praise; they said the exercise was 'embarrassing' or 'pointless'. But some of these critics were the most affected, bit by bit, towards a more positive self-view. For instance, one who said in week 6, 'It makes no sense big-noting myself', said in week 12, 'The personality questions helped me in that by telling myself I am better or more so that I thought I was, I started acting that way (and consequently am) ... I found this immensely useful.'

Many students exuded enthusiasm for personality questions from the start, and typical of the responses to the self-appreciation questions in week 6 were these words: 'jubilation' (Frank), 'really stoked' (James), 'peachy-keen' (Mike), 'tremendous' (Jenny) and from Linda, the sometime cynic, 'stimulating ... perplexing ... wonderful ... entertaining ... revealing'. Overall, I think the wider scope of learning induced by the personality questions contributed as I had hoped to students wanting to attend the workshops. As Ronis (7) put it, 'It's getting to the stage for me that I just have to go along on Thursday morning [to the workshop] to be with the people and talk a bit and I feel good.' So, people kept coming. The attendance rate was well above the minimum requirements, and I had no drop-outs.

By the end of the course, in summing up their responses, students strongly backed the personality questions as an important part of the workshops. Typical comments were: Linda (3), 'I was more-or-less learning about the people involved and applying those discoveries to a better understanding of people in general', and Paul (13), 'I have enjoyed the workshops very much. It has been a completely new learning experience ... joining the social and learning aspects of education.' In fact, a number of people said we should have done more personality questions and more with them: 'Gary (13), 'On personality questions ... there should have been a lot more ... we could have learnt more about ourselves (and I was learning more about myself) ... and been more able to identify where we stood in relation to the subject', and Kevin (13), 'It could be that understanding people is the key to history ... I think because we did stress this aspect we were really able to get to the personalities concerned ... understanding others through understanding self comes in here. I don't think we went far enough on this.'

6. Two responses to the course in general
Below are two quotations from others to sum up the Mexican history course. The first is part of a student's final journal, and it does, I believe, reflect on issues

of autonomy without the writer having that in mind. It is by a woman not previously quoted in this article.

> I would like to give my impression of the workshops ... The stuff about one-to-one I feel is very important. I like being able to have an uninterrupted space in which to express myself; and I can't help feeling that this is universally important, if the space is to be used constructively. I like being able to pause and think about using the most appropriate word etc, knowing that my expression cannot easily be cut off by interruption from the other person. The listener is forced, to a degree, to take in a *wholeness* of information and vibes, and I've found this to be valuable both as a listener and as a speaker. There also seems to be value in a spontaneous reaction from the listener which can only occur in open discussion. Thus, I think a blend of the two approaches as we have mostly been doing lately, is a good compromise.
>
> The concept of the workshop as a personal and group exercise in learning made it seem important to study the characters and events of the Revolution in a real way – not just in order to be able to regurgitate facts and figures to pass an exam or to write an essay. Reading and discussing historical issues which are seen as personally important leads to an increase in perception of the reasons behind historical happenings. In turn, the new perception can be applied critically to current situations ... In summary, it seems that the workshops are extremely important in allowing and encouraging a *real* work effort, but that other factors such as pressure of other courses and lack of time retard their better use.

The last quotes are from a colleague in the School of Education who wrote a paper on the workshops from an independent reading of the journals:

> On teacher direction: a few students did mention they'd have preferred a bit more structure, for example weekly assignments – but the journals of about half the students showed that they were using these for just that kind of task, working through the history learned during the sessions and from reading and reflections between sessions: there was no clearly discernible common 'line' in the history (which one might expect from a group of students heavily influenced by a particular tutor).
>
> ... A fairly common pattern was an early dissatisfaction with David for offering too little guidance – students' worry about not being 'right' initially inhibited them from expressing their opinions freely. All but two of the students seemed to me to exhibit a marked growth in self-direction and confidence as the semester progressed.
>
> ... The students mostly showed an awareness of bias and selectivity in historical writing, their own as well as authoritative sources, and of the need to evaluate evidence in the light of this; they did not seem to mind risking their own opinions, which were quite diverse.

Repercussions

I had started my workshops at the beginning of the Australian academic year, in March 1973. Later that year two other colleagues set up their own style of workshops, based more on an encounter approach. The next year we gave papers on what we had done, and several others began experimenting with related structures. As of 1978 about half our department (of over 50 members) have adopted some aspects of the original workshops.

The profusion of workshop techniques has proved to be a two-edged sword. Few people apart from me like using one-to-one, yet so many of the other aspects of workshops are correlated to it that selectively to exclude it creates new problems. While the good teachers continue to be good, and develop their own approaches according to their own personalities and objectives, and while others miss the best opportunities of a technique but do well enough, some have turned everything into a new and increased set of burdens and dissatisfactions.

For me, one-to-one is the most exciting learning technique I know. Something of its potential for autonomy lies in the nature of the questions, but by and large, whatever the question, the structure alone guarantees autonomy; as people develop their sense of the technique they realize that they have space and support to do with a question whatever they like – even entirely reverse it or ignore it. Yet it is a very difficult technique, very demanding. Students (like myself and others at Jeff Love's group) need firm direction to get into it, yet paradoxically the firmer the control the greater the freedom. I think the only justification for it, as a highly structured format, is that it works.

The confidence I evolved that it would work, and how, came from my direct experience of it in Worcestershire. For many of my colleagues, any confidence at all in it comes from articles and from recommendations by my ex-students. Backed only by such second-hand experience they approach the method diffidently, in a spirit of trying it on. Often they do not explain the concepts behind it; and no one that I know of, in trying it as a teacher, has been firm about its practice (alert postures, direct facing, clear set-up of questions and use of names, strict non-interruption, partners thanking each other, clear delineation of time spans). Often, too, their questions are not adequately conceptual. So, loosely faced with a technique that is both difficult and embarrassing, students opt out of it. Most do not try hard, but await a chance for complaint and release because they sense (or know) the ambivalence of the lecturer. This is to be expected, surely – much the same as they would opt out of any difficult written task, like an essay, if they were invited to see how they liked it and given the choice not to proceed with it. As workshops proliferated I have had students come to me in their third and fourth years who have experienced attempts at one-to-one in other groups and deeply disliked it, only to find, if properly introduced, encouraged and protected in it, that it could prove exciting.

Some teachers hold one-to-one together as a form of paired discussion with open-ended time. I recognize that such discussion does have a value of its own; clearly it allows better space for the development of a type of competitive articulation than is available in strict one-to-one. But it is a very different technique; and it misses out on a lot of the benefits of one-to-one. In paired discussion people can deplete each other's energies by interruption as much as they might build them up; if one person initiates non-directed and personal chat, his partner can confirm him in this (whereas the responsibility in one-to-one is

147

more clearly on the individual to do useful work in his given space); the theory of rationality as expounded at the beginning of this paper receives no chance; and judgements (rather than self-judgements), put-downs and manipulation can occur.

The worst problem, however, lies with teachers who go halfway and then give up. In a spirit of enterprise they set up two-hour or three-hour 'workshops', but then rather quickly abandon either one-to-one or small groups as a main technique – perhaps because they feel uncomfortable or out of control. They then come to rely overwhelmingly on the traditional full-group discussion. Old patterns occur, with teachers talking most of the time, or with directive chairing, with selective approval and disapproval, and the shunting of students through hoops towards ends very few contribute towards or understand. The tedium of one-hour tutorials now becomes extended over two or three hours. Consequently some students have become bitter about the whole process.

Lastly, the potential of journals is easily destroyed if they are converted (as has happened frequently) into simply another directed writing task. As I saw it, they were extra work over set requirements, so there was no need to labour them. They were to be spontaneous feedback on individual one-to-one experiences, something where students could enjoy writing and in which they could vent their emotions – especially criticism of the learning methods. I never liked being abused, but in another sense I appreciated the open information as part of knowing what were the various realities of workshops for all students. And I accepted, too, that discharge of personal problems might be important to students, and for me to recognise what was affecting their approach to academic work. Some teachers, however, made journals a specific academic task, for instance a summary of set reading with later additions according to historical understandings gleaned in group work, all followed up by the return of the journals with judging comments. There were students who used this system well, but others, already on the lower rungs of academic achievement, found it a troubling chore and a further contribution to their sense of inadequacy. Several students, then, have cursed me for the introduction of the idea of journals, occasionally for the way I use them, but overwhelmingly for the more rigid use of them by some other staff.

Out of all this, especially on how the groups are run, I have come to believe that staff need experiential training in various experimental teaching methods. The chances of effective change from reading articles, especially with a technique like one-to-one, seem to me rather low.

Conclusion: on autonomy

To discuss adequately either the possibility or the value of autonomy in tertiary education would, I believe, necessitate starting with issues like free will and determinism and going on to what I would want to achieve for myself, for my students and for society as a whole. It is all too difficult to explore briefly here. However, I have a few simple guiding prejudices.

First, I have come to believe that, for myself at least, it is wrong to ask students 'What do you want to do?' as a starting and controlling point for a learning programme. They are either too inexperienced or too conditioned for that to be liberating. I believe that by putting on a course I have a responsibility to lead and to use my abilities and experience to offer valuable material and ideas.

Secondly, students cannot know without training *how* to do something. It is not giving a person autonomy to throw him into water without teaching him how to swim. Such an approach grants him neither success nor satisfaction. Skills are most rapidly learned where most conscientiously taught, and where structures are set up to allow for their practice.

Thirdly, however, there is a dilemma. I believe the acquisition of knowledge and skills under imaginative leadership gives great joy to students. Most are happy to be led, if where they are led is satisfying. And if they want to be, teachers can easily be alert and sensitive enough to set up interesting coursework. Nevertheless, I believe teachers have a responsibility to themselves, their society, and their students' long-term interests, to tackle the harder task, to generate autonomy. I want students to become self-aware and honest, able to confront the world adequately, to make their own judgements, and to recognize and respect their own considered (not manipulated) needs. And yet again, I do not want that autonomy to lead to arrogance or rampant individualism. I want it to be wed to sensitivity to others and willingness to cooperate and assist.

There is no simple position to take on all this, either philosophically or practically. I keep being trapped into wanting students to have autonomy but to adopt the values I believe in. Even, for instance, an attempt to generate autonomy in people who do not want it illustrates one of many paradoxes in the education game. What I sit back on is some sort of intuitive balance. Perhaps it is like Freire's idea that the best environment is one in which in the final achievement no one has taught another and no one is self-taught. I believe that workshops with one-to-one and open journals can be one way of creating such an environment.

Chapter 9
'Parrainage':
Students Helping Each Other

Marcel Goldschmid,
Chaire de Pédagogie et Didactique, Ecole Polytechnique Fédérale, Lausanne, Switzerland

Introduction

A number of attempts have been made in the past few years to counteract some of the problems the typical modern university is faced with: large classes, lack of contact among students and between students and faculty, passive teaching methods and inadequate study methods.

Peer counselling programmes in particular (eg Gentry, 1974; Wasserman *et al*, 1975; Wrenn and Mencke, 1972), have emerged, whose objective is to enhance the affective climate and enable students to be assimilated into the university. One could also argue that in order to improve instruction in higher education, it is essential that students be trained in a variety of specific learning skills to enable them to participate effectively in innovative as well as traditional forms of instruction (Goldschmid and Goldschmid, 1976a).

I should like in the following article to describe a peer-counselling programme which we call parrainage. It aims to develop both a favourable climate in the university and students' learning skills.

Origins and objectives of the parrainage

The parrainage was initiated by a professor of mechanical engineering and myself in autumn of 1973 in the mechanical engineering department (Goldschmid and Burckhardt, 1976).

In this programme, more advanced students act on a voluntary basis as counsellors to first year students in a variety of areas. For example, they offer their assistance in practical matters, such as questions of housing, transportation, stipends and loans, as well as academic problems, such as study skills, curricular choices and vocational orientation. More generally, the objective of the parrainage has been to help incoming students adapt to their new environment and provide them with a favourable climate at the beginning of their studies.

The assignment of *parrains* (the term used for third and fourth year students) to small groups of three to four first-years, was based as much as possible on their nationalities, mother tongue and regional origins in order to facilitate the first contacts. The parrains had offered their help spontaneously, although as it turned out later, it was possible to offer them a small stipend at least during the first two years of the programme.

Once the parrains were recruited, the *filleuls* (first year students) invited and the counselling groups formed, the two academic staff members met regularly with the parrains (about once or twice a month) in order to discuss their experiences and problems with the students they were counselling. During these meetings the parrains also indicated situations which they felt were beyond their capacity to deal with, ie either complex personal problems of their counsellees or serious difficulties the students had encountered with their teachers. In such cases, the professor of mechanical engineering would talk to either the students or professors concerned in order to try to remedy the situation. The parrains also wrote monthly reports about their meetings with the filleuls in order to inform us of the progress being made.

The first encounters with the newly enrolled students (about once a week) were usually initiated by the parrains and were devoted to practical problems, such as the functioning of different student services and the library. Numerous problems of adaptation were identified in the meeting and the records kept by the parrains during this phase clearly indicated the importance of a counselling scheme. The students, often being away from home for the first time and, in many cases, having come to a foreign country, were disoriented and unaccustomed to the structure and working methods encountered at the university. The large classes, in particular, created a feeling of impersonality and difficulties in establishing personal contacts. The academic backgrounds of the students also represented a factor of uncertainty and anxiety, many wondering whether they were sufficiently well prepared to meet the demands.

One of the tasks of the parrains consisted of offering reassurance and practical help during this difficult period. Another was to provide information about their field of study. Although the students had enrolled in mechanical engineering in line with their preference, they often had only a vague idea about the profession. In fact they were rather disappointed by the apparent lack of relationship between the courses they were taking in their first year and their perception of the work of a mechanical engineer. The senior students, who had been confronted with the same problems earlier on, were able to orient the new students, for example by telling them about the courses they were taking and the projects and fieldwork they were presently involved in.

These first group meetings which had been organized by the parrains were gradually replaced by more spontaneous and informal contacts. In fact, later on the parrains frequently met with their filleuls upon their request, often on an individual basis when personal problems were revealed. As it turned out some of these 'personal' problems were shared by other first year students and could therefore subsequently be discussed in the group.

First results

In general terms, the monthly meetings with the parrains and their reports clearly confirmed the need for such a programme and demonstrated the effectiveness of the parrains' interventions. More specifically, one could cite the improvement in the affective climate and the contacts among students (much as Heiney, 1977, had found with a peer-counselling programme in psychology), as well as the resolution of a number of practical problems, such as housing or transportation.

Based on the parrains' reports, the professor of mechanical engineering was able to intervene successfully with some of his colleagues in matters of teaching as well as with individual students who had motivational or academic problems. Occasionally, the parrains also addressed themselves directly to the tutors in order to remedy a specific problem, such as the lack of instructional materials or consultation time with teachers in certain courses.

Another area where the more senior students were able to help their younger colleagues concerned working- or study-methods. Examples included more effective use of the library and preparation for exams, as well as more efficient note-taking. In fact, the parrains' reports revealed that a majority of students were at first unable to take notes which they could use later in individual study.

We also attempted a statistical analysis at the end of the first year by comparing the grades in mechanical engineering at the end of the first semester for three consecutive years (the two preceding ones without parrainage), in order to determine whether or not the parrainage had an effect on the freshmen's academic performance. The results turned out to be quite favourable to the scheme: the grade point average was higher and the number of drop-outs smaller in the year with parrainage. Furthermore, the number of failing grades (below six in a 10-point scale) was considerably lower (4.6 per cent for the year with parrainage and 15 per cent and 12.5 per cent respectively for the two preceding years). Nevertheless, it should be pointed out that these statistics do not necessarily indicate that the improvements were due to parrainage. In view of various grade fluctuations in other departments, one cannot exclude the possibility that other factors might have contributed to these changes.

Finally, it should be mentioned that the parrains had identified several cases of students who had been so discouraged that they were thinking of dropping out, but who with the encouragement and assistance of the parrains and the professor were able to persevere and pass the exams successfully. These observations are in line with the results obtained by Brown *et al* (1971) who were also able to help potential college drop-outs through a peer-counselling programme.

In view of the positive outcome, the department of mechanical engineering decided to continue the experiment with another professor and a new group of first year students and parrains in 1974-75. The structure and procedure adopted were much the same, but in addition, a short guide with practical recommendations for the parrains was prepared by two parrains and one filleul of the first year (Audemars *et al*, 1977).

After the first and second years, we conducted a survey by means of a questionnaire in order to ascertain the reactions of both parrains and filleuls (Brun, 1976). The parrains (23 of 24 responded) felt that the parrainage had helped them improve their interpersonal relations, gain a sense of responsibility, become more conscious of first-year problems and acquire a better perspective on their studies. The parrainage was thus clearly perceived to be helpful to the parrain was well, not just to the filleul. The literature on peer teaching (Goldschmid and Goldschmid, 1976b) supports this finding: the student counsellors benefit themselves considerably, ie peer-teaching is by no means a one-way 'philanthropic' exercise: all the parrains indicated that parrainage should continue. Among the problems, they thought that information about the parrainage given to new students was inadequate, and that the programme started too late.

A majority of the filleuls (49 of 84 responded) also reported great satisfaction in the affective area. Most of them acknowledged the help they had received with regard to practical problems, study methods and information about the school, the professors and vocational questions. Relatively few (less than 20 per cent) stated specific complaints: some wished for more contacts with the parrains and others felt that the parrainage could have been more efficient (eg started earlier, better information, etc). Only 6 per cent of the first year students said they would *not* be willing to be a parrain in their fourth year.

Evolution of the parrainage

In view of the general satisfaction of the students in mechanical engineering during the first two years, the student association (Agepoly) decided to extend the parrainage to all departments of the university. They also insisted on operating the programme themselves without the help of the professors. In 1975-76, the Agepoly was able to recruit over 70 parrains in eight of the nine departments and in principle assign every first year student to a parrain. Unfortunately, because of a lack of cooperation among the students, various delays and organizational inefficiency, the parrainage did not function adequately in all departments. Some of the freshmen, for example, had not been informed of the parrainage and some of the parrains were not properly instructed as to their role. It was obvious that such a large enterprise involving several hundred students strained the organizational capacity and manpower of the student organization.

Our third survey (Chaire de Pédagogie et Didactique, 1976a; Champagne, 1976) which was carried out in all departments concerned (filleuls: N = 338, respondents = 105 or 31 per cent; parrains: N = 76, respondents = 46 or 61 per cent), nevertheless revealed that a large majority (80 per cent of the filleuls and 70 per cent of the parrains) felt that the parrainage met a real need at least among a portion of the first year students, especially those from abroad and other regions in Switzerland. A number of respondents also indicated that it was not necessary to assign a parrain to each new student, ie that it was sufficient to make a parrain available to those who wanted one. (This was in fact the procedure which was adopted in the fourth year.) Among the most serious problems the survey pinpointed was the late start of the programme. Many respondents felt that the parrainage was most useful at the very beginning, ie in the first weeks, and much less needed later on. Furthermore, both parrains and filleuls complained about the infrequent contacts between the two groups, leaving the new students with doubts about the efficiency of the programme and the parrains with considerable frustration and disappointment since their services were apparently not wanted. A third deficiency in the new structure was the relative lack of direct interventions by the class counsellors (one professor in each department) who had played such an important role in the first two years of the programme.

Another set of questions in the survey concerned the students' attitude to study methods (Chaire de Pédagogie et Didactique, 1976b). A large majority (81 of 105 first years and 31 of 45 parrains) stated that the university should offer the students the opportunity to improve their work and study methods. Among the *subjects* which many would find most useful (in decreasing order of frequency) were the following: how to write a report, how to carry out a project, how to present a report, developing study skills, memorization, documentation, public speaking, and preparing for exams.

As to the *form* of this training, by far the largest number (close to one-third of the respondents) would prefer to have access to a manual on these subjects. Close to one-fifth would prefer an information centre; somewhat fewer would prefer regular courses; and about 10 per cent each, seminars, mini-courses and workshops.

Finally, in the fourth year (1977-78) the parrains were only assigned to those first year students who had indicated that they wanted access to a student counsellor. Again the student organization was largely responsible for the information and orientation of both incoming students and parrains. The results as indicated by a fourth survey (Talbot, 1978) were similar to those obtained in the third year, when the parrainage was first generalized to the entire univeristy: organizational problems and infrequent contacts were listed most frequently among the problems, but again a majority indicated that the parrainage was useful and those who participated were satisfied with the results, especially in the affective area.

Conclusions

This programme of peer counselling has now been running for several years and has been regularly evaluated. On the whole, it appears that the parrainage meets the real needs of a sizeable portion of first year students, in particular at the very beginning of their studies. Besides improving the social climate and contacts among the students, such a programme can contribute to the solution of practical problems, such as housing, tranportation and social services. It can also enhance the development of study skills and working methods. In short, the parrainage constitutes an effective self-help organization directed at getting students off to a good start. It is also an inexpensive operation, an advantage which, in a time of budget constraints in higher education, is by no means negligible. Successive student groups can – on a voluntary basis – serve as student counsellors, after having benefited perhaps from the help of older colleagues when they began their own study. Each generation then in turn assumes the responsibility for helping the other. The parrains also profit from the experience and besides establishing better personal relations, further deepen their understanding of their subject matter and future profession.

Our experience also showed that close cooperation between professors and students in the running of the operation greatly enhanced its success. In fact, without institutional resources and connections, the programme's reach is very much curtailed and its continuity in fact questioned from year to year. It is necessary, therefore, to strive for a delicate balance between student initiative and responsibility on the one hand, and the provision of sufficient institutional structure and support on the other.

Chapter 10

Student Autonomy in Learning Medicine: Some Participants' Experiences

Barbara Ferrier,
Professor of Biochemistry, McMaster University, Hamilton, Ontario
Michael Marrin and Jeffrey Seidman,
Formerly medical students, McMaster University

The introduction and first two sections of this chapter were written some years ago. The medical student authors are both now pediatricians, and the objectives and structure of the medical programme referred to have undergone some changes (Neufeld, 1983). However, the basic principles of the educational approach remain the same.

Introduction

One of the stated objectives for students in the McMaster University MD programme is 'to become a self-directed learner, recognizing personal educational needs, selecting appropriate learning resources and evaluating progress'. In order to graduate, students must meet this as well as the other objectives; student autonomy in learning is therefore not an option but a requirement. The objectives were developed to ensure that the school's graduates would have the qualities, knowledge and skills necessary to provide them with the flexibility, awareness, and attitude to learning thought to be necessary to meet future health care needs. The programme is based on an interdisciplinary problem-based method in which students work in a sequence of small groups throughout its three-year (31 months) duration. It is of considerable complexity and cannot be fully described in this article. A rather comprehensive description of it at an early stage was published (Journal of the Royal College of Physicians of London, 1972), and aspects of its subsequent development and of some particular features have been described in many publications (Ali *et al*, 1977; Barrows and Mitchell, 1975; Barrows and Tamblyn, 1977; Ferrier and Hamilton, 1977; Hamilton, 1976; Neufeld and Barrows, 1974; Pallie and Brain, 1978; Sibley, 1978; Sweeney and Mitchell, 1975; Walsh, 1978).

Since the emphasis is on small group learning, the students must not only be able to direct their own learning, but to do so in a way which is compatible with the learning objectives of the group and its other members. They must also accept responsibility for facilitating the learning and evaluating the progress of their peers. Thus, the autonomy which they must acquire is a conditional one. They cannot allow their own objectives to interfere with those of the group, and collectively the group must ensure that all its members meet the programme objectives.

These programme objectives are general and descriptive. They specify no core content or factual requirements. The programme is divided into sequential segments which last for periods of up to ten weeks, and which have conceptual objectives. For each segment students are allocated to new tutorial groups consisting of five students and a tutor, and each group has to decide what methods, models, examples and strategies they will use to allow its members, individually and as a group, to achieve the objectives. In each segment, problems in various formats, clinical experiences and a variety of resources are offered from which students may select. They may also identify other problems, negotiate other experiences and find their own resources. Thus the students have some minimum objectives to achieve, but how they achieve them is their responsibility. They may also add to these objectives. Evaluation of progress towards meeting the objectives is finally the responsibility of the tutor, but students are expected to share this responsibility and actively assess their own and their peers' performance during the programme. The written summary of student performance, which is done on completion of each segment of the programme, is a summary of observations made by all participants on the level of performance in tutorials, associated activities and problem-solving exercises.

An attempt is made to select students for the programme who will perform well in this setting (Ferrier *et al*, 1978). As well as appropriate personal qualities and academic ability, potential in problem-solving ability and self-directed learning is sought. There are no course prerequisites for admission and nearly all students have completed at least three years of university undergraduate education before entering. The very small number of exceptions to this are students who are at least 24 years old who have demonstrated adequate performance in university extension courses and have shown evidence of creativity and leadership in community service.

On entry into the programme, students have to adapt immediately to an educational system which is strange to many, and to a complex organization involving several hundred faculty members, many of them in different hospitals. To help them to adapt, three days at the start of the programme are devoted to orientation, with emphasis being put on key aspects of the system. Students from the second year plan these events in the light of what was, or would have been, useful to them. These students also take on most of the tasks of introduction and familiarization during the days of orientation. Different sessions are devoted to group learning, problem-based learning, and self-directed learning.

The text of the session on self-directed learning is given here (I) and it will be

157

followed by a commentary by two second-year students (II). One of these students had no prior experience of programmes which required self-direction in learning. The other had had a considerable experience and his remarks will therefore relate to the specific problems of adapting this style to medicine and to the McMaster programme. As a conclusion, a summary of what is known about the outcomes of the programme will be given (III). Explanations given in italics are additions made for clarification for the present purpose and were not part of the original talk.

I. On self-directed learning and setting personal goals: a tutor's view

(A tutor is assigned to a group of five students for each unit of the programme. The tutor is responsible for guiding and evaluating the work of the students in that unit.)

When the students planning orientation asked me to talk to the new class about setting objectives, personal goals, and personal assessment, they asked me to do so as someone who had tutored for several years in Phase 1 (*initial 10 weeks of the programme*). I agreed to do so on that understanding, and what follows, therefore, is my opinion only, based on my experience and not on any educational theory. You will all find it obvious. I hope you will find it acceptable and useful.

In the programme you have just entered, you will be expected to get involved in your own education, and that of your peers, at a very personal level. You will have to make major decisions about the design, the style, the implementation and the evaluation of the programme you follow so that you can get the most out of it. The involvement of each of you as a person rather than as an intellect is inevitable for several overlapping reasons. First, the school's objectives require this. This is put explicitly in the objective which requires that you 'recognize, maintain and develop characteristics and attitudes required for a career in a health profession – these include: (a) awareness of personal assets, potential, limitations, and emotional reactions; (b) responsibility and dependability; (c) ability to relate to and show concern for other individuals.' This objective is taken up in the Phase I objectives which include the need 'to develop competency in ... self-directed learning, small group learning ... to develop a self-awareness of and ability to cope with individual strengths, weaknesses and emotional reactions'. This means, bluntly, that if you do not meet these objectives you will not be considered to be suitable to graduate. A second reason for your personal involvement is the fact that the emotional climate dramatically influences the effectiveness of learning. If you cannot assess this and, if necessary, change it, you will not have the best conditions to work under. The third reason is that you will find that the personal interactions in the small groups, in which you will work, will become intense.

Self-directed learning

You are now largely responsible for your own learning progress. One very important aspect of self-directed learning is the development of self-evaluation skills. There are three components to self-evaluation: you need to be able to assess where you are when you begin a task; you need to be able to monitor your progress as you proceed; and you need to know when to stop. I want to look at each of these components in a little more detail.

Starting condition. Assessment of your starting condition should review your knowledge, skills, attitudes and personality traits. Your pre-existing knowledge should be relatively easy to assess. For those of you without a biological science background, you may feel this is glaringly obvious, but I suggest that everyone has knowledge gaps that should be identified. You may not have had an introduction to the behavioural sciences, or you may have no awareness of the historical, social, political and economic realities of health care. Many people tend to underrate themselves in the area of their knowledge, especially those who do not have a science background. Perhaps this is because they are reluctant to apply knowledge from life experience to 'scientific' or 'medical' situations. One student who had no science background before studying medicine, when faced with some simplified problems of measurement of rate and flow in the cardiology-respiratory unit, hotly denied the ability to solve them. Yet, when translated into problems of driving a car or filling a kettle, the solutions were obvious. In this case, the knowledge lacking was the knowledge that what was already known was validly applicable.

Assessment of your learning skills is important because many of you will be faced with the task of re-organizing your methods. What worked for you in the past may not work in medicine. You will have to cope with vast areas of knowledge and vast areas of ignorance, and methods of presentation which may be verbal, photographic, diagrammatic, schematic, mathematical, or any mixture of these. Some of the questions which you can ask yourself to help define your skills are given in the Phase I manual as *Inventory of Learning Habits*. In this inventory of questions, Phase I tutors have rated the possible answers from undesirable to highly desirable to give you some guidance about what they have found to work well. Assessment of your attitudes should particularly include those towards group learning. Your past experience in this will no doubt have influenced your attitudes and this influence should be identified.

Personality traits are often said not to be relevant to education. But I suggest that in all education, including the isolating and structured programmes which many undergraduates experience, final achievement, even when represented by numerical grades, is very greatly influenced by personality. Emotional stamina would be one such trait, compliance would be another. In the small group learning setting here, the importance of personality in learning is magnified. For example, inflexibility will not only limit your experiences and impair your learning, but it will impair the atmosphere of the group, and hence the learning of the other group members. Virtually all aspects of your personality will become relevant considerations.

Measuring progress. Measuring your own learning progress will be new to many of you, who have been able to rely on external judgement in the past. I would like to emphasize that self-evaluation does not have to mean evaluation carried out alone. It means that you are to be responsible for gathering the necessary information on which you will make a judgement about your performance. There are a variety of tests available for you to use to assess your knowledge. You should also use your tutor, your peers, your student adviser (*an adviser is assigned to each student on entry, and is responsible for monitoring the progress of the student through the entire programme*), and your senior mentor. (*A senior mentor, a selected second year student, is assigned to each tutorial group in Phase I. The role of the senior mentor is to help the new students adjust to medical education at McMaster and to assist in the successful operation of the Phase.*)

Students are, perhaps rightly, very conscious of what they do not know, and what they have not managed to do, but all too often they do not realize what they do know and what they have accomplished. It is important to register your development so that you do not get disheartened. As well as keeping fact-files and notes and references, you should try to record your acquisition of skills such as mastery of a new vocabulary, and changes of attitudes. Think about your experiences both good and bad and try to analyse what you learn from them. Remember that you can learn a lot from bad experiences so try to be resilient without losing sensitivity. This advice to be analytical could lead you to be too self-conscious so try not to lose your spontaneity either.

In assessing how well you are doing, you need to be able to accept and respond to criticism, the most important type of which in this context is self-criticism. If you find something in yourself which you genuinely criticize, or if you can accept criticism from others without making excuses or being defensive, you should consider this to be a sign that you have a good sense of your own worth and that you therefore have an acceptable base on which to work in this respect. You should all believe that the school has already judged you worthy of being given this chance. You are not here by mistake.

As well as monitoring your own progress, you have to be able to generate your own satisfaction, since the rewards in this system are largely intrinsic. Those of you who have been high grade achievers in the past may miss this more than you now suspect. If rewards for performance are not institutionalized, the positive regard of your peers becomes very important. It is therefore important for you to express this regard when you feel it. There is a danger in this system, I think, of students over-reacting to what they take to be negative signals from faculty members. Like everybody, faculty members can be moody, distracted and forgetful. In spite of that, I believe that you should trust that faculty members are well-intentioned towards you.

Knowing when to stop. The problem of knowing when to stop will remain with you all your lives, because you will always have access to more information than you can cope with. The strategy to adopt is not to aim to become super-efficient information processors, but to develop confidence in selecting problem-specific information. At first, many of you will find it impossible to be confident in stopping work in an area where it is all too obvious that you have left much undone. You should rely on others to help you: your tutor, resource people (*experts in relevant disciplines who are assigned to be available for consultation by tutorial groups or individuals*), student adviser and senior mentor can all be consulted. Your peers in your tutorial group should also be involved in developing a consensus of what is a right amount of any subject for the group members to know at any time. Since group members have different academic backgrounds, the appropriate amount of knowledge for all members will not be uniform. You will find that if you work with all these people you will gradually develop a sense of what is enough 'for now'. It is important to keep reminding yourself that problems will recur in slightly different forms throughout the programme, and your clinical life. You will have the opportunity to increase what you know at each recurrence.

In relation to the problem of knowing when to stop, you should adopt a pragmatic use of time. Set goals for what you want to achieve with your available time, even quite small blocks of study time, and try to stick to your plans even though great areas of your ignorance become apparent in the course of your work. You should also resist the temptation to re-allocate time to esoterica.

Learning in a small group

The setting of your own goals and the monitoring of your progress which are components of self-directed learning, have to occur in a situation which has its own constraints. The education programme which you are entering requires you to work as a member of a small group. This will provide a wide variety of benefits, but will add to your responsibilities. As I have already said, your goals must be compatible with those of your group, and you will be expected to accept responsibility for the learning of the other members of your group as well as your own.

For groups to be functionally effective, the members must be challenging and critical of each other, as well as being supportive. Criticism can only be usefully exchanged when there is an atmosphere of trust, and it takes time for most groups to develop this trust. This happens more quickly when group members are concerned not with the question, 'Can I trust them?' but rather with the question, 'Am I behaving in a way that shows they can trust me?'

Trust must go beyond the group however. You will be happier and more successful if you trust the intent of the people who run the programme. Great efforts are made to help students in any kind of difficulty. However, the school has a responsibility which overrides its responsibility to its students. Its graduates must not fail in their competence, reliability and honesty, as they deliver care in the future. Of course, any medical school has this responsibility, but here you are asked to share it, and you should not condone or ignore imcompetence, unreliability or dishonesty in your peers.

As a member of a group, you will almost certainly find yourself sometimes behaving in ways which do not help the group's functioning. Even the most skilled and experienced group members have lapses. You will find yourself

161

being defensive of your ideas and of yourself. Of course, there are many ways of expressing defensiveness. Sometimes it takes the form of immediate counter-attack. 'I don't agree with you' quickly becomes, 'You're wrong' and then, 'So what's your problem?'. A more muted counter-attack is the affected surprise, 'Nobody ever told me that before'. The defence of prior knowledge becomes, 'I knew you were going to say that'. You may meet people who will tell you that their angry and argumentative response to criticism is due to former experience in 'academic debate'. You may find it difficult to resist the temptation of bolstering your apparent strength by showing up others' weaknesses and avoiding your own areas of weakness. Common ways of doing this are to ask questions which demonstrate knowledge rather than a desire for knowledge, and to project an image of composure which is a veneer of confusion and trepidation. I believe that it is impossible for most people, students and faculty members alike, to avoid such behaviour completely. But you should try to minimize it and be alert for when it happens, so that you can try to identify the reasons for it and ask yourself why it was necessary for you to behave in that way.

You will share the responsibility of evaluation of all the members of your group. It is sometimes said that evaluation by peers becomes too personal, and a matter solely of liking or disliking. You should remember that performance is being measured, not the person. However, the school's objectives require an evaluation of some aspects of performance which are very personal, and discussions of personality often become inevitable. Degrees of liking and disliking among group members are not relevant issues for evaluation, but the attributes of both the observer and the observed which are the basis for these feelings are relevant. A form called Individual Group Member Assessment is included in your manual to guide you in assessing your own and your peers' performance. The roles of the student, tutor, and senior mentor in relation to evaluation are also given in your manual.

Formerly, if you worked as individuals, nobody else suffered if you were unpunctual or irresponsible in any other way. Now your group will be directly affected by such behaviour. The demands of responsible professional conduct apply to you now as a result, and you cannot look on your time in medical school as time to make gradual adaptations in behaviour. If you were formerly unpunctual or unreliable or uncooperative in any way, you will be expected to change rather abruptly.

Setting goals
By being here you have all accepted the school's objectives, so the goals I am talking about are those which go beyond, or are additional to, these. Any individual goals will have to be compatible with those of the school and of the tutorial group you are working in.

When you think about this, try to think about all areas of your life; about how your being in medical school will affect your family and your friendships. Do not minimize the stresses which will be put on them: start now to plan how you are going to protect what is important to you. I would urge you not to get totally immersed in the world of medicine. If you are to meet the school's objectives you will have to be able to sense the needs of the community. You will not be able to do this if you are out of touch with all but the medical community. You should also be sure to safeguard time for mental and physical recreation. Students here work very hard, even compulsively, and 'time off' all too often disappears. Self-directed learning can turn into an enslavement by one's own demands and fears.

Sometimes it is easier to make a start by setting negative rather than positive goals. Most of you have probably seen things you did not like in the health care system, or if you have not you certainly will. From your experiences you can probably identify behaviour you do not want to lapse into or adopt, and situations you want to avoid. Keep your individual goals under constant review. As your knowledge and experience increase, the nature of your goals should change accordingly, perhaps to be defined more precisely, perhaps to be adapted, or perhaps to be completely replaced. Do not limit yourself by getting locked into your first goals.

The ability to identify goals for yourself is very much a matter of practice. Many of you who have not had to do this often may be feeling quite threatened by this talk of personal objectives. You may not have any special goals that you are aware of, and be perfectly content to accept the school's objectives without expansion or elaboration. That is quite acceptable for now, but you should certainly develop specific plans to meet your own interests and needs as you proceed through the programme.

This programme will, to a large extent, be for each of you what you make it. You should not be concerned with just getting through but in getting the most out of the opportunities available to let you develop in ways best suited to your temperament, skills and needs. In addition, you should do what you can to make the experience the best it can be for your classmates. To do this, you will have to get involved with the programme and with your peers. They need you.

II. Students' reactions

Reactions of a student from a conventional undergraduate programme
Before I was asked to contribute to this chapter, I had done quite a bit of thinking about the changes which I have had to make in my methods of learning since coming to medical school, after completing an honours programme in biology at this university. There are four different kinds of adaptation which I can identify. They are the changes necessary in moving from a research-oriented approach to a more practical and applied one, the changes necessary in the style of studying, the need to develop the ability to approach, on my own, subjects about which I know nothing, and the need to develop greater integrative skills. I will describe my experience in relation to each of these in the following paragraphs.

In my undergraduate programme, emphasis had been placed on the ability to analyse and criticize original research, to understand the importance of experimental design and to weight conclusions drawn from results. I was therefore used to approaching a problem by going to the most recently published original research, and although I quickly realized that this led me in medical studies to too much detail and too narrow a view, I found that I did not completely overcome this tendency until the end of Phase II (*the second ten weeks of the programme*). By that time, I had learned where to look for good review articles or summaries. By going to these first, I saved time which would otherwise have been spent on tracking down original papers, and avoided the tendency to go into too much detail. I also found that I had become comfortable in accepting that I could not get a detailed knowledge of all I was studying. Although my undergraduate education did make this adaptation necessary, at the same time it helped me to make it. My knowledge of biology enabled me quickly to conceptualize possible mechanisms, and gave me the confidence to make good guesses as a starting point for exploration.

In the lecture system which I had been used to as an undergraduate, I had been accustomed to reading relevant material quickly before each lecture, and having the identifying and sorting out of what was essential done by the lecturer. Now I spend much more time on reading about a topic. I re-read several times and underline, before I can be sure that I have isolated all the important concepts. I felt reasonably confident about this by the middle of Phase II. Each student works independently to some extent, but our tutorial groups are crucial to us for checking that our concepts are accurate. As an example, in my present group we posed the question of what two laboratory tests are the most important in the initial diagnosis of diabetes. All the group members researched the same area and acquired the same information, but individually had different perceptions of what considerations were relevant in answering the question. A very lively hour of information exchange, challenge and rethinking was necessary, before all the group members had agreed on the answer and on the qualifying statements attached to it. This kind of exchange is most fruitful when the question of what information is essential is raised, when the information and the concepts generated are confirmed and when individuals' contributions are integrated and augmented. I have found that in only one of my tutorial groups did these benefits not result. They are dependent on the attitudes of the group members and their willingness to share their knowledge and question their own and other people's concepts.

From my undergraduate education, I was also used to being introduced to new subjects by lecturers. I did not have to worry about defining the dimensions of the subject or identifying a starting point. Now I have to be prepared to start alone on any appropriate new subject. The approach which I have used and which took me until the end of Phase II to get comfortable with, is to ask simple questions, one at a time, at the start. The questions gradually get more complex as the framework of a concept is built up and then filled in. This takes time and a lot of patience, when the urge is to find out everything at once. It suits my style to get some knowledge of the anatomy of the relevant area or organ as a starting point. This provides me with visual references for further information. More recently, I have been finding that the embryological development of relevant tissue or organs is often my best starting point.

The final adaptation which I made was the easiest. I had to accept responsibility for integrating knowledge, which formerly I could rely on lecturers to do. Indeed, I can remember specific examples of this happening in lectures and many pieces immediately falling into place. For me, it was enough to know at the start of the medical programme that this was necessary. I was able, with deliberate effort, to make connections to expand my understanding, and to relate new knowledge to my pre-existing knowledge. I try to do this with the information I have gathered in individual study before tutorials, and the work of the tutorial reinforces this.

Now, at the end of Phase III (40 weeks made up of four units of organ system study), I am able to see what changes I have made. I find the increased degree of my personal involvement in my studies to be fun and I enjoy the chance to be a detective. The need to defend one's information and one's concepts makes them more of personal possessions.

Reactions of a student with previous unconventional, self-directed educational experience

I was an independent ('freewheeler') student long before arriving at McMaster Medical School. My high school – Nohant School – comprised a band of 40 teenage outlaws. These renegades from convention abandoned their respective schools and established a small, private sanctuary of learning, which they ran, without benefit of budget, building or paid faculty, for five school years. Nohant 'hired' a faculty of 25 volunteer teachers from the community at large, established headquarters in a public library, and held classes most evenings in private homes. Each of the 40 students carried one-fortieth of the responsibility for the smooth function and good government of the operation, and 100 per cent of the responsibility for the implementation and success of their own personal learning programme. No student was obliged to show up at all, ever. No student – this, by decree – had to do anything he or she didn't want to. The dictum we came to prefer, as we matured philosophically, was that all students at Nohant were free to do anything they *did* want to do. Mostly as a result of the unfettered enthusiasm of our staff and students, and the excitement generated by the adventure, much was accomplished, both in terms of the growth and development of the participants as human beings, and in terms of cold, hard, provincially recognized academic accomplishment.

My undergraduate programme, Integrated Studies at the University of Waterloo, Ontario, amounted again to a licence to do as I pleased. The programme was twice the size of Nohant, but was still completely student run, through weekly school meetings and committees, whose jurisdiction extended to the hiring and firing of faculty, dispensing a considerable budget, student programmes, and other issues bearing on the operation and growth of the programme. The only compulsory requirement was that each student submit a summary, by the end of the year, of the year's academic activities. Otherwise, students were free to 'go where they would, do as they wished': they could study the violin in Vienna, literature in London, biology, philosophy, journalism or mathematics. One of my own years in Integrated Studies was spent in Montreal, with Dr Hans Selye, founder of the theory of stress in human disease, and the year following I became a co-worker in an amateurish but successful attempt to develop an injectable treatment for malignant tumours in rats.

One of the first things that struck me on arrival at McMaster was that adjusting to independent learning could still be difficult for students from conventional programmes. Seeing it again reminded me very much of my days at Nohant, and the growing pains we all went through. New students invariably suffered a period we called the doldrums. Realizing that one was in a school which allowed unqualified freedom to do as you pleased made the idea of doing absolutely nothing absolutely irresistible for a time. Many a carefree afternoon was spent languishing in the sweet clutches of freedom. Over endless cups of coffee, and uproarious conversation, we toasted the end to repression, to being told what to do. Then, for each person in turn, came 'the morning after' of the victory celebration. This was the day on which the individual awakened to the realization that doing nothing was not freedom; that in fact we were being controlled by our need to prove our autonomy – defining ourselves by the hold our enemy no longer had on us. That is, we still saw ourselves as what we weren't, but not by what we were. This was the moment of truth; when we had to accept as *proven* that no one could tell us what to do. We then buried once and for all our vanquished enemy, disposed of the half empty coffee cups, revved up the generator and got down to work. The successful 'freewheelers' came to understand that being truly free meant doing things because one was free to. With the externally imposed structure, reward and punishment systems gone, we resolved to build our own internal structures, and become genuinely self-directed. A.S. Neill recognized the 'pre-free' or doldrum stage in students at Summerhill School in England. He estimated that it took from three months to ten years for his students to become successful self-starters.

During my first several months at McMaster the often-voiced complaint from some students was that there wasn't enough work to do. They felt that, having been geared up in anticipation, medical school was providing nothing to sink one's teeth into. It was, in short, too easy, which made some students very uneasy. What these newcomers to independent learning didn't know was that while they were going through their 'pre-free' period, wanting to be *told* what to do, other, more autonomous students (from whatever background) were having the most arduous, busy time of their lives, having fired their *own* starter's pistol. This was partly a function of some students having no background in biology or physiology, and being panic motivated. But more so a reflection of the two different attitudes; the one, fostered by conventional education, of awaiting orders from the top in order to begin learning; the other, engendered by successful independent programmes, or acquired naturally, of self-motivation.

So, according to A.S. Neill's schedule, somewhere between three months and ten years post-entry begins the process of self-actualization. Another stage often intervenes, sometimes at Nohant and often at McMaster. This is the penance stage. It occurs when a remorseful student decides that he has just frittered away several weeks/months of precious time in unproductive leisure. By this time he has accumulated a veritable mountain of unresolved, merciless guilt. As a form of penance, the guilt-ridden student makes a solemn and serious vow to work himself to the bone, burn the midnight oil, put his nose to the proverbial grindstone. The problem arises when this otherwise valuable energy resource is harnessed to some almost fruitless task. McMaster students, for example, may sign Lehninger's *Textbook of Biochemistry* out of the library, and attempt to 'work through it', chapter by chapter. This allows one to trade suffering for guilt. It seldom, however, results in much productive learning. Proponents of problem-based learning claim, and I agree with them, that in order to be of real value, knowledge should ideally be gained in solving a specific problem; then, in order to be retained, this knowledge should be exercised in solving other problems. The trouble with chapter reading as a learning style is that it involves trying to gobble up reams of information passively, without actively using this information. Instead of having questions, and searching out the answers which are thereby incorporated into one's thoughts, it means working through pages and pages of 'answers', never having asked the questions to begin with. Certainly there may be something to gain in chapter reading, but as the 'penance' worker often finds, as he throws down Lehninger in despair, there is no limit to the information one can find to 'gobble' and one can very easily choke on it. A certain amount of chapter study is useful in acquiring background, say in a new area. Few people go through our system without it (not even freewheelers). But this is distinct from the penance activity of throwing oneself headlong at some impossible task in the name of working hard, rather than working well.

Barbara asked me to offer comment on the adjustment of students in the programme, and myself, to McMaster medicine. The biggest problem I've faced at McMaster is the loneliness of the long distance runner. For many of us, it has been a dawn-until-midnight routine from day one – six days a week, 11 months a year. Not every minute is brain-breaking, but it's all medicine, without let-up. I've all but run out of friends, abandoned hope of ever falling in love, and am now a little uncomfortable in the company of 'outsiders'. It has become hard to let loose, relax, and be frivolous and warm with people, having become so accustomed to 'life in the monastery'. As Rod says, when one finally takes a night off to see an outsider, one unconsciously begins taking a health history and physical, which is the relationship we have become most comfortable with. This skill has a limited value in social settings. I don't know if anything could change all this; with all the long hours and seclusion I still don't feel I've accomplished anything *near* the learning I should have so far. But some days the loneliness and struggle make me nauseous. At other schools, students face exam pressures and the endless boredom of lectures, none of which I could ever tolerate, nor do I see these as constructive. But McMaster can be its own brand of hell on earth, and when you stand alone it's just you and the flames. Loneliness and anxiety are rampant in the programme. I guess really they are in life also.

Lauren was saying the other day that two years in the programme changes a person; that by the end you almost don't recognize yourself. She claims to feel uneasy at the morning mirror, not knowing whose teeth she's apparently brushing. The greatest personal changes for me were induced by working in tutorial groups. Tutorials are the learning focus of McMaster medicine. In them, five students and a tutor 'problem-solve' each other to near delirium. With several days' preparation, the group works through explaining a given health history to the best of their acquired knowledge.

One doesn't win favour in tutorials by saying nothing. Nor will a group tolerate a member who dominates the proceedings. Somewhere between the two extremes lies the elusive happy medium. Groups are much like life, in which, as Martin Buber says, 'Secretly, and bashfully, every person waits for a yes'. I have wanted, like a bear wants honey, my groups to recognize my thinking as right and correct, and praise my memory. Performing well in tutorial is all that has mattered for me at McMaster. From this I derive all my sense of self-worth and personal value. I don't sleep well the night before, and do so the night after only if all goes well in tutorial. In a programme which allows little or no time for love or friendship on an extra-curricular basis, the tutorial group becomes co-workers, friends, lovers, family – the individual's only mirror of himself for two long years. The group's bi-weekly meetings come to represent much more than mere academic forums. Whether the group likes you as a person on a particular day determines to a large extent whether you like yourself in any given week. For example, the other night I had dinner with my friend (... ...). An otherwise jolly and warmhearted person, on this particular evening he was the picture of melancholy. Something was bothering him, and it hurt so much he couldn't even discuss it. Twice over dinner his eyes grew red, and I sensed him holding back the tears. Later that evening, some checking around turned up the problem. Someone in (... ...)'s group, whom he had looked on as a friend, had commented in the day's 'evaluation session' that he had made them feel uncomfortable since the group began. He was devastated. And N.B., my friend is no fragile youngster – he's a graduate in engineering, been all but married once or twice, and even lifts weights. In 'real life' the comment wouldn't have flattened my weight-lifting friend, but in the vulnerable, 'need love' condition of a McMaster medical student, it was nearly lethal.

Another thing Lauren commented on the other day was that tutorials challenge one to be maximally assertive and minimally aggressive. I agree strongly (but nicely). My foremost goal in tutorials has been to learn to speak with such self-assurance and cogency of thought that no one would dream of contradicting me before thinking twice, yet at the same time to perform in such a way as not to make any other group member feel intimidated, put-down, or inferior. This is the real art of tutorial success: to be respected, and at the same time liked by one's peers. The assertive/aggressive balance is a delicate one in the best of groups where the sensitive issue of what one knows and has learned is always in the air. The need to develop confidence in myself has made me more assertive than ever before in my life. The need to be liked prohibits building up my own sense of worth at the expense of someone else's feelings. In a group without trust, this is an impossible challenge.

One of my groups consisted of five almost incompatible students, with a thoroughly disreputable tutor. The tutor intimidated everyone, and played our feelings mercilessly one against the other. Why should he, one might wonder: but why are people ever unkind? A stronger group might have weathered him, but ours broke ranks. It established a mood of every man for himself from the beginning, and what both fascinated and annoyed me was that the quality of the tutor had such an impact on how the students related to one another. This tutor has had a similar effect on all his groups. Winning his approval meant joining in a game of mental fencing in which, by fair or foul, one was meant to jab at one's opponents, and if possible render them sensitive and off balance by hurting their feelings. A group which might otherwise have stood a chance was lost in constant one-up-manship and scrapping. Twice the group met in private to consider why they weren't getting along. Both times we recognized that somehow the tutor had undermined our sense of trust in each other. This helped immeasurably, although it was too little, too late.

I consider this trust issue an important one in all my groups. It means a lot, for example, for someone to say in the first meeting of a group, something to the effect that they feel a group is a place where one should never be afraid to be wrong, because we're all here to help each other in any way we can to maximize the learning experience. This sets an important tone – to have the thought expressed is crucial. It is not enough to assume that everyone knows this. It is similar in my mind to dealing with patients, who, like students, are in a very vulnerable position. On the evening of an operation, it's important for a patient to be told that events are planned for the day after the operation. The patient knows he will probably wake up after the operation is over, but it is often important to hear from someone else what one already knows. Groups which don't establish an atmosphere of trust, and don't respect each individual's need to be right once in a while, don't work, in my experience.

What I have forgotten to say, but naively assumed the reader knows, is that despite my complaints, the learning and growth I have undergone at McMaster have provided among the most satisfying moments of my life to date. I am feverishly loyal to the programme, and consider it one of the most profoundly successful educational experiments ever.

III. Outcomes of the programme

The question of whether the public can be assured of the competence of graduates of programmes in which student autonomy in learning exists, is usually posed in relation to professional education. The immediacy of the question is tempered in Canadian medical education because the licence to practise medicine is awarded by a body independent of the universities and is based on performance in a written examination and successful completion of at least one year of internship. It is still, of course, of vital interest to those involved in medical education at McMaster to know how well the programme has met its objectives and the needs of its graduates in practice.

Graduates' opinions

Surveys of the first six classses made some years after their graduation showed a generally high level of satisfaction with the programme (Woodward and Ferrier, 1982). Among the strengths identified were self-directed learning, problem-based learning and independent study. Lack of definition of core material and the anxiety level created were reported as deficiencies. It is interesting that these strengths and deficiencies are related in that lack of definition of core material and consequent anxiety may be a necessary price to pay for self-directed learning.

In response to questions about their preparedness for internship in comparison with their peers from other schools, the McMaster graduates reported themselves, as was hoped and expected, as better prepared in areas emphasised by the programme, such as independent learning, problem-solving and self-evaluation. They also found themselves equally prepared in knowledge. Thus although our medical students express fears that they will be less prepared than graduates of other schools, these fears are not borne out.

More recently we have wondered whether opinions of more recent classes might differ from those of the first six. Over the years classes have grown larger and have higher proportions of women, and the curriculum has undergone some changes. A survey of three classes ('78, '80, '82) that represent a stage of stable class size (100) and proportion of women (50%) has shown that perceptions of these graduates are very similar to those of earlier classes.

Graduates' performance

To obtain a licence to practise, physicians in Canada must pass an examination set by the Medical Council of Canada. This examination has a portion that emphasises basic knowledge, tested in multiple-choice format, and a portion that emphasises the handling and solution of problems. Graduates of McMaster have usually performed slightly below the national average on the first portion and above the national average on the second.

To be certified in a medical or surgical speciality, medical graduates must pass examinations of the Royal College of Physicians and Surgeons of Canada. The first attempt pass rate of McMaster graduates in these examinations is higher than the national average.

Assessment of the performance of four classes of McMaster graduates (1977 – 1980) in their first postgraduate year by their supervisors has been studied. The supervisors compared their performance with that of graduates of other universities and, in general, the McMaster graduates were rated as being better. When assessment of comparison groups for the classes of '78 and '79 (ie contemporary graduates of other medical schools) was studied, this was also found to be positively skewed, although less so than for the McMaster group.

Instruments to measure performance of physicians in independent practice are only now being developed, so this final test of competence cannot yet be applied. However, the results of interim tests described here have led us to conclude that, in general, McMaster graduates are at least as good as those of other North American schools.

Graduates' career choices

Although records of McMaster graduates' careers have been maintained, only recently has it become possible to find out whether they differ in career choices from graduates of other Canadian universities. The Canadian Medical Association has set up a data bank containing information on the career paths of holders of current Canadian licences, and this allowed for the comparison of McMaster graduates with groups of their contemporaries (Ferrier and Woodward, 1986). A striking result of this comparison has been the detection of a much higher interest in academic medicine in the McMaster group, as reflected by numbers involved in research and in classroom teaching and by proportions of salaried physicians employed by universities.

Any explanation of this must be speculative at this stage, but several features of the McMaster programme have been considered as contributing factors. Self-directed learning around problems may have forcefully shown students that many questions are unanswerable with present knowledge, and may have given them the interest and the confidence to seek some of the answers. It is also possible that the close faculty – student relations that result from the small-group learning and from the students' seeking help from individual faculty members may have provided for potent role modelling. Other medical schools which have had innovative programmes (Western Reserve, University of Calgary) have also noted a high interest in academic medicine. Perhaps such programmes attract students who are interested in education.

Autonomy in learning as a student can, it is hoped, lead to habits of life-long learning in practice. In a rapidly changing profession such as medicine, this will prove to be a crucial component of maintaining competence. Studies to determine how McMaster graduates compare with others in this respect are being planned.

Chapter 11

The Negotiated Learning Contract

Catherine Tompkins,
School of Nursing, McMaster University, Hamilton, Ontario
Mary-Jean McGraw,
School of Nursing, Laurentian University, Sudbury, Ontario

A wise educator once wrote:

> If he is indeed wise he does not bid you enter
> the house of his wisdom, but rather leads you
> to the threshold of your own mind. (Gibran, 1923, p 56)

Leading students to the wisdom of their own minds and setting them free on their own learning journeys remains a challenge facing modern educators. Searching for teaching methods that will enrich the autonomous experience for learners has become an endless quest. We have turned to the negotiated learning contract as an effective tool for developing facilitative relationships with students in an undergraduate nursing programme. Our experiences in using contract learning to foster the development of student autonomy will be the focus of this chapter.

Learning contracts can be used in a variety of ways within the formal educational system. However, we have found that one of the most valuable is in situations where students learn from experience. Thus, we use them as a plan for student learning in clinical practicums. Through these learning experiences nursing students develop knowledge, skills and attitudes relevant to their future role as professional nurses in a variety of hospital and community-based clinical settings.

Contracting as a framework for lifelong learning

The literature describes the learning contract as both a *product* and a *process*. Donald's definition of the learning contract as a product is as follows: 'A learning contract is a document drawn up by a student and his instructor or advisor, which specifies what the student will learn, how this will be accomplished, within what period of time, and what the criteria of evaluation will be' (1976, p 1). This focus on the contract as a document greatly diminishes its value as a powerful strategy for enhancing student self-direction and autonomy. We have seen this emphasis on the product lead to teachers and students focusing on producing a perfect document to the detriment of meaningful learning outcomes. Rewriting and recycling the piece of paper can rob students of the time and energy that could be better spent pursuing their learning goals.

We believe that the focus of contracting should be on the process instead: the relationship beween the student and teacher and the negotiation that occurs throughout the learning experience. Therefore, we define contracting as a continuously renegotiable working agreement between the student and teacher which emphasizes mutuality in decision-making and student self-determination in relation to learning outcomes. For it is in the 'contract work' or the actual process of negotiation that we have found that skills for autonomous learning can develop. This assumption forms the underlying premiss of this chapter.

In our explorations with contracting we have discovered the following advantages of this process in promoting student autonomy.

(a) Contract learning provides a framework for allowing students to discover the meaning of nursing content for themselves, an important aspect of the socialization process into our profession. This is accomplished by students manipulating learning experiences to meet their own needs and interests and by risk-taking within the safety of a supportive student – teacher relationship.

(b) The contracting process results in learning which is relevant and meaningful to the learner, thus increasing motivation. It also heightens motivation by placing responsibility for learning where it belongs: with the student. The excitement and challenge generated within the students as they create and implement their own learning experiences results in achievement of outcomes far beyond those seen in a more traditional approach to learning.

(c) As modern educators our goal is also to help nursing students gain skills in learning. At a time when rapid changes in society and the health-care workplace necessitate lifelong learning, new practitioners need to develop skills necessary for educating themselves: skills in problem-solving, in defining learning needs, in identifying learning resources, in assessing individual learning styles, and in negotiation. We have found that through the learning contract many of our students have developed these skills.

(d) The process of contract learning also acknowledges individual learner differences in a way that few other teaching methods can. It effectively recognizes and builds on differences in students' backgrounds, needs, aims, strengths and deficiencies, while meeting the educational requirements of a course or programme designed to produce a competent professional nurse.

(e) Contracting encourages learners to tap a wide range of resources and alternative strategies for learning. This reduces their dependency upon the assigned faculty, exposes them to resources outside of the university, encourages peer consultation and challenges them to stretch their imaginations in identifying and negotiating relevant learning experiences.

This list is by no means exhaustive. Certainly many other educators have documented similar advantages in their research related to contracting. *Using*

Learning Contracts by Malcolm S. Knowles (1986) provides a detailed description of their use in a variety of educational situations and outlines both advantages and disadvantages of contracting based on the experiences of a number of teachers in higher education. The above list does, however, highlight what we feel are the key educational features of contracting that have evolved from our experiences with the process. Personal outcomes for both teachers and learners involved in contract learning add another positive dimension and will be examined more closely later in the chapter.

The process of contracting

The process of contracting can be complex, and, without some kind of sequence or order, negotiation of a learning contract can be an overwhelming and rather bewildering process for novices – both teachers and students. Having a predetermined structure for the stages of the process helps both participants feel more secure, provides a road map for the tasks requiring negotiation and discussion, and highlights the key decision-making points.

In structuring the 'contract work', we have found the eight stages described by Sloan and Schommer (1975, p 199) helpful in guiding novices through the process. The components and stages of the contracting process are outlined in Figure 1. An example of contracting between a fourth-year nursing student and a faculty member will now be described to clarify these stages. Figure 2 illustrates a portion of the completed learning plan.

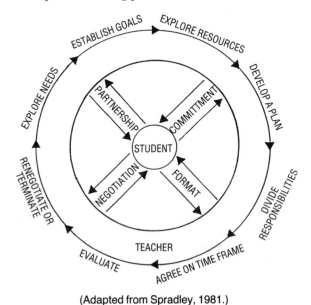

(Adapted from Spradley, 1981.)

Figure 1 *The concept and process of contracting.*

SAMPLE LEARNING CONTRACT

Student .... Maureen D.   Clinical Setting....... Doctor's Office
Course .... N4J7/4K7   Date.............. 19 Sept – 8 Dec

OBJECTIVES	STRATEGIES AND RESOURCES	EVIDENCE	CRITERIA AND MEANS FOR EVALUATION

Develop knowledge about the normal anatomy, physiology of the female reproductive system in the pregnant woman and to apply this knowledge to the development of skill in the physical assessment of the pregnant woman
 	
Eg – palpate fetal position,
– auscultate fetal heart,
– measure fundal height.
 	
Modification of Objectives
To develop knowledge of psychosocial and normal physiology of the pregnant woman.
 	
To increase skill in physical examinations, interviewing and teaching of the pregnant woman.
	1. *Books* – Literature
	A & P
	Interviewing books
	
	2. *People*
	Office nurse
	Office physician
	Adviser
	
	3. *Videotapes*
	Reproductive system
	Interviewing
	Pre-natal teaching
		1. Written summary of anatomy and physiology in chart form with a verbal explanation of content.
		
		2. Direct observation of physical assessment skills by clinical staff.
		
		3. Tapes of interviews.
			1. Evaluation of charts by my adviser as to:
			  i) Degree of clarity and comprehensiveness of charts.
			  ii) Degree of understanding of subject matter as illustrated by my oral explanation of content of charts.
			
			2. Evaluation by myself and a clinical staff member of physical assessment and interviewing skills according to following criteria:
			  i) Degree of accuracy in taking physical measurements and assessment of fetal position.
			  ii) Degree of confidence shown in approaching physical assessment.
			
			3. Taped interviews and direct observation to be evaluated according to the following criteria:
			  i) What degree of confidence is demonstrated?
			  ii) Do I demonstrate ability in assisting the patient to find ways of dealing with her health problem?
			  iii) Do I give appropriate information to the patient about her health problem? (including resources available.)

Legend for Evaluation of All Criteria

to a great extent	above average	average	some-what	not at all

Figure 2

175

Maureen is a nursing student in the final year of an undergraduate nursing course. She is in her early twenties and worked as a secretary after completing 13 years of primary and secondary school education prior to entrance into the university nursing course. Maureen is working with her adviser, Suzanne, in completing the expectations for a clinical practicum in a physician's office. Suzanne is a faculty member who has taught for several years using more traditional methods of interaction with students including group seminars, lectures and direct clinical supervision. Contracting as a method of facilitation is a new experience for her, and both she and Maureen attended a faculty and student orientation programme prior to initiating the contracting process.

1. Exploration of needs

In the first meeting between Maureen and her adviser, the focus is on the establishment of a climate for mutual negotiation and an assessment of Maureen's unique needs, strengths and background she brings to the learning situation.

It is at this time that the teacher and learner begin the groundwork for later negotiations by providing realistic visions of how they plan to work together throughout the contract. Communication is the lifeblood of the contracting relationship. It provides the vitality and nourishment necessary to foster a healthy student – teacher relationship, and it is through these early communications that trust is developed and tested. Without this trust, students may say what they think the teacher wants to hear and develop contracts which do not truly reflect their needs and interests.

Occurring throughout the process, negotiation is the key to ensuring that the contract is tailored to Maureen's needs, is flexible and can be modified to meet her changing learning goals. Negotiation can be defined as 'the total set of processes whereby actors [Suzanne and Maureen] in pursuit of common interests [achievement of course and individual objectives] try to arrive at a settlement or arrangement with each other' (Martin, 1976, p 6) Martin identifies two preconditions for negotiation which we believe are crucial for successful implementation of the contracting process.

(1) negotiations must be centred on shared interests;
(2) although one party (the teacher) has the power to realize her aims, she is reluctant to use it. (p 6)

It is essential that the teacher enter into and implement the contracting process with values that are congruent with this philosophy. Otherwise, negotiation will not take place and the learning contract will simply become Suzanne's plan for Maureen's learning – ie it will be an implementation of the traditional teaching model.

The initial meeting between Maureen and Suzanne took place during the first week of the autumn term.

176

Before this first meeting Maureen had reviewed the course requirements and visited the setting for her clinical placement, a physician's office. In preparation, she had made an assessment of her learning needs. This requires the learner to consider both the activities of the clinical area and the course requirements and reconcile these with her own needs. Maureen came to the meeting to discuss this and the development of her learning contract with her adviser. As part of this meeting, her adviser is responsible for initiating a climate of free communication and support and providing for freedom of expression ... Maureen's needs determine the nature, content, and scheduling of the meetings; her adviser acts as a resource person and learning facilitator, reviewing the relevance of her objectives for the course requirements and providing an opportunity for later modification or change.

This initial meeting represented for Maureen and Suzanne a situation that required negotiation to clearly define Maureen's learning needs. We feel that it is important to emphasize here that although Maureen had her own perception of her learning needs and interests, these had to be congruent with the 'givens' or requirements of the clinical course. In a nursing programme, these represent the standards that must be attained for professional accountability. Negotiation at this point in the process provided the forum for blending Maureen's unique needs with these programme 'givens'.

While Suzanne possessed power related to her designated role as adviser, she shared this power with Maureen by allowing her active participation in the needs assessment process. Thus, the conditions for negotiation were met and the contracting process was initiated.

2. Establishment of goals

Discussion and agreement between student and teacher on learning goals becomes the focus of the second stage of the process. Once needs and expectations are outlined from the perspective of both participants, these must be translated into statements that can provide the direction for learning strategies, and be the guideposts against which student progress can be measured. Putting these goals on paper also signals a commitment to the contract, and for some students this may be intimidating. In this case it is best to start with a single objective and work through the process slowly. Contract work can also be completed verbally at first, moving later to a written form as learner confidence increases.

Dangers to be avoided at this stage relate to the degree of challenge for the learner. In the extreme, goals that present too much or too little challenge can be destructive to student motivation, but Suzanne should not be afraid to allow Maureen to make mistakes, explore her limits and gain self-awareness through the consequences of her decisions. Letting go is sometimes the greatest challenge for the teacher.

Once Maureen had created a vision of herself satisfactorily performing in a particular field of activity, the activity was broken down into the specific contractual outcomes she would pursue.

The focus for the initial meetings with Maureen's adviser related to her first objective: to develop knowledge about the normal anatomy and physiology of the female reproductive system in the pregnant woman, and to apply this knowledge to the development of skills in the physical assessment of the pregnant woman.

Maureen's concern related to the achievement of skills in the physical examination of the pre-natal mother. Her plan was to involve the experienced clinic nurse in evaluating her knowledge and performance. But, when she discussed this proposal with the nurse, a conflict arose: the nurse wanted to focus on the technical details of the examination rather than the total needs of the patient which Maureen assumed would include the emotional as well as the physical aspects of patient care. Maureen wanted to explore alternative ways of meeting her objective with her adviser. The way they chose to do this was through role playing ... Through this process, Maureen was helped to identify strengths and weaknesses in herself, in the nurse and in the situation ... With continued analysis of this clinical situation, Maureen readjusted her learning focus. Now that she had defined her own strengths more clearly, she was able to accept broader learning challenges and reassess her objectives, and was able to seek out an interdisciplinary learning situation with a physician – nurse team in the same office which would be able to meet her objectives more effectively.

In this situation, Maureen and Suzanne continued to use the negotiation process to clarify how Maureen's interests and goals would be met within the limitations of the clinical situation. It was important at this stage that Maureen had a sense of ownership of the contract and that Suzanne valued the learning goals in relation to the course and programme objectives. The dynamic nature of the process which reflected mutual problem-solving and commitment resulted in a motivating and realistic contract for Maureen.

3. Exploration of resources

This stage involves further definition of what the teacher and the learner will offer to and expect from each other to meet the challenges of the contract goals. It can also include brainstorming and fact-finding to identify appropriate learning resources such as peers, agencies, books, workshops and other professionals. It is at this point that students can be actively encouraged to express their uniqueness and creativity.

In our example, Maureen's negotiations with the clinical setting, other nursing staff, and professionals illustrate this searching approach. In this stage, Suzanne's role was to assist Maureen to identify and approach potential learning resources in an open and creative manner. As in the example, the relationship should allow each participant to become more familiar with the other person and to gauge the depth of the commitment to and understanding of the goals. Dialogue should help clear misunderstandings based on unstated assumptions, and further develop trust.

4. Development of a plan

Once the alternatives have been explored in terms of resources, negotiation centres on identifying the specific methods and activities for achieving the stated goals.

> A variety of ways for achieving the knowledge component of [Maureen's] first objective were explored. Maureen rejected the idea of writing another formal paper, of presenting a case study, or of giving a formal seminar; she preferred to do a project that would be creative and stimulating. Her adviser engaged her in a brainstorming session to help her expand the range of projects from which she could select. The result was the development of a number of charts that integrated anatomy and physiology of the reproductive system.
>
> Maureen was encouraged to consult with some of her student peers who were also developing audio-visual resources or who had some contacts that would be useful to her in completing her project.

At this stage, power struggles can ensue as teachers frequently view selection of learning strategies as their domain. Negotiation must continue to reflect shared power and decision-making and maintain student-centredness. Letting go of traditional values and roles is a central ingredient in successful implementation of this component of the process.

In our experience, the payoffs of letting go and freeing the learner to move beyond the constraints of teacher-determined assignments have been tremendous. Student-designed projects have demonstrated innovations that bring new perspectives to nursing practice and immeasurable reward and satisfaction for both learners and teachers.

As Maureen worked through the first four stages of contract development, a cooperative and supportive atmosphere also promoted collaboration and consultation between herself and other nursing students. In the traditional approach, formal interaction between learners is minimal, and competition may result as students compare their achievements in relation to external rewards rather than focusing on individual progress. In contracting, this peer consultation is a planned and valued component of the learning process.

5. Division of responsibilities

If the relationship between student and teacher is progressing well, there should be a growing consensus about the roles and responsibilities of each in the learning process. Now these need to be explicitly interpreted within the framework of the contract, negotiating and labelling the activities for which each participant will be responsible. We believe it is important to recognize at this stage that contracting does not mean that Maureen learns *independently*, rather that an *interdependent* relationship is developed between Suzanne and herself.

In our example, Suzanne agreed to act as a resource for the knowledge component of the first learning goal. She also agreed to act as evaluator for the charts. Maureen maintained responsibility for the execution of learning activities, and the monitoring of the contract time frame. She also assumed responsibility for updating Suzanne regarding progress in meeting her learning goals, presenting revisions for negotiation, and setting agendas for meetings with her adviser. Shared responsibilities were identified as the establishment of evaluation methods and criteria, input into the assignment of the final grade, and the periodic review of the teacher – student relationship.

6. Agreement on time frame

Setting limits for the contract in terms of length of time includes establishing a critical path for each goal. Dates for completion of learning strategies and for submission of evidence of achievement of learning goals are identified. This stage also involves defining the number of contacts between teacher and student and the extent of time commitment each is willing to make to the process. This stage may be controlled in part by the length of the course but also allows for individualized student pacing and mutually agreed-upon student access to consultation with teaching staff. While frequently subject to revision, the contract can serve as an excellent tool for student time-management, priority setting, and accountability. Maureen and Suzanne agreed to meet every two weeks for one hour throughout the duration of the contract.

7. Evaluation

Besides stating what the student will do, and by when, the contract specifies what the learner and teacher will accept as evidence that the learner has achieved her goals. We believe it is important for periodic formative evaluation of progress towards goals to occur at agreed-upon intervals. Are the goals being met? If not, do they need to be revised to be more workable? Is there a new problem or need that must be met? Are the course objectives being met satisfactorily?

It is at the stage of final or summative evaluation (assessment of student achievement of the learning goals) that many of the more traditional values about teaching and learning can resurface and problems with power distribution may arise. In our experience this component of the contracting process can pose the greatest difficulties for both learners and teachers.

The word 'evaluation' has a very strong emotional component and the process is often seen as threatening for both participants. We have witnessed two negative extremes in implementing evaluation. For students who have had little experience with self-evaluation, the ability to look within themselves and determine their strengths and limitations is a difficult and threatening exercise. They may feel more comfortable deferring to the teacher, a perceived authority, for feedback regarding their progress and achievement. The other extreme may arise if teachers take control at this stage and impose evaluation. In this situation, teacher behaviour is no longer congruent with the message conveyed throughout the development and implementation of the earlier phases of the contract. Until this point students have been encouraged to share the control and responsibility for their own growth, and as a result have worked towards strengthening their self-concept. Suddenly the bubble bursts as teacher control surfaces. Student self-concept becomes threatened, and this may lead to resistance and a resultant lack of internalization of the feedback provided.

We have found that the need for teacher control at this stage often relates to the following concerns:

(a) the establishment of criteria and means for validating evidence;
(b) the potential for lowering professional standards,
(c) the subjectivity of the evaluation process,
(d) the discrepancies between teacher and student expectations.

In contracting, the emphasis in evaluation must remain student-centred. The concerns identified by teachers can be minimized by a clear understanding of roles and course requirements at the course outset and frequent teacher – student consultation throughout the process. With the focus on redefining student learning needs, and with an emphasis on assets rather than deficits, evaluation can be viewed as a more positive process by learners. Control is shared between the student and teacher, allowing both parties an opportunity to evaluate learning outcomes.

Grading, however, remains a complicated and thorny issue and it is at this point in the process that teacher control is most protected (Knowles, 1986, p 149). In our programmes it remains the responsibility of staff to ensure that standards and professional requirements are being maintained within the negotiated order of the contract, and to assign a final grade to student performance. Students indicate what level they perceive their performance reflects; however, it is the teacher's ultimate responsibility to interpret the course and programme expectations in this final stage in the process. If the negotiation process between the student and teacher has been clear and open throughout the earlier stages of contracting, this final step will not be a difficult one as expectations will have been clear to both participants from the beginning.

If several teachers are supervising learning contracts in a course, as is often the case, it is important that the approach to assignment of grades to contract achievement be mutually defined by them and agreed upon before the negotiation process begins with the students. This will ensure consistent assignment of grades throughout the student group, even though individual contracts may reflect very divergent ways of meeting the course expectations. A method for resolving teacher – student conflict outside of the relationship may need to be established for the purposes of conciliation and mediation by an 'objective' third party if differences cannot be resolved. This will ensure that the rights of both the teacher and student are maintained while consultation is sought. Although this is rarely necessary if a sound climate of negotiation and trust has been established, it can avoid negative outcomes related to the grading process that may ultimately effect how willingly both the student and teacher will be to enter this type of agreement again.

> Consultation with Maureen progressed to the ways in which she could demonstrate the achievement of her learning objectives. She presented evaluation scales which could be used to assess her performance by herself and clinical staff in the physician's office. These related to physical examination, charting, and counselling skills ...
>
> In addition to this aspect of assessment, an overall course grade is required, and students have the opportunity to negotiate for the grade they are aiming for. Initial discussions regarding grading revealed that Maureen wanted to work towards a 'B' grade. Prior to completion of the term, Maureen was asked to review all her learning, continuous assessments, and course requirements. She was encouraged to examine the modifications made to her learning contract which reflected not only increased knowledge and skills, but creativity and initiative. It was agreed, mutually, that Maureen had achieved an 'A' grade.

8. Renegotiation

Agreement to modify, renegotiate or terminate the contract can be initiated by either participant. Continuous or formative evaluation of student progress, the time frame, learning needs and the teacher – learner relationship can lead to refinement or changes in the learning goals or outlined strategies. This opportunity for renegotiation gives the contracting process its dynamic quality; however, guidelines need to be established early in the process for the timing of renegotiation and any course 'givens' in relation to the finalized plan. This will ensure that the focus is not entirely on the development and modification of the contract, to the exclusion of the implementation of the learning plan. Maureen and Suzanne agreed that renegotiation could occur until the ninth week of a 13-week term, at which time the finalized plan was in place and the evaluation process was clearly defined.

Preparing for contract learning: changing roles and changing rules

When we enter any teaching situation, both we as teachers and our learners possess a set of expectations and assumptions about roles. Both Maureen and Suzanne entered the contracting process with a unique set of past experiences, values and role definitions which shaped their expectations.

Traditionally, the teacher role is perceived to be one of the transmitter of content, and implies an 'expert' orientation. The teacher then assumes and maintains responsibility for all components of the teaching – learning situation, and the climate reflects this authoritarian stance. In contract learning, Suzanne's role shifted from that of directing and transmitting knowledge to facilitating learning and collaborating as a co-learner with Maureen in the learning process. The climate thus changed to reflect this more informal and supportive relationship. This redefinition of the teacher role is not easy. Expressions of anxiety, fear and inadequacy in making the transition to the role of learning facilitator are common.

Students must also make a shift in their perceptions of their roles as learners. Dependency is a major component of the traditional learner role. Students are perceived, and perceive themselves, to be dependent on the teacher for planning, implementing and evaluating the outcomes of the learning process. They thus become dependent, passive recipients of the transmitted content. When expected to move from this traditional role, students frequently exhibit anxiety. They want the security of knowing that they will receive the content required to pass their examinations and qualify them to meet their career goals. A guarantee of this is not always apparent as they begin contract learning.

To engage effectively in the contracting process, Maureen had to make shifts in her perception of: (a) her view of the teacher; (b) her view of herself as a learner; (c) her view of her peers and their role in her learning; (d) what knowledge is; and (e) what learning is (Herman, 1982, p 127). In order to help both teachers and learners make the necessary changes in perceptions of their roles for contract learning, opportunities for self-assessment of required competencies and orientation to the contracting process are essential.

A one-day faculty and student orientation programme, attended by Suzanne and Maureen and other teachers and learners in the clinical course, used the contract-learning model to allow participants to experience the process and to increase their understanding of this learning mode from a learner perspective. A self-diagnostic tool such as the one presented in Fig 3 allowed Suzanne to assess herself in relation to the relevant teacher competencies for contract learning. The student self-diagnostic tool presented in Fig 4 helped Maureen in the same way to assess her learning needs. Based on the needs of the entire teacher and student group, as identified through these two forms of assessment, the orientation workshop was structured to acquaint all participants with adult learning principles, role expectations, negotiation skills and peer and self-evaluation. The workshop was highly interactive to allow an opportunity for the development of working relationships between students and teachers, student peers, and teacher peers.

Teachers discussed the following questions in an attempt to identify the skills they would use in their roles as facilitators of learning.

1. How can I help learners understand my role as facilitator and gain an understanding of self-directed learning?
2. What methods will I use to involve learners in decision-making for planning their learning?
3. How can I assist learners to assess the gaps between their present level of knowledge and competencies and the required level?
4. How can I help learners translate their learning needs into realistic objectives?

McMaster University School of Nursing
Ad adviser self-diagnostic tool for student-centred learning in Year IV
(for new advisers)
RELEVANT COMPETENCIES

Adviser: ....

		SELF-RATING			
	Don't know	Weak	Fair	Strong	
I. SELF-CONCEPT					
A. Climate Do I have the ability to:					
1. create a climate of trust and mutuality between teacher and student, as joint inquirers.					
2. understand the differences in assumptions about learning and the skills required for learning under teacher-directed learning and self-directed learning and the ability to explain these to others.					
B. Diagnosis of Needs Do I have the ability to:					
1. involve student in self-diagnosis of learning needs, personal and professional, and in the development of a learning contract.					
C. Evaluation of Learning Do I have the ability to:					
1. help students develop criteria for evaluating their learning experiences.					
2. help learner to measure his/her own competencies.					
3. initiate opportunity for feedback from					

II. EXPERIENCES						
Do I have the ability to:						
1. draw on past experiences of learner and relate to new learnings.						
III. READINESS						
Do I have the ability to:						
1. utilize students' interests as learning priorities.						
IV. STUDENT-CENTRED LEARNING CONCERNS						
Do I have the ability to:						
1. facilitate learning by focusing on the students rather than subject matter.						
2. diagnose and consult with peers regarding student-centred learning problems.						

Figure 3

(Adapted from: Knowles, 1980).

WELSH COLLEGE OF MUSIC & DRAMA LIBRARY

185

	I possess these competencies to the following degree:			
	None	Weak	Fair	Strong
1. An understanding of the differences in assumptions about learners and the skills required for learning under teacher-directed learning and self-directed learning, and the ability to explain these differences to others.				
2. A concept of myself as being a non-dependent and self-directing person.				
3. The ability to relate to peers collaboratively, to see them as resources for diagnosing needs, planning my learning; and to give help to them and receive help from them.				
4. The ability to diagnose my own learning needs realistically, with help from teachers and peers.				
5. The ability to translate learning needs into learning objectives in a form that makes it possible for their accomplishment to be assessed.				
6. The ability to relate to teachers as facilitators, helpers, or consultants, and to take the initiative in making use of their resources.				
7. The ability to identify human and material resources appropriate to different kinds of learning objective.				
8. The ability to select effective strategies for making use of learning resources and to perform these strategies skilfully and with initiative.				
9. The ability to collect and validate evidence of the accomplishment of various kinds of learning objectives.				
10.				
11.				

(Taken from: Knowles, 1975)

Figure 4 *Competencies of self-directed learning: a self-rating instrument*

5. What kind of help will I give learners in designing their learning plans to meet their objectives?

6. What is my responsibility for assuring quality of the learning activities?

7. What is my role in judging the quality of evidence of accomplishment of learning objectives and in presenting these judgements to learners in a manner that enhances the learner's self-concept as a self-directing person?

(Knowles, 1975, pp 34 – 7)

The format of the workshop also allowed students and their advisers to consider the following questions which were key to the development of their relationships:

(a) How can we develop a trusting relationship over the year?

(b) How can we promote clear, open communication?

(c) How can we acknowledge each other's interests and feelings respectfully?

(d) What actions promote growth in a non-threatening manner as a student or teacher?

The contracting method can be successfully implemented with students at varying levels of expertise but the teacher role needs to be altered to provide support for the student learning how to learn. Content and process objectives need to reflect realistic expectations for student performance based on their assessed learning needs and progress within the programme. The student's proficiency in use of the contracting process will provide guidance to the teacher for tailoring their role in giving direction and structure to students who are less sophisticated in carrying out the learning tasks. The workshop provided the opportunity for teachers and learners to develop realistic expectations regarding their roles, which formed a solid base for effective working relationships throughout the contracting process.

Opportunity was also available to clarify expectations regarding grading in an attempt to anticipate and prevent some of the problems which could arise in this area as described previously.

Although an effective orientation programme is essential when introducing contract learning within an educational institution, ongoing support for both teachers and students is also required for its success. Confronted with challenges as they move through the contracting process within the climate of a newly defined relationship, some traditionalists may retreat to the safety of teacher control and a regression to the 'old ways'. It is thus important that provision be made for ongoing support and encouragement for both teachers and students beyond the orientation. This will help them depart from the *status quo* and become more confident in changing their approach to learning.

We believe that it is not enough simply to desire a change in the teacher – learner relationship, and that there must be an appropriate innovation for teaching such as the learning contract at hand. Both Suzanne and Maureen had to believe that they had or could get the influence, the skills, the time, the materials and resources and the personal rewards necessary to begin the contract work. In a process that is new for both the teacher and the student, this 'unfreezing' is critical for role change to occur.

The shift from the traditional educational model to contract learning places demands on both teachers and learners as they are required to modify their perceptions and role-related skills. As Griffin cautions, using the *techniques* of self-directed learning, including contracting, without changing *values* will 'give self-directed learning yet another "black eye" ' (Griffin, 1982, p 40). Maureen and Suzanne's success in implementing the contracting process reflected their ability to make this shift. With Suzanne's facilitation, Maureen moved from a passive receiver of content to a proactive and responsible collaborator in the learning process. Contracting thus became a model for shared accountability between teacher and student.

The impact of contract learning for teachers and learners: personal reflections

Before instituting any innovative method of learning, it is important for educators to examine carefully the implications that this approach may have for both themselves and their learners. In our experience, students' responses to learning through contracting can be categorized under three main areas: independence behaviour, cognitive achievement and self-directed, autonomous learning. The conclusions presented in this section are based on our experiences and observations only, but reflect many of the findings of Lehman (1975) and Chickering (1972 cited in Lindquist, 1975), who conducted empirical research on this topic at Empire State College in New York.

We have found that independent learners view contract learning as superior to traditional methods of teaching, and as much more valuable for personal and professional growth. They experience feelings of confidence and competence and of being challenged to do their best thinking. They welcome the opportunity to plan and direct their own learning, and require little encouragement to plunge into the process.

More dependent learners, on the other hand, do not find this learning method as rewarding – at least when first introduced to the approach. They experience feelings of frustration at the lack of structure, anxiety regarding teacher expectations and the evaluation process and confusion regarding what they are doing and how they will show evidence of achievement of course objectives. Without considerable support and encouragement through the process, they may develop unimaginative contracts and experience feelings of boredom and disinterest. They tend generally to be more tense and worried throughout the implementation of the learning contract, and some demonstrate resistance to the process. The level of structure these students require to engage successfully in contracting must be carefully assessed, and support must be provided as they struggle with taking on a new learner role. This structure can be provided by advisers, but the involvement of peer support for more dependent learners has also been found to be helpful in creating an environment in which risks can be taken and learner confidence can develop. Once this confidence does develop, however, many of these students indicate that the freedom and individuality inherent in the contracting approach open up new worlds to them.

We have also observed that students 'learn how to learn' using contracting and become more adept and comfortable with the process as they gain more experience with its use. Becky Jill Hollingsworth, while a student at McMaster University, made the following comments about learning how to use the contracting method.

> In the beginning it was very painful. Anxiety levels ran high, causing many fears and rude remarks about contracts ... As time went on, the process took on new meaning and became easier ... Year 4 was a joy! Faculty and students, alike, had reached a level of comfort, even affection, with the contract. We had learned to write it with ease and use it with confidence. It had become the indispensable tool it was meant to be, which made our learning uniquely our own.

Newsom and Foxworth (1980) suggest that contract learning may in fact assist more dependent learners by promoting the development of an internal locus of control, thereby moving them to increasing levels of independence. Our experience in working with learners at different stages in the nursing programme has led us to believe that this may indeed be true.

In the area of cognitive achievement, we have found that through contracting many learners attain objectives far beyond the course expectations. The opportunity and encouragement to be creative and to truly 'own' the learning experience leads to educational outcomes which are highly satisfying to students. We have also seen that the application of 'book learning' and factual information to real nursing situations leads to an increase in the amount of time many students spend in analysing, synthesizing, evaluating and applying knowledge rather than memorizing facts. Through these higher level cognitive processes they develop role-related competence.

In working through the contracting process, learners also develop the confidence and skills required for self-directed, autonomous learning. To quote Becky Jill Hollingsworth once more:

> We would be hard put now to sit passively through hours of lectures, for we are 'active' learners. Telling us what we should learn would not go down well, for we are in tune with ourselves and are aware of our learning needs. We set our own pace, for each of us is different, with different life experiences and styles, responsibilities and needs. We are 'mature' learners in the true sense of the word, and we will not stop learning or growing when we are handed our degrees. This is only the beginning of the rest of our lives, and we intend to take advantage of the opportunities life offers. We know how to go about that because we have learned how to learn through being self-directed.

189

We believe the confidence and enhanced self-esteem reflected in Becky's statements are not only important for the personal growth of our learners, but are essential qualities in developing the role of the professional nurse.

The impact of contract learning on students is thus apparent in many ways. For faculty, the experience in working with contracting can be both joyful and threatening. The impact of the contracting process on teachers can be summarized under two main areas: the development of a new role definition and skills, and teaching rewards.

Knowles (1986) perceives that teachers must redefine their roles to 'serving primarily as designers and managers of procedures for helping learners acquire the content and only secondarily as content resources' (p 246). We have found that the relinquishing of the content expert role and the resultant change in authority leads to a sense of loss and anxiety for some teachers. Comments such as 'It would be so much easier to just tell them what I know and where to find the best resources', and 'It's hard sometimes to be the non-expert tutor – my students seem to know more than I do about a lot of things!' can be heard in the faculty lounge.

The use of the contracting method also means that teachers must be aware of available resources and a variety of approaches to learning and evaluation. The one-to-one interaction between teachers and students not only allows staff to use their communication, questioning and negotiation skills effectively, but also exposes weaknesses in these areas more openly than more traditional teaching approaches. Thus contracting demands that teachers use their skills in different ways, and provides an opportunity and impetus for professional development.

Some teachers express concern regarding the amount of time contract learning involves and the impact of this on their own professional development. When contracting is first introduced, it will indeed require more time to conduct the negotiations with students and to feel comfortable with the process. This is particularly true when working with junior or more dependent students who may have some adjustment problems related to expectations for increased self-direction. Institutional support, by adjusting expectations on teaching loads for those using this approach, is thus essential for the successful implementation of contract learning. Other teachers report that contracting is an ideal way because of the flexibility inherent in its approach, to meet the educational needs of busy adult learners who have many external commitments.

The uniqueness of each student's learning contract provides constantly changing experiences for teachers. The repetitiveness often seen in a more traditional teaching model is thus not an issue in contracting. The variety of evidence presented by learners provides a stimulating and interesting facet to the teacher's role.

Finally, the relationship that develops during the contracting process allows teachers to get to know students more as individuals and to invest more of themselves in the teaching-learning process. Although this may be threatening to some traditionalists, many of our colleagues value the opportunity to develop a meaningful relationship with their learners. In contracting, teachers and students join together as co-learners – gaining from each other through the shared inquiry process.

In conclusion, this chapter has presented an educational alternative that the authors feel offers an exciting and innovative process for developing student autonomy. The *relationship* between the student and teacher and the *negotiation* that occurs throughout the contract learning experience have been described as the key elements for achieving content relevance and meaning for the learner, student creativity, lifelong learning skills, and active acknowledgement of learner differences. The process as illustrated here can provide a structure for the 'contract work', in which rich rewards can be found for both parties involved in negotiating and implementing the learning process. Through careful planning and advanced preparation for the changing roles and rules inherent in contract learning, the transition to this form of facilitation can be more readily achieved.

We hope that you will discover, as we have done, that this learning strategy, built on both genuineness in relationships and shared accountability, can provide an approach that demonstrates in a very real way caring for individual learners. By setting them free at last on their own learning journeys – to the threshold of their own minds – may you too be set free.

BON VOYAGE!

Acknowledgement

The authors wish to extend their gratitude to Professors Mary Buzzell and Olga Roman of McMaster University who contributed the chapter 'Preparing for Contract Learning' to the first edition of *Developing Student Autonomy in Learning*. With their permission, we have used their example of a fourth-year nursing student, Maureen, to illustrate the stages of the contracting process. Much of the material presented in relation to the orientation workshop was also taken from their chapter. Their support and encouragement to expand upon their original work is gratefully acknowledged and appreciated.

Chapter 12

Struggling with Self-assessment

John Cowan,
Director, The Open University in Scotland (formerly Professor of Civil Engineering, Heriot-Watt University, Edinburgh)

Introduction

In the three years prior to writing this chapter, I experimented with self-assessment in an engineering course (Cowan, 1984) – and I felt that I was thoroughly baptised with fire in the process. I made many mistakes from which I should have learnt a lot; I encountered problems and pitfalls beyond all my prior experience of university teaching; and I glimpsed sufficient promise of the potential of self-assessment to sustain and enthuse me in what has undoubtedly been a period characterized by difficulties, struggles and frustrations.

It will be obvious that I cannot contribute here as a researcher or as an educational authority. But I can share with those who have yet to experience self-assessed courses what it is like to be exploring this possibility for the first time – and I can give an account of my own experiences which may save others from having to rediscover the wheel.

I can offer an account of innovation in which I tried to pass responsibility for assessment, and for the learning which both preceded and followed assessment, to the students themselves. I cannot separate self-assessment from the other features of this innovation, since they were interdependent. So I must present as complete an account as possible, in order to be understood; and I leave it to you, the reader, to concentrate on what is of interest to you.

What did I do?

In November 1982 the Royal Society of Arts recognized my experimental first-year course in Properties and Use of Materials (Cowan, 1987) under their Education for Capability Scheme. The success of this course as an extended feasibility study of 'Independence in Learning' had led to the incorporation of all of its main features in a major revision of the established first-year course of the same name. Those who had shared with me in the development years came together to celebrate, and in the midst of that (mainly undergraduate) gathering, a gate-crashing second-year student asked 'Why don't you do something like that for us – next year, when you teach us Design?'. 'Why not?', I responded readily, with a clear recognition on both our parts that I found the idea attractive.

Soon 12 students (from a class of 60) had volunteered for a 'learning agreement' approach to the study of Design, and my discussions with them quickly centred on how this would be assessed, with the implication on their part that I would be responsible. 'Why can't *we* take responsibility for that? I thought the idea was to let *us* make the decisions', protested one of the 12. Immediately I prepared to express the obvious objections to the idea of a self-directed and self-assessed scheme in a major subject at a late stage in the course. But, by a curious coincidence, I had only the week before been reading Carl Rogers' rewrite of *Freedom to Learn*. I had been much influenced by the new sections in that text; and I could almost see a sad smile on his lips as I prepared to squash the suggestion that students could ever take responsibility for assessing their own development.

Tentatively I asked myself 'Why not?', and found no convincing answer. So conscience won – and I met with my volunteer group on several occasions before the end of their second year to draw up an agreement (which we called a learning contract) for a self-directed and self-assessed course. I must admit that much of the fine print of this agreement came from me. The students really had no detailed appreciation of what lay ahead for them, and found that they could not plan for it in a meaningful way. For neither they, nor any other students in the department, had any previous acquaintance with this type of learning situation, which made it difficult for them to anticipate what might be involved. I was in a somewhat similar position; so fortunately I restricted the draft agreement to general statements of procedures – which was to allow us considerable freedom later.

Our agreement specified (in only a little more detail than I will give here) that:

(1) Each student would have complete control over the weekly choice of objectives and over criteria and assessment. Even if requested, I would not do anything which could influence the decisions taken – although I should facilitate the processes involved if I were invited to do so. Other students would comment on objectives and outputs, but they too would have no other influence on the assessment.
(2) Each student would give and receive comments on the objectives and activities of others when asked to do so.
(3) Each student would carry out a formal self-appraisal (in a manner which we did not specify) twice during the academic year, exposing the same to comments and questions and making reasonable response to these – even if only to explain the grounds for rejection or disagreement.
(4) The students would make their learning available to other members of the group on request.

Introducing and consolidating a self-assessed course in my department called for a complete change in my role as a university teacher. The old authoritarian strategies, which had served me well when I controlled assessment (and hence the hidden curriculum), were rendered totally inappropriate. I now took authority only for the decision to pass authority to the learners, and then I had to devote time and effort to learning my role in this entirely new situation. For I still had a responsibility to facilitate learning and development. Although I had deliberately passed over to the learners the authority for the direction of their learning and for the appraisal of it, I could not regard this as an abdication of my responsibility as a teacher – which I now had to work out and define in these strange new circumstances.

I am attracted to the definition of teaching as the deliberate creation of situations from which learners cannot escape without learning. This philosophy implied that it was my responsibility to create self-assessed situations in which purposeful learning should take place. I had to do this on a large scale (when I devised the course structure); but I also had to arrange it on a small scale in my individual contacts with the learners, whom I could no longer pressurize through the medium of assessment procedures. When I began, I had no clear idea of how either of these responsibilities should be implemented.

Early rewards

I eventually rationalized the effect of self-assessment on my teaching (Boyd and Cowan, 1985) in terms of recent researches into student learning (Marton *et al*, 1984); but that was a relatively late review. My memory (and record) of the early months of the innovation is of an unshakeable and probably irrational conviction on my part regarding the quality of a self-assessed learning experience. The arrangement which I had established only seemed to me to fail or to stumble because of my ineptitude as a facilitator.

Before the six months had been completed, I observed striking and tangible changes in the behaviour of some of the learners with whom I worked. As a result I was powerfully sustained in my desire to improve my competence as a facilitator of learning in this type of situation. The improvements were so convincing that it never occurred to me after that to question the potential of self-assessment as a component of the total experience which is higher education. Indeed, in each of the three years in which I have offered self-assessment, I have been rewarded by seeing quantum leaps in the learning and development of some of my students – which I have never observed when I have taught in the conventional way, however much my students have matured steadily over the years.

The finest fruits of self-assessment are splendid, and of that I have never been in any doubt. The problem is to nurture and harvest them.

Immediate problems

1. The students didn't know where or how to start

I should perhaps have planned an introductory or transition phase, during which they could have explored possible objectives, ways of reaching them – and the whole concept of setting realistic and meaningful criteria. Instead they were dropped in at the deep end, from the beginning of the first week.

2. I tried too hard to be non-prescriptive

I should have taken more authority for providing the structure within which we would work – and I should have differentiated more clearly and carefully between the features of our agreement which were renegotiable (or open to unilateral rejection) and those which were immutable.

3. I had no notion of how to facilitate fully autonomous learning, or self-assessment

I knew that it meant being non-directive and non-prescriptive, which implies that I knew about not doing much of what I had done hitherto as a university teacher. But I didn't know what I should be doing in place of these omissions.

Three years on I must admit that I still feel very much on my own with regard to this problem. I still find it difficult to plan effective facilitation of learning in which I should not direct or otherwise influence the learner. And I find it even more difficult to help learners to develop the ability to judge their own learning, without conveying something of my own values in the process.

4. For the above and other reasons, many issues troubled me week by week and almost hour by hour

I should have set up some mechanism for debriefing and co-counselling before the course began, in order to improve the quality of my *ad hoc* responses to the calls for facilitation during the academic year. Facilitators need to be able to unpack their facilitation, examine it, and profit from that experience in the face of the next immediate demands on them.

The activities of the first term

In many ways the first term (of ten weeks) appeared to be a disaster. The weekly group meetings, which we had decided would permit exchange of learning and experience, were stilted, arid and unmotivating. I had had high hopes that these would be a focus for an emerging confidence and maturity on the part of the students, and that they would assist in the movement towards autonomous learning. But, after about six weeks, they were abandoned by common consent.

The weekly study proposals (which each student prepared) were often thin, inadequate or even downright trivial. The students didn't seem to know how to decide what to do; and they wandered aimlessly from one topic to another. With only few exceptions they (predictably, perhaps) produced fragmentary outputs of poor quality. And all of this, of course, was in stark contrast to our preliminary discussions before the year began, during which the students had outlined their plans on a grandiose scale, and ideas for worthwhile topics of study had proliferated. It was clear that something had gone badly wrong between intentions and reality.

Relationships between students, and between students and staff, were strained and often antagonistic. Yet, curiously, the group never faltered in their commitment to the concept of the course. In that first term I twice attempted to make it possible for students to revert to the conventional course (which was being followed by the rest of the class, with me as the teacher). Both were quickly and firmly rejected by every volunteer member of the experimental group. We had a curious group loyalty – and still have. I suspect this depended on individual trust in a facilitator who didn't try to take back authority when a learner abused it; but perhaps I am being optimistic.

I was obviously curious and apprehensive to discover what would happen in the end of term assessments. For rigour and high standards had been conspicuous by their absence in almost all the commenting and appraising and decision-making of the first term.

(Here, perhaps, it is appropriate to mention that I kept – and have used here – extremely detailed personal records in which, during the first 15 months, I separated descriptions of events from accounts of my own feelings, reactions or deductions. The comments which I make in this chapter are based on these notes and not on my long-term memory.)

The first formal assessments

Each student had agreed to prepare a statement outlining what (s)he had done, how much (s)he valued it – and how (s)he had reached that decision. I was then to read each statement, try to understand it – and react, in a manner which the agreement did not specify. I determined to challenge incomplete or unsubstantiated data, to point out logic which was fundamentally unsound, and to ask genuine questions of clarification. I also resolved that I would not challenge or discuss values which differed from my own (although, in the event, I discarded this resolution when I found that some students appeared to me to be harsh in their writings on themselves).

Four of the 12 members of the experimental group entered the process of self-assessment with failure ratings in this important subject, although two of them were eventually to reconsider these decisions. Several of the self-appraisals were brutally self-critical on factually accurate grounds. All were thoughtfully introspective.

I regret to admit that I discussed the assessment documents more than I had intended – in the case of three students only, but that was still three too many! On the other hand I volunteered no opinion or challenge in the case of the top-rated student, whose mark was completely incompatible with his own description of his work during this term and with the criteria which he chose to define in association with his goals. That fortunate abstention was to provide me with a useful lesson in the following month.

Comment

You will gather that, at the end of the first term, I was far from optimistic about our progress. Indeed the records I made immediately prior to the interviews of the self-assessment period showed quite clearly that I considered the experiment unsuccessful, and felt that some – though not all – of the responsibility for this lack of success lay with the students.

Certainly I was clear then that the situation could only be rectified by the learners. I intended to carry on merely because I had made my commitment to the agreement and intended to adhere to it – in spirit as well as to the letter – despite the fact that the students, in my opinion, had not honoured their initial commitments (even after we had discussed this criticism frankly together).

Interestingly I note that I was troubled at that time by the loneliness of facilitating self-assessed learning where, as never before, I found it impossible for a teacher to be 'one of the group'. The intimacy with learners in a course of this type is of a very special kind, but it has marked dissimilarities from friendship, or even the companionship which all of us need at testing times.

The activity of the second term

Term 2 began, to all intents and purposes, just where Term 1 had left off. We made only one change in our procedures, and no changes in our agreements or overall philosophy. But that was the only similarity to what had gone before – as was to be apparent fairly quickly.

More than half of the students radically changed their ways of working and the type of objectives on which they concentrated. And at this point – having already spattered my narrative with more generalisations than are even justified by the limitations of space – I feel obliged to give detailed examples of the changes which were planned and implemented by the learners, without consulting or informing me.

The most significant was that all opted for *me* to offer weekly comment on their objectives and outputs. This differed from the original format of the agreement, in which it was clearly intended that a different person would do this each week for a given learner, and that most of the commenting would be provided by fellow-students. In making the change, all of the learners were adamant that they would feel no obligation to accept all or any of my comments; and none of them wished me to direct their learning or suggest objectives and criteria. But they had a definite wish to receive rigorous comment; and at least five of the group made it clear, as they commissioned this comment from me, that it was to be purely formative – suggesting how they might meet their self-set goals, particularly with regard to the quality of their thinking.

However, this change in procedure was less significant for me than the changes in behaviour which I observed and noted, in these weeks and thereafter. These changes can be usefully summarized in the following comments, in which I have used fictitious names, except where the students concerned have already published an account of their experiences (Boyd *et al*, 1984). One of the women is thus 'disguised' as a male!

(a) Three students (Ade, Helen and Russell) joined together with the shared goal of improving their effectiveness in the processes of analysis and synthesis, which they now identified as the real priorities in design education. They prepared a schedule for regular working, with a weekly period allocated to activities whose form would be suggested by me as the facilitator, in response to a brief from the trio defining aspects of the process which they felt worthy of further development or scrutiny. They firmly adhered to the discipline of this self-prepared schedule for the remainder of that term.

In the first term Ade had worked erratically on a random selection of topics, most of which were concerned with applying Codes of Practice in the design of structural elements. Helen had grasshoppered around a number of topics associated with the design of timber structures, ranging from Code of Practice design and manufacturing processes to common structural forms and samples of total design calculations. Russell had used a straightforward design problem in structural steelwork as a vehicle for identifying, comprehending and using (rather badly) the relevant subject matter and concepts which he tended to abstract from a curious selection of textbooks.

It is clear that the Term 1 objectives for the members of this group were random, unrelated, determined week by week, and mainly concerned with understanding and with some application of that understanding. Their Term 2 objectives, in contrast, were integrated and process-centred, predetermined, and at a higher level on the Bloom scale (Bloom *et al*, 1956) than their objectives in Term 1.

(b) Three others collaborated until their objectives for the term had been formulated, and then, by common unexpressed consent, they went their own ways.

In Term 1 Jim had been little more than a parasitical observer of the shallow efforts of Bob (who was *not* a member of this second-term trio). Bob had opted to follow through a published example of bridge design, trying to learn from it, as he went along, what he needed in order to believe that he understood. In Term 2, Jim, who had observed Bob's activities with little involvement, identified as his essential starting point the thorough analysis of problems, design briefs and strategies. He sought some assistance from me as his facilitator in devising a personalized scheme for non-directive but formative self-appraisal. His work rate – and his standards in self-criticism – changed dramatically at the beginning of the second term, and continued to rise steadily thereafter.

The second member of this trio, George, had worked alone in Term 1 and had convinced himself, until self-assessment time, that he had satisfied the letter of our agreement by digesting a disjointed assortment of straightforward topics from a range of undergraduate textbooks concerned with the design of structural elements. In the second term, while settling for the same type of goals as the third member (Ewan), he was much more precise with regard to the scheduling of his work, and more demanding in specifying criteria about the depth which he required in his understanding of what he chose to study.

Ewan was a shrewd but not particularly successful student who had spent Term 1 in a disastrously over-ambitious effort to carry out and evaluate a design of striking complexity. He had floundered badly on every aspect of this task, ricocheting from one activity to another after the failure of each previous week. In the self-assessment period he (privately) decided to go right back to the beginning, and establish as thoroughly as possible a competence in what he defined as the basics of the design of structural elements.

The most determined personality in this trio was the ex-parasite, Jim. It was he who had rated himself above his fellows in the self-assessment, who had not been challenged, and who therefore moved into the second term in a somewhat exposed position. Ewan and George had, in contrast, mortified themselves in the self-assessment – to an extent which had provoked me to disagree with the harshness of their criticism in relation to the data upon which it was based. I have often wondered what happened in the planning discussions which this trio had together, and have wished that I could have been a fly on the wall. I have no idea of what happened then, and I would never ask.

(c) Colin, Frank and Leslie all worked individually; I only group them together here because each made relatively little change in his tactics as he moved from Term 1 to Term 2.

Colin had thought a lot in the summer preceding the learning agreement course about what he wanted to do; and he saw no reason to depart from his half-completed schedule, which he had derived from syllabuses for conventional courses and had followed through steadily and consistently in the first term.

Frank had unexpectedly failed in his second year, and had incurred a heavy resit penalty in the summer before the experiment began. He, too, had had a predetermined schedule and a steady work rate since the beginning of the course, although his schedule centred on a particular (but not unduly complex) design problem.

Leslie also decided to follow through a design problem. He was as ineffective and lost for most of the second term as he had been in Term 1, when he had worked on fragments of isolated topics which he seemed to choose for no clear reason and where I saw no sign that his learning had been taken to a conclusion, or had even significantly advanced.

(d) Having neatly grouped the first nine students in trios, I now find it impossible to classify the last three under any one heading, unless I describe them as 'Assorted'.

Since his first undergraduate year, Bob had been a methodical worker with a liking for self-directed individual study, which amounted to passionate insularity. He had performed ineffectively in Term 1 (perhaps because the absence of structure left him floundering, or perhaps because his unfortunate partnership with Jim was alien to his natural style of working). By Term 2 he was ready to proceed with objectives similar to those of Colin, Ewan and George – but in a different area, and very much on his own.

Notice, then, that there were four students in the total group who all opted for something similar to a conventional syllabus in Design of Structural Elements, except that fewer topics were to be studied in more depth than in a conventional course, and some topics, as a consequence, were excluded. In Term 2 Bob did his best to ensure that external inputs to help him to be aware of omissions and lack of rigour would be identified – although he never aspired to make identification of these weaknesses one of his main aims, or part of his self-appraisal.

David had devoted Term 1 to the unstructured study and discussion of points which he had identified at the beginning of the course, or previously, as important, relevant or interesting. He now negotiated with me a demanding and regular tutorial interchange. This was to be centred on study papers which he would prepare while focusing on one topic in depth, and attempting to integrate textbook learning, design practice, research knowledge and Code of Practice provisions. He was much more concerned with developing his ability to study in these types of area (and to master his learning in depth) than with particular subject coverage. He specified clearly a format for discussion in which, within the dyad, we would reach no conclusions and make no judgements – other than about the subject matter.

Ian had spent the first term in an idiosyncratic exploration of a wide range of topics, which he considered fundamental to a total approach to the design of dams. In Term 2 he identified two fundamental aspects of engineering behaviour which he had never understood in the past, and had deviously (and successfully) sidestepped. He now considered it important to master these topics; and he called for facilitation, which was not to be instruction, to help him to achieve his objectives in his own way (which was strikingly idiosyncratic).

It will be apparent from the above statements that significant changes in the choice of objectives and criteria, and in the approaches to learning, took place for at least half the members of the group following the first formal self-assessment.

Changes in my Role

In many ways Term 2 was to prove more difficult for me than Term 1. In the first term the students had been very concerned with their own problems – what to study, how to work, how deeply to go into various issues, and so on. They had therefore used me mainly as a sounding board on which to shape up their vague ideas; or as a living index to available resources; or as someone to whom they could express criticisms or frustrations.

In Term 2 (in most cases) our relationship changed. Most of the students now knew what they wanted – and what they wanted of me, within the terms of our agreement. And the demands which they made often left me groping desperately for effective responses.

The cooperative trio (Ade, Helen and Russell) were my most difficult clients. They would pinpoint an aspect of process ('How can we generate more and better viable options to any design problem which we encounter than we manage to do at present?'); and they could ask for one (or preferably more) possible activity which would occupy their effort for a morning, and take them to a point where they would be ready to decide how they should proceed thereafter. Consequently I found myself designing short workshop activities for them, usually at 24 hours' notice, and all with goals more difficult than any I had tackled before, in such circumstances or otherwise. My remits were also complicated by the fact that these clients usually wished to run any of my suggested activities for themselves, and to have the freedom to amend my outlines as they saw fit.

However, each student in the total group presented a different demand in a different situation – as far as I was concerned. Even the four individuals who were following a semi-conventional but personal syllabus, with restricted coverage and increased depth, did not present similar demands in a given week or over the term, taken as a whole.

The needs of David, Ian and Jim were critical to their chosen direction of development, and outwith my prior experience as a teacher. Ian called on me to disregard all my learning and teaching experience, in order to help him along his (to me) curious route to deep understanding. David's objectives, if he had been able to formulate them, centred on sharpening the mental abilities used by a designer (irrespective of course content). He demanded purposeful progress and tangible outcomes, in circumstances where I was only a resource person and frequently had no clear impression of his objectives, since he regarded questions of clarification as tantamount to external influence on the direction of his learning. In these circumstances facilitation was a particularly tough challenge.

Jim set great store on analytical logic – which, again, he wanted to strengthen and extend in his own terms and to his own standards. He also wanted to achieve this with minimal contact with me – and desired that contact to be in a form which he could reshape for his own purposes. That again made an ongoing process of facilitation quite tricky.

My only possible strategy in such circumstances was to identify with each learner in turn. I had to listen hard to the learner's account of his or her objectives and their origins, and I had to feel and express that need in her or his vocabulary, without allowing my own thoughts or priorities or reactions to intrude. I also had to relate to the learner's prior experience in the area concerned, and then identify ways in which new learning could be related to that prior learning.

It will be apparent that, during a very demanding term, I was having to learn a great deal about responsive facilitation. I had, and still have, much further to travel along this particular way before I become an adept facilitator of either self-directed learning or self-assessed development. The latter demand, in particular, was to prove a real challenge. As the course proceeded, I found myself increasingly confronted with demands to facilitate processes of self-appraisal and the setting of criteria, without becoming involved in a particular appraisal or the criteria on which it would be based. In these situations

I was entirely on my own in conceiving what were, for me, innovatory responses.

The final self-assessments

Students and facilitator now saw assessment more distinctly as a process in which objectives, criteria and performance should be identified and compared as objectively as possible – by the learner. But knowing what we were trying to do did not make it any easier for the students to carry out self-assessment, or for me to facilitate it.

We had agreed that data and the reasoning which led to a judgement would be offered to me for comment, while the marks which had been chosen by the learners would be presented in sealed envelopes to be opened only after any intervening discussions had been completed. The marks would, however, be open to modification at any time by the learner concerned.

I could thus express no comment on marks – then or now. Indeed I believe the most important point I have learned about facilitating self-assessment is that I must never allow myself to formulate my own judgement of the mark or rating which a student should receive. I may express comment on discrepancies between the agreed and actual processes of self-appraisal, or fundamental weaknesses in the logic implicit in the reasoning. But, without access to all that the learners know of their learning, any judgements of mine can only be shallow and unhelpful. Consequently, in the situation I have described, it was essential that the students regarded my comments as no more than the reaction of a detached observer, to which they were free to react, or not, as they wished. In this first experience of a self-assessed course I had still to learn – and practise – the full implications of this important principle.

The cooperative trio were the first to embark on the final self-assessment. They came together with ample time on hand, and called on me for an activity that would help them to define what they meant by 'assessment' and 'criteria', and to determine for themselves how they should approach this final part of the course. It then took them a while to devise a process which satisfied them, and to work through it. Although I had no detailed knowledge of what they had done, I was confident – perhaps unjustifiably – that they would carry out their self-assessments thoroughly and objectively. So I didn't see any point in discussing process or reasoning with any member of the trio, and I said so. This came as a surprise to them; Helen and Russell were to make slight upward revisions in their final marks, which perhaps tells us something about the influence I might have had on their self-assessments. However, the marks from all three went forward as final decisions, without any involvement on my part.

In three cases (Colin, David and Leslie) the statements which were presented to me were lacking in objectivity. They included no review of performance which mentioned data, and consisted of the pure value judgement with regard to overall quality. Two students (Eric and Jim) had set no criteria by which to distinguish between various standards of performance. Two other students (Bob and Frank) produced conscientious reviews, but with a few ragged edges which needed a little more attention to make them complete. George and Ian, on the other hand, produced statements based on reasoning and data which fulfilled the commitments made under the agreement.

My reactions to the nine remaining students therefore varied from a quick response to an extended debate. Generally, however, our discussions were brief, because the only matters on which it was valid for me to comment were deviations from the procedure which was contained in the agreement and in our expansions of it. The students concerned then redrafted their appraisal in a form, and with conclusions which we had not touched on in our discussions; the final appraisal was therefore not submitted for further comment, and each student received the original or amended marks which they chose to award to themselves.

Evaluation of the scheme

After the summer vacation my 12 guinea-pigs rejoined the rest of the class for their final year Design work. Immediately they found themselves in small groups, working full-time on a range of 2-week design projects.

The ex-learning-agreement students found that they had patchy coverage of the relevant subject matter, compared with their fellows. Some had concentrated on structural steelwork, others on reinforced or prestressed concrete, or on timber. Some had devoted considerable time to the behaviour of struts, or members which would fail in shear, or connections; others had given these matters scant attention and had concentrated on more general topics. But most if not all had learnt in the interim to interpret Codes, to use textbooks and to think through problems from first principles. With one exception (Leslie) the ex-learning-agreement group, working in an open-book situation similar to real life, were judged by my colleagues to be at least as competent as their conventionally taught classmates on the topics which had been covered in the conventional course syllabus, and had often been forgotten over the summer vacation. And the self-directed learners proved more resourceful and effective in dealing with topics which were unfamiliar to all students in the class.

My own personal evaluation of this experiment really began 15 months earlier, when I carefully noted the class position of each of my group at the end of their second year. When the same class, minus the drop-outs, completed their final degree examinations at the end of their (conventionally presented) final year, I repeated the exercise. I found that the 12 ex-learning-agreement students, one of whom had been first in the second year, moved up the class of 60 by an average of almost 15 places. I found this encouraging, Hawthorne effect or not, and particularly so in view of the relatively poor performance of one student (Leslie) who nevertheless improved his class position.

(At this point I should perhaps mention that the volunteers for the learning agreement experiment were, fortuitously, of mixed abilities. Their spread of marks in their second year roughly corresponded to the spread within the total class group.)

203

The quality of self-assessed learning

The most fundamental outcomes from this experiment concerned the nature of learning in a situation where the learners set their own criteria and monitored their own performances. Involvement in the setting of criteria led my group inevitably to a higher level of commitment (Boyd and Cowan, 1985). For you can hardly be other than committed to objectives and criteria if you have chosen them for yourself, without external influence.

The monitoring of learning, which entails thorough identification and comparison of performance with criteria, stimulates a questioning approach to both elements in the comparison (Boyd and Cowan, 1985). This is a major step towards the adoption of a deep learning strategy. Consequently the project completely altered the quality of learning for those concerned, although it was naively conceived and inexpertly facilitated, as I have admitted.

For my part, I had learnt that the potential of self-assessment is massive. However I had also learnt much about the obstacles that encumber reality and render it difficult for a teacher to realize the potential of this approach immediately. In particular my self-assessed course showed the need for:

(a) A well designed framework or programme which delegates authority firmly, yet provides guidance through (non-directive) procedures which will assist but not direct learners in situations that are totally strange to them. These procedures must be likely to prove effective (in furthering the purpose) and efficient (in minimizing wasted effort).

(b) Formative interactions between peers.

(c) Creative facilitation of process without influence on product, objectives or criteria. This should be available both in respect of learning about the subject matter and of learning about how to assess one's worth.

(d) A non-directive transition into self-directed and self-assessed learning, during which learners should probably select their opening objectives.

(e) An obligation to assess objectively, linked to an explanation, or perhaps a joint exploration, of what that requirement entails.

The next year

Now I realized that I didn't want to teach design conventionally again, and I wanted to widen the scope of self-direction and self-assessment. Fortunately my department was on the verge of introducing a subject called interdisciplinary studies. This was to be part of our third-year curriculum, and the staff who were responsible for the course structure had no preconceptions about what it should involve, or how it should be taught. My offer to switch courses and run interdisciplinary studies was accepted with alacrity; and this despite the fact that I made it clear that learners would have an opportunity to concentrate on the development of interdisciplinary competencies which they themselves would identify as important, and which were not covered elsewhere in our course.

Interdisciplinary studies was a compulsory subject for all our third-year students. It occupied two timetabled and two private-study hours in each week of an entire academic year. I responded to the five points which I have listed in my above review by making the following arrangements:

(a) The course framework was fully detailed. (The detailed documentation unfortunately generated more problems than it solved, mainly for semantic reasons. It was describing a situation and experiences of which the students were as yet unaware.)

(b) Formal self-assessment procedures involved only students. The staff played no part unless one student was challenged by another for failing to satisfy one of the (few) course requirements. In that case the staff might adjudicate, but would not assess. (There was to be a disastrous lack of rigour as the class group settled comfortably to relatively undemanding standards in their criteria.)

(c) The colleagues who had expressed an interest in assisting me were briefed carefully on a style of facilitation which might be expected to be successful. (With one exception they either gave up in the face of the first real demands to facilitate process, or they reverted to teaching authoritatively.)

(d) The greater part of the first term was devoted to a carefully planned transition towards self-directed and self-assessed learning. (Most students fretted at this extended transition, and were irked not to be able to start almost immediately, prepared or otherwise.)

(e) The assessment procedures were carefully specified and published in detail. (This documentation conveyed little to the students, for whom many of the concepts were unfamiliar and much of the explanations misleading.)

It will be clear from my cryptic comments in parentheses that the second year of development encountered more problems than the first had done. In my opinion this happened because

- □ the course was compulsory
- □ the numbers (of students and staff) made it impossible for me to have personal contact with everyone
- □ my well-intentioned changes encountered reactions which I had not predicted (although they also had considerable beneficial effects, which tended to be accepted and to pass unnoticed, even by me)
- □ the first formal self-assessment (at the end of Term 1) could not focus on much self-directed work, because relatively little had taken place by then. It was therefore not a fruitful development experience.

What were the outcomes?

The complete year's work led to dramatic changes in educational maturity for the majority of the group, in the opinion of external assessors who were brought in to review the folios, interview the students and offer formative evaluation of the course in general terms. Individual learners chose a wide range of objectives, which I will illustrate by mentioning briefly a series of examples taken from separate individual programmes.

Several small groups formed to concentrate on deepening their understanding of how people interrelate in work situations. They wished to use that understanding to bring about tangible improvements in their group project work. In contrast some individuals opted to find ways of working more effectively – and thereby of achieving significantly higher standards than before in a variety of tasks. Others, with a rather different goal, wished to discover how to work more efficiently – so that they could achieve their desired results in less time, or with less effort, or both.

Several students collaborated with the goal of developing their ability for effective professional dialogue (as in meetings and interview). And one passionately enthusiastic individualist raised his awareness of current affairs – and of their relevance – by a powerful effort of sustained self-discipline and frequent self-appraisal.

Similarities

In both pilot-scheme experiences:

- my self-assessed students (taken as a group) rated themselves lower in the self-assessed subject than they did in their other subjects, which were assessed by members of staff.
- students who awarded themselves astonishingly high marks in the first formal self-assessment did not repeat their apparently self-satisfied behaviour subsequently – despite, or perhaps because of, the absence of challenge.
- Students who harshly appraised their weaknesses subsequently improved in the class ranking order in the self-assessed subject and elsewhere.
- Self-assessment provoked declaration of intensely personal and highly critical needs, in situations which frequently verged on the confessional.
- Self-assessment had a powerful role in changing the quality of learning and of learning aspirations for many of the students in the class, even in subsequent subjects which were taught conventionally.
- Effective facilitation of demanding objectives, which were mainly concerned with process, was crucial.
- Undergraduates showed themselves able to cope with demanding objectives, self-direction and self-assessment.

The next revision

Having identified scope for improvement, I consequently made changes in the next revision of interdisciplinary studies, to be offered in the third year of my developing experience. These changes were intended to ensure:

(1) Structure – without there being confusing complexity in the documentation.

(2) A short induction phase, followed by actively self-directed learning in the first term.

(3) Facilitation based on interactive peer groups linked to one member of staff.

(4) Involvement of both staff and students in facilitating formative and summative self-assessment procedures – without the judgements of the learners being influenced directly or indirectly.

(5) Brief and comprehensible requirements for the assessment procedures.

At this point, however, I find myself running too far ahead in my narrative. Although I could write in similar detail about the third experimental year, in which self-assessment is now working relatively smoothly, I should remember that my original aim was to write only about the first steps, because the readership for whom I have a special concern are those about to take the first steps with self-assessment – and therefore those in most need of elementary practical advice.

Elementary practical advice

As a result of the mistakes, failures and problems which I have described, I now feel able to set out advice which I wish had been available to me when I started. Here, then, is my statement of advice which is still relevant to me in my present state of professional development, and which I hope will also be helpful to others with less experience:

(1) Make a wholehearted commitment to the fact that self-assessment should be undertaken only by the learners themselves. You would note from the earlier stages of my narrative that, if you or any of your colleagues retain any involvement in this process, the weaker and less determined students (at least) will quickly look to you for your opinions, guidance or even covert direction; and any prospect of developing genuine self-assessment will disappear.

(2) Define the limits at the outset. Make it clear what cannot be changed, what must be done, and where freedom begins as well as what it encompasses.

(3) Take authority for establishing and maintaining procedures. Nothing much will be gained by requiring complex interactions to determine these procedures, in a situation where the students already have many difficult and novel challenges to resolve – and they should not be diverted from their main purpose. Only if students already have experience of self-assessment can it be extremely valuable for them to take part in the debates which establish procedures for a subsequent course.

(4) Express the required procedures briefly, carefully and simply. They must be unambiguous, easily and quickly understood by the inexperienced, and

easily followed. They must also be devoid of inference about the selection of objectives or criteria or learning strategies.

(5) Make provision for formative as well as summative assessment. Learners profit from every aspect of involvement in feedback and its self-generated equivalent.

(6) Involve both the students and the staff somehow in setting up the assessment procedures. Students learn from their involvement; and staff exemplify through their involvement what is meant by 'rigour', 'criteria' and 'logic'. Note that, by this recommendation, I refer to the formulation of the procedures before the course begins and not to the application of these procedures to particular learning or development.

(7) Exclude any circumstances in which judgements about the comparison of criteria or performance can be made or implied other than by the person concerned. Self-assessment must be the independent responsibility of the person assessed.

(8) Find out for yourself (by trial and error, and review and extensive meditation, and preparation) how to facilitate learning and assessment without influencing the outcomes – or, since that is an impossible ideal, with a slight effect on the outcomes. This will usually mean that your discussions with learners will concentrate on improvements in processes rather than on the standard of products.

(9) Expect to encounter a depressing lack of rigour in a student group until after the first formal self-assessment. The influence of this experience becomes significant once the learners have found out (sometimes almost to their surprise) that you really meant it when you said that they would be free to choose their own marks, and judge their own performances. For some reason which I do not fully understand, it is this exercise of independence – especially when some part of it is not done well – which prompts a learner to aspire to improve.

(10) Be willing to hang on until the 59th minute of the eleventh hour for the shallow-minded or trivial to see the light and make progress towards setting themselves worthwhile goals and criteria, for which they will then plan appropriate work styles. In my experience this transformation can occur literally in the closing stages of a course, and perhaps even after the assessment has been accepted. It seems to happen, paradoxically, because the teacher has not reclaimed authority. And, if it should not come about, there is nothing any teacher could have done which would have brought about a change in values on the part of the learner – so my suggestion is worth trying.

(11) Believe in the data which are presented to you, unless you know from first hand that they are incorrect; your function is to strengthen procedures, and not to confirm conclusions or check data.

(12) Always believe in your students and in their ability to do better with self-assessment than they could do in the conventional pattern of education. Your confidence in their exercise of authority is one powerful

influence pushing them to use that authority wisely and creatively.

(13) Identify with each learner. Adopt the learner's vocabulary, concepts and strategies. Question – but only when you want to know or to clarify; challenge only when you cannot follow; point out procedural weaknesses only to help the learner to eliminate them.

(14) Don't advise; don't direct; don't express opinions – except about the procedures followed by learners.

(15) Always accept the final judgement, whatever it is – and never with your tongue in your cheek. It is your trust in their ability to assess themselves which prompts them to be responsible, in their own ways – although not necessarily in yours. And it will be your openness to consider judgements other than your own which will help you to mature as a genuinely facilitative teacher.

Finally

(16) Respond only to those items of advice in this list which you judge to be consistent with your style and situation – and with your definition of 'self-assessment'.

Postscript

When I sent Dave Boud the first draft of this contribution, he asked me bluntly how I had persuaded my department to accept self-assessed grades. The answer which I gave him was in five short statements.

First and foremost I admitted that the pilot scheme took place without anyone, other than my head of department, really noticing what I was doing until it was all over. The students were volunteers who trusted me to rescue them if the idea proved unworkable. And my head of department was reassured by the success of the previous experiment, which had been enthusiastically received by the assessors from the Royal Society of Arts.

Then, in the second year of the development (when we introduced an obligatory self-assessed course) I was very fortunate in that I was agreeing to take on a course which nobody else wanted to handle, or knew how to handle. That is not the kind of situation which anyone else can contrive for themselves, and so I think the lesson to be learnt from this important point is that innovators need to be devious strategists, and to exploit the circumstances of a particular situation.

Within a year it was obvious that the 12 learning-agreement students had done extremely well in their conventionally taught final-year subjects, and that our external assessors were impressed by the work of the better students in the third-year interdisciplinary studies course. So it then made sense to ensure that professional people, whose opinions would be heard and respected beyond the bounds of the department, as well as within it, had an opportunity to form their own judgements and convey their enthusiasm about what they were doing to all concerned. Consequently, once the third-year IDS students entered their final year and began to go for interview, I found myself in a situation where the students reported that their prospective employers regarded the IDS course, and their commitment to it, as a main selling point during interviews.

All of this, I suppose, adds up to the fact that this innovation, like any other, got off the ground because an individual had a commitment to it, found ways to make it possible without provoking opposition, and demonstrated outcomes which were sufficiently convincing to forestall any attempts to interfere with the consolidation of the development. If you can't manage to satisfy these tactical requirements, I am afraid it doesn't matter how educationally creative you are as an innovator, you are unlikely to be permitted to survive. Consequently the last point which I mentioned to our editor was that I have a thick skin – and I didn't mean that comment facetiously, incidentally. I was merely reflecting on the fact that any facilitator who can withstand the backlash from self-assessed learners should find it relatively simple to deal with the reactions of his colleagues, which will be mild in comparison. If you are minded to explore self-assessment, don't expect any easy passage – but do expect rewarding outcomes.

Good luck.

Chapter 13

The Experience of Independent Study at North East London Polytechnic

John Stephenson,
Head, School of Independent Study, North East London Polytechnic

In the first edition of this book I reported in detail on the ways in which we had introduced independent study into undergraduate courses at North East London Polytechnic (NELP). The School for Independent Study at NELP has now been in operation for 13 years and is in a strong position to report on its experience.

This chapter presents a summary of our main observations based on that experience. It includes our thoughts on the kinds of conditions that make independent study successful, the apparent educational benefits for students, and a description of some of the resource implications of running such a scheme within a conventional public institution. It draws on material collected from former students and begins with a summary of the School's background and origins.

Background

Independent study continues to grow and flourish within the School for Independent Study at North East London Polytechnic where students have the opportunity to plan their own programmes of study to diploma, honours degree and masters degree levels using expertise from any part of the polytechnic. There are currently over 700 separate student enrolments and they collectively comprise about 9 per cent of the total polytechnic. Students are working on their own programmes in engineering, science, computing, business, management, art and design, education, environmental sciences, humanities, community, and the human sciences. Many have planned programmes which cover more than one of these areas.

Independent study is not a fringe aspect of each student's work. It is not an option for Friday afternoon. It is their total experience. Students are responsible for the planning of the content, learning mode, pace, location, and assessment criteria. Their proposals have to be fully and coherently expressed, and are exposed to internal and external scrutiny before they can be used as the basis for the public awards for which they are intended. Final work is submitted for internal and external assessment before the student can be considered for the award required. The Council for National Academic Awards (CNAA), the body responsible for all UK public sector awards at Diploma of Higher Education, Honours and Masters Degree levels, recognizes the students' achievements and provides the appropriate certification.

Independent study was not our original intention. It grew out of our plan to provide educational ways of helping students become generally competent through the mastery of problem-solving techniques. These skills could not be taught, only learned. If possible, the context in which they were learned had to be as real as possible, and nothing was more real than the students' need to get the most out of their higher education. It therefore occurred to us that the most effective ways in which students could develop these skills was for them to formulate the problem of their own higher education and to plan their own programme of study as a solution to that problem.

Independent study was therefore seen as the central learning process for the development of general competence. In order to 'formulate the problem of their own higher education' students had to be clear about where they were and where they wanted to be. The 'solution' was the course which would take them from one to the other. From these beginnings has grown a form of education characterized by students, in mutually supportive groups, evaluating their previous experiences and learning, identifying their strengths and weaknesses, exploring the implications of their longer term personal, academic or vocational intentions, setting learning goals appropriate to their own needs, taking responsibility for the implementation of their plans and proposing the criteria and means of assessment.

The school was originally established as a central unit drawing specialist tutorial support from the faculties of the polytechnic. In successive polytechnic reorganizations it has been part of the Faculty of Humanities (at the time of the First Edition of this book), and of the Faculty of Human Sciences, and is now once again a free-standing central unit. All independent study students are registered in the School for Independent Study and are placed for part of their time in the specialist area most relevant to their studies.

The school has 23 full-time equivalent academic staff providing personal tutorial help for student planning, the monitoring of student progress and a wide range of support workshops. It draws on a similar number of specialists from the polytechnic as a whole to support student specialist studies. Nearly all of the school's own staff have transferred from the specialist areas, being attracted by its distinctive way of working. Two recent appointments have been of former independent study students. Otherwise the staff have had no formal training in independent study before they arrive. They are helped by experienced tutors to learn as they go along. There is independent study for tutors as well as for students.

The educational experience

It is difficult within the confines of a brief chapter to convey the sum total of all our experiences. A whole book would be necessary for that. A number of key features are explored here.

Programmes are planned around themes or problems relevant to the students themselves

Tutor-planned courses are invariably subject based, and students are required to follow a programme of lectures and reading, or learn basic skills, according to an arbitrary definition of relevant content usually justified in terms of 'the needs of the subject'. Since students by definition are not guardians of a subject, independent study students tend to start somewhere else, namely themselves. They usually build their plans around a theme or problem with which they can personally identify and which can be judged in terms of the theme's relevance to each student's previous experience and future intentions. A valid programme of study readily emerges on 'the stone in the pond' principle. Such studies are rarely criticized for being as narrow as the theme itself might suggest; frequently students have to be counselled against including too many contextual studies for the time available.

One obvious benefit of planning their learning around a problem or theme relevant to their own needs is that students never lose sight of the relevance of any area being studied. Motivation is therefore consistently high, particularly if the theme/problem arises directly out of the students' own assessment of their previous experience and their longer term aspirations. For instance, a student who wished to convert a lifetime's experience as a waiter into a business career built a programme around the theme 'Business and Organisational Problems of Catering Establishments', which included aspects of business accounting, banking, the law, and staff management relevant to the problem of running small-scale businesses. Fieldwork in successful London restaurants provided the focus for bringing it all together. In such cases, the study is actually about the student and for the student. It is difficult to separate the theme from the learner.

Here is a sample of some recent problems or themes which have been built into honours degree programmes:

The influence of marketing techniques in British politics
The role of the word processor in the primary school
Automatic control systems in robotics and in jetfoil
The impact of the World Health Organization Special Programme on tropical diseases
The development of three-dimensional images using print techniques
Black children and self-identity in the British school system
The computerization of engineering calculations in oilfield drilling
Neuroactivity from a biochemical point of view
The advent of fibre optics and its impact on society

In each of these cases, the justification for its approval has not been the more traditional one of whether teachers think it is a convenient vehicle for the acquisition of skills and knowledge of which they approve, but on the basis of a rationale submitted by the student related to the student's own view of knowledge and the student's own personal circumstances. Instead of the academic establishment saying 'Your proposal does/does not accord with our definition of a valid programme of study in [say] Business Studies', our Validation and Registration panels are able to say 'Given your experience in this field, and your longer term intentions, we can see you have focused on an appropriate theme which, if developed in the way you describe, will provide the basis for a worthwhile educational experience leading to the award you require'. Students are in a weak position to argue with the former judgement and therefore have no power. They can debate the latter because *they are* their own experiences and intentions. In preparing their proposals, students must therefore be thorough in their appraisals of their experiences and intentions, and be coherent in presenting a rationale which relates their proposals to where they are and where they wish to be.

Students are capable of putting togther a wide range of specialist support and resources.

On a conventional course, students expect the host department to provide what is required to complete the course successfully, either through its purchases for the library shelves, the expertise of its staff, the equipment in its workshops, or the facilities in its studios.

All our students are provided with a specialist supervisor from the most appropriate department, but because the students are in control they do not feel confined to one department. They seek out what is most useful. Their host department is usually satisfactory for the predictable and routine, but often the most appropriate expert is working out in the field or in another institution. One former student told me that she found one particular book so stimulating that she rang up the author to discuss certain points. The author was both surprised and flattered to be so approached by an undergraduate from the other end of the country. The student was invited to visit, had a lengthy tutorial, followed up many useful leads, and stayed long enough to establish working contacts with research students working in the same field.

Another student, working on the history and practice of portrait painting, was finding the help from the polytechnic too bland. She wrote to six leading portrait painters to ask for advice. She received many helpful replies and had a lengthy telephone discussion with the most prestigious of the painters. Another, studying the role of the arts in the school curriculum, has discussed her work with the country's leading expert on art in education, prominent writers on pupil motivation, local authority art advisers, and specialists on current ideas on the structure of the brain.

Students of computing seek out the most relevant hardware, often in other institutions and businesses. Students of politics serve as research assistants to Members of Parliament. Literature students have attached themselves to theatres and production companies. One student, studying Third World Development, attached herself to one of the few specialist research centres in British universities as an unpaid research assistant. She joined postgraduate workshops and seminars and arranged a lengthy field placement in Peru. She used two other major libraries and attended workshops in yet another university.

Not being fed reading and assignment lists, students have to create their own. They learn early on how to use the library's reference system and to convert their specialist interest into reading lists. Library assistants are there to be used, not feared. Students eagerly seek out conferences and workshops, mainly outside the polytechnic. It has not been an uncommon experience for myself, as a regular conference attender, to meet our own students at these events.

The benefits from students having to negotiate their own resources are obvious. Students perceive themselves to be in control of their studies and in a position to command the best or the most helpful support and advice. Many work beyond 'run of the mill' departmentally prescribed fare. They are alive to wider issues and the wider context of their work, and they learn to find their way around their topic. In the process, they develop a high level of personal competence.

The above examples are typical rather than exceptional. However, less adventurous students also work effectively on their own assignments under the supervision of a polytechnic specialist.

Payment for such specialist support is only occasionally a problem. Outside specialists welcome intelligent discussions of their work with interested students from other institutions. Often they are impressed by the student's initiative in approaching them. Where a longer term association is required, the provision of some unpaid research assistance is much appreciated. Access to specialist resources is often accompanied by some unpaid work in exchange. The main problems have been with specialist short courses with a high enrolment fee. Sometimes full-time students can get an extra grant from their local education authority, sometimes they pay for themselves, and sometimes the polytechnic pays out of its educational visits budget. In all cases, the contact is negotiated in advance by the student.

Implications for tutors

Each student has two tutors, a personal tutor with responsibility for helping with the student's overall development and a specialist tutor to help with the specific field of study. Their roles and how they fulfil them are important issues. Tutors can so easily subvert or frustrate the student's independence if they don't understand, don't believe in this approach, or are not prepared to give it a go.

The best specialist tutors share an overwhelming desire to see other people learn, combining the roles of servant, general practitioner helping to diagnose learning difficulties, challenger, critic, expert, therapist, and, above all, supporter. Each function is relevant at different times. The transition from traditional teacher to being an independent study tutor is most easily made with the simple acceptance that the student is, and should be, in control. Our experience has been that many tutors are capable of independent study tuition while retaining their more traditional roles on other kinds of course.

A key factor in encouraging specialist tutors to take independent study students is that tutors find it a refreshing and stimulating experience to work with students who are committed to what they are doing. Students ask questions, bring information, take initiatives, seek advice, and welcome suggestions. They are encouraged to use their tutors as resources, and tutors respond well. It is a release for tutors as well as students. Tutors learn from their students.

On some occasions resource constraints bring about change. A brief exchange between a potential new specialist supervisor in engineering and myself:

Tutor: At a staff–student ratio of 12:1 and a maximum tutor student contact time of 15 hours a week I can only give this student 36 minutes of my time every week.
Me: (sympathetically) It's a bugger!
Tutor: (long pause) I can't possibly teach her everything or lecture her!
Me: (more sympathetically) I can see that.
Tutor: (defiantly) She'll have to do most of it herself! She can come to me for advice and help but she'll have to get on with it.
Me: (resignedly) OK. Try that and see how it goes.

That was the sum total of that tutor's staff development. He worked very well with the student concerned and was genuinely surprised at how well she did. Growth in tutor commitment to independent study often comes from positive experiences with students.

The difficulty for some tutors is that their self-esteem is heavily bound up with their traditional role as 'the authority'. If students can do better by doing it themselves, then what does that mean for the tutor's self-respect? It is not always easy for some tutors to reply to student questions with 'I don't know but I can suggest ways of finding out', or to see their role as helping the student to ask appropriate questions rather than to give information. Often, tutor direction is done in the guise of protecting the student from the possibility of failure. We have learned that some tutors are not capable of exposing themselves to the possibility that what students can do may be better than what they as tutors can provide. Fortunately, over the years we have found over 150 specialist tutors who are able to cope with students running their own programmes. This number is about one-third of the total polytechnic establishment and has been achieved by student example and by negotiations almost as casual as the example above. We don't know what proportion would respond to a more concerted staff-development drive.

The role of the personal tutor, the one who is responsible for helping students articulate their own needs and plans and monitor their own progress, is similar but further requires the considerable facility of being able to establish an effective and mutually supportive learning community. This is explored in more detail in the section on risk and self-confidence (below). Such tutors have to be recruited more carefully. They are usually drawn from our experienced specialist tutors and are invited to work with us for a short while before they finally commit themselves. Once they join us, we place them within a community of four or five experienced personal tutors with whom they will work closely. From then on they learn as they go along, supported by their colleagues. Successful personal tutors have come from all discipline areas, including science, engineering, business, art and design, humanities and the social sciences. What they have in common is an interest in student development, an ability to listen, and a capacity for accurate empathy.

The importance of risk and self-confidence

Independent study requires students to make a major commitment for a period of anything up to three years. Where their proposed studies arise from their own assessments of their past experiences and future intentions, they have great meaning to their lives. In such circumstances successful completion is important in more ways than just gaining the award. Having to take responsibility for devising and then completing those studies puts students at considerable risk. There is no one to do it for them. It is down to them.

Some students are used to taking responsibility for their own actions but very few have had experience of doing it in higher education. Their commitment to their own educational development often outreaches their confidence in their ability to do it themselves. In a real sense they are moving into what for them is unchartered territory. Their future is on the line. The presence of risk is real and has to be acknowledged and appreciated by both students and tutors.

Some students avoid taking risks and pursue safe and familiar programmes of study, often under close scrutiny from a specialist. They get less out of it. The greatest benefits are experienced by those who accept the risk and go for what they really want. Their growth is more than just in terms of the specific knowledge and skills peculiar to their field; it is in terms of their belief in themselves and their own personal power.

Risk-taking is particularly a problem for the diploma students, nearly all of whom are 'under-qualified' mature students entering higher education for the first time. Often the risk is in exposing to others or committing to paper one's self-doubts, aspirations, beliefs and intentions. Who are you to be deciding what is right for you in higher education? How will you be perceived? Is it all right to think of yourself in this way? Are you as bad as you think you are? Is it really OK to have these aspirations in higher education? Will they laugh at you for wanting to do this? Will you be taken seriously? Students on conventional courses can hide these thoughts behind the anonymity of the class and the regime of the syllabus. For independent study, they are up front, exposed to scrutiny from peers and validators.

217

Support from fellow students and personal tutors therefore plays a crucial role in the early stages. It is important that each student is made to feel that it is all right to share private reservations and explore dreams and aspirations. We have found it pays to provide students with the security of a safe community within which these explorations can take place.

Groups of 12 to 18 students meet regularly with an experienced tutor whose job it is to encourage and facilitate student confidence and initiative. Confidence comes mainly from being taken seriously by peers and tutors. Students learn that they really do have something to contribute. Acceptance by peers and representatives of the culture to which they are aspiring, if handled well and if sustained, gradually builds up student confidence to plan and then to go for the programme required. In a recent survey of former students, the following comments were made about this aspect of the experience of independent study:

> totally liberating
> an emotional shower
> I discovered that others had had the same kinds of problems and I realized I wasn't
> alone
> I was amazed to discover that people valued what I had been doing
> I realized that I had something of value to say after all
> It helped me to understand better what I had done previously and how my plans
> fitted in with that
> It was valuable to share one's concerns with others

These feelings of acceptance, of being more at ease with themselves, of understanding more of where they are at, give students the confidence to look forward on their own terms. In the spirit of Carl Rogers, they have to *be* before they can *become*. The provision of an accepting community is therefore given the highest priority for those embarking on the planning of independent study programmes.

Ironically, the mainly bureaucratic procedures for validating student plans, initially set up to guarantee their educational credibility, have a considerable educational benefit for the students. First, they encourage students to delve more deeply and to be more explicit about themselves, thus giving them more opportunity for the empowering experience of acceptance from relevant others. Secondly, successful validation is saying to students 'You are OK as a student; it is acceptable for you to study this in this way. We will recognize your achievement if you complete what you yourself have planned.' As a result, the students' confidence to 'see it through' grows. The more the students have put themselves at risk in their planning, the more empowering is the experience of validation.

Many kinds of students are capable of independent study

Of the 700-plus students in the School for Independent Study, the youngest is 18 and the oldest is 65. The dominant age band is 23 to 33. Sixty per cent are women and about 35 per cent are from ethnic minorities. Two-thirds originate within daily travelling distance of the polytechnic, and 90 per cent of the entrants to the diploma (the largest programme) have educational and other qualifications other than the normal minimum entry requirements for higher education in the UK.

These crude statistics hide a rich variety of backgrounds, experiences and reasons for studying. There are able school-leavers attracted by the opportunity to do something different, school-leavers who can't get into other institutions, early school-leavers returning to higher education after a period at work or with a family, people trying to find a new direction or commitment in their lives, successful self-made people wanting to distance themselves from their work and make more sense of it, premature retirees and unemployed people looking for retraining or new interests, employees looking for updating and further expertise, and those just interested in study for its own sake. All of these categories are potentially capable of planning and completing their own programmes of study.

Not all of our students come to us solely because of the attraction of independent study. Some, because of personal constraints or the lack of conventional qualifications, have little effective choice. They too do well. Our experience suggests, after over 2000 examples, that most people are capable of studying independently if they want to or if they have to. Some colleagues in other institutions comment that independent study is fine for 'certain types of student' but not for theirs. Recently, we have extended the opportunity for independent study to Chinese students from Hong Kong. They have coped extremely well in spite of their tradition of formal teaching and tutor control.

The students who have greatest difficulty are those who are unable to articulate intentions in spite of a great deal of help from their groups, or who cannot perceive themselves as in any way being able to influence their own lives. Many such students eventually succeed after much persistence by others. Often they have deep emotional problems which require specialist help. I suspect that it isn't that independent study is unsuited to them but that the strict time scale imposed by the higher education calendar gives insufficient time for them to establish a state of personal readiness. Being able to embrace the possibility of effective personal initiative seems to be a precondition for progress on the programme; the role of the personal tutor and the supporting communities is therefore to provide the conditions under which that can happen. If students in difficulty eventually do discover that they can take initiatives which influence their own lives, the effect can be electrifying. Even if they don't complete their studies, developing an awareness of their own personal power can be reward enough.

Students can achieve high levels of performance

All students' final work is scrutinized by external examiners approved by the Council for National Academic Awards. These examiners are chosen because of their subject expertise and their experience of standards in higher education in general. All examiners have commented that some of the work they have seen has been of the highest standard. 'Publishable', 'highly distinctive and original', 'thorough and challenging' are some of the comments we have received. One celebrated case is of a student who for two and a half years had not been able to make contact with a specialist supervisor in the Polytechnic. One did not exist so we had to find a caretaker supervisor. The student's final piece of work was judged by an experienced examiner as being the most refreshing, original and perceptive analysis she had read from an undergraduate. Such comments are not rare.

One interesting characteristic of the independent study approach is that final achievements appear to be unrelated to prior educational success. On the degree it is common for over 50 per cent of a year group to achieve upper second or first class honours. This is much higher than the average for British higher education. Within that number, many of those gaining the highest marks had had no previous record of academic success either in schools or in post-school education. What appears to make the difference is the high level of commitment, motivation, identification with the study, personal investment, and awareness of the relevance of all the components of the course. These are inevitable consequences of requiring students to put together their own programmes and to articulate for the benefit of validating and registration boards how the various course components and activities fit into a coherent whole.

Its relevance to continuing education

Allowing students to plan programmes which build on their distinctive educational, vocational and other experiences is particularly valuable to those students who for some reason have had to interrupt their normal education or who need to move from one institution to another.

Admission with advanced standing is possible where students can show how their proposed course makes use of relevant experience and capability. One student wanted to study management and organizational development on the strength of her lengthy experience building up and managing a growing and complicated nationwide voluntary services unit. A professional jazz musician of 40 years' experience wanted to 'make sense' of the music he had played and the styles he had experienced. He wanted to become a tutor for the jazz guitar. Both were admitted directly into the final year on the strength of their plans to build their courses on their considerable experience. Both got first class honours degrees. There are many other examples.

Building programmes on each student's actual experiences also facilitates credit transfer without loss of time. Credit transfer is currently in fashion but conventional course structures always seem to put up barriers. 'Only students who have studied x can cope with our second-year programme, or can join our third year.' Conventionally students can and do transfer but they risk losing time. Modular structures aim to facilitate transfer and are on the increase but they are not free from similar restrictions and the resultant total experience for the student can be fragmented.

The facility for credit transfer through planning a distinctive course which builds on previous experience has been exploited by: a student who successfully completed two years at York University but who felt that the University's third year would be of less use to him; a Dartington Hall student who at the end of his first year felt that his drama-based course needed to have a more community-based emphasis; Hong Kong students whose Higher Diploma qualifications were undervalued by British universities and who have been able to get honours degrees after only one year's further study; holders of Higher Diplomas from UK institutions who have been able to convert them into degrees by independent study after only one year; and holders of a variety of professional and other qualifications who have been able to slot in at the most appropriate year.

Its relevance to in-service education and training

The availability of the one-year honours degree and the masters programme has opened up the scope for in-service development by independent study. Potential students struggling with new and challenging problems in their place of work can build tailor-made courses which give them access to the most appropriate polytechnic expertise. Such plans can be discussed with the employer who might sponsor the student because of the obvious payoff for them from improved performance.

Many such examples are in education. One student working with Bangladeshi children has put together a school-based programme of study designed to improve his understanding and skills in multicultural teaching with special reference to inner-city environments, and has received employer support. Other teachers are learning how to cope with the computer or are updating their scientific knowledge and have secured release and financial support from their schools. Similar three-way agreements between student, employer and the polytechnic have been arranged in the paramedical field, in engineering and in management. The attractions for both learner and sponsor are obvious: relevant programmes with maximum return.

Learning outcomes

It has not been surprising to discover that one of the main benefits to accrue has been the acquisition by students of valuable specialist knowledge and skills. This has been particularly true of those students who deliberately planned a programme with a specific vocation in mind and who pursued their studies as close to the field as possible. These students are generally established in a career and are doing well.

Neither is it surprising to learn that all successful students report experiencing a great boost in their confidence and self-esteem. To some extent this is true of students on most courses, but independent study students report their feelings of well-being with much intensity. It is very closely linked with a strong sense of

221

personal identity, either as an individual or as a worker, or both. This partly comes from the experience of always having to think through what they were doing and why they were doing it as an integral part of their studies.

There is also a suggestion in some of their reports that the origin of this strong personal commitment lies in the extent to which independent study actually 'puts the individual on the line', at risk. Coming through the programme successfully is more than just a reward for doing well; it is a total vindication of 'what I did, how I did it, and why I was doing it', ie

> It was recognition for what I had achieved for myself.
> First and foremost it is knowing that I'd done well as a result of my own personal achievement.
> I wasn't doing it just for the certificate; I was doing something that was part of my life.
> It's being able to say 'I did it my way.'
> When I came out with flying colours, I knew that it was me that had been validated.

The consequences of this greatly advanced feeling of self-respect and self-identity are many. It has been a major factor in encouraging the students to commit themselves more fully to their chosen lifestyle or career. One student who was a waiter in a fish and chip shop before coming to the school now owns a chain of very successful restaurants and other businesses. When asked why he couldn't have done that without coming to the school his swift reply was 'I wouldn't have had the nerve.' He is totally clear that he is a businessman, not a restauranteur, and this clarity of identity and his commitment to it have enabled him to cut his way through the day-to-day hassles to identify what is really important and to go for it. His success in his independent study showed him what he was and proved to him that he was capable, not just clever.

There are many similar examples. The student mentioned above who talked to artists is now totally committed to her art work. She is now an 'artist', not 'a housewife who paints'. It dominates her life and 'nothing is as important enough for me to give it up'. Another, previously a journalist, has set up his own newspaper for which he is the proprietor, chief reporter, editor, and business manager. His work is totally engrossing. Another, who previously wrote poetry in the secrecy of her own room, now publishes her work and uses it in a hospice as a means of helping people to articulate their thoughts 'in order for them to get the dying right'. Her commitment to this lifestyle is complete: 'There is no amount of money that could take me away from this. I would do it for nothing.' Another student who had previously pursued a wandering and flippant lifestyle, says 'For the first time in my life I am doing something to which I am totally committed.'

Another consequence is a growth in self-competence. Knowing that you were able to take on the academic establishment and come through is enormously empowering:

I now feel that I can cope with anything.
Things that would previously have been disasters I can take in my stride.
I know I have the strength to see it through.

It is this feeling of self-efficacy which is enduring and transferable to new and more challenging situations. An interesting manifestation of this inner strength has been an improvement in personal relationships and an interest in helping others to do things for themselves.

These are just a few of the reported outcomes of successfully completing higher education entirely by independent study. It is impossible to assert that they are exclusively the product of taking responsibility for your own work. However, the frequency and strength with which these points are volunteered suggests some sort of connection.

It also links in with the work of others. The humanistic psychologists, Carl Rogers and Abraham Maslow in particular, would not find these observations surprising. William Perry (1970), Jane Loevinger (1976) and others who have studied stages of personal development would recognize characteristics of their higher orders. David McClelland's work (see Klemp, 1977) on achievement motivation and its relevance to the world of work would help to explain the success of some of these students. Arthur Chickering (1981) has written at length on the educational implications of the ideas of these writers, and concludes that the only way forward is to reverse the pattern of teacher control and student passivity.

I have come across a small number of former students who have not been successful in the way they had hoped, in spite of completing their studies. In each case peculiar personal circumstances have intervened. Nevertheless some general points emerge, mainly to do with the polytechnic's own inability to make adequate provision or through subversion of student plans. In one case, a strong-minded tutor persuaded a gentle mature student that if the student wanted an honours degree she should concentrate her course on traditional subject matter, not on what she really wanted to do. She completed the course more as a chore, not really gaining satisfaction or personal growth. Another experienced considerable frustration because of the polytechnic's failure to deliver its part of the contract in terms of appropriate resources. A third focused her plans towards her need to get a well-paid job and away from her true interest. She feels she did not take full advantage of the opportunity.

The challenge to the professions

Independent study is a direct challenge to the established professional bodies. They control entry to their ranks by imposing requirements on feeder undergraduate courses. These are frequently expressed in terms of numbers of hours in specified classes. The consequence is that educational preparation for the professions is dominated by teacher-controlled routine contact hours and acquisition of pieces of knowledge and skills. The idea of student-planned courses runs directly counter to their formal requirements.

The irony is that the professions themselves are asking for more of the personal qualities displayed by independent study students. They want recruits who can accept responsibility, learn for themselves, show initiative, communicate with others, get on with things, and who know what they are about. When some of our independent study students have submitted themselves for consideration, they have been told they haven't spent enough hours in front of a teacher. The professions just cannot, or will not, see that the very means of control which they exercise are preventing the development of the qualities they say they want. This is particularly true in the older and more established professions. Independent study students have successfully established themselves in the more 'relaxed' professions and are doing exceptionally well precisely because of the extra personal qualities gained through independent study (McKenzie *et al*, 1985).

Resource issues

Independent study at North East London Polytechnic is resourced on exactly the same basis as the polytechnic's other activities. The primary control is the staff–student ratio (SSR). Our agreement with the polytechnic authorities is that we should accept the same SSR as the average for the polytechnic as a whole. In recent years that has risen from about 8:1 to the present 13:1. In practice, because of our growth and staff shortages, we work at over 15:1, ie way above the actual polytechnic average.

In fact, as the polytechnic's financial squeeze has intensified, as illustrated by the changing SSR, so has the number of independent study students increased. The greater the squeeze, the more rapid has been our growth. At a time when over 200 academic posts have been lost, such growth could only have been accommodated if it had been cost-effective. And it is.

There are many reasons for this. They are generally related to the flexibility inherent in the independent study system. For instance the polytechnic can recruit students who wish to plan courses in fields where there are surplus staff but no established course. On the other hand as some specialist areas are squeezed by the non-replacement of staff, recruitment to that area can be reduced. With monolithic pre-planned courses which depend on minimum class sizes of 13 for each component, a polytechnic's profile can easily become fossilized, not fluid. In recent years it has been possible for us to recruit more students with interests in science and fewer students with interests in law in response to changing staff availability. This flexibility is much valued by the polytechnic.

As staff–student ratios are pushed upwards, so is the pressure for a greater proportion of the work to be allocated to students. The earlier example of the engineering tutor forced by resource constraints to change the method of tuition is not an isolated case. The School for Independent Study is better able to do this than other more traditional schools.

Continuing education, credit transfer, and education for groups such as the unemployed, the unqualified (*access*), the aged and ethnic minorities are all currently in fashion. As the country's age profile changes and the proportion of conventional 18-year-olds declines, so will these other groups become still more important. It will no longer be possible to make bland assumptions about the educational needs of whole cohorts of students. The dominant characteristic will be the variety of students and their many and varied experiences and intentions. Independent study is therefore a valued feature of the polytechnic, hence its growth in times of shortage.

At the operational level, the unit of currency is a student full-time equivalent (SFTE). One full-time undergraduate is worth one whole SFTE, and one part-time student is worth 0.4 SFTE. Each SFTE at our current staff–student ratio (SSR), and at an average of 15 hours a week tutor contact time, can command just over one hour a week of individual tutor time. For the planning periods we retain 0.6 of an SFTE for each diploma student. This enables us to provide one tutor for support groups of about 18 students. The tutor will use the time in a combination of whole-group activities, smaller set meetings, and individual tutorials.

The remaining 0.4 SFTE is available to the specialist tutor. As the earlier example shows, this can amount to about half an hour a week. In practice, students get on with their assignments and have longer tutorial sessions once every two or three weeks. Students can also attend any other regular activity on any course in the polytechnic, in the same way that they can use any book in the library. If specialist tutors have a number of students, they can introduce shared activities such as collaborative learning or student-led seminars.

The undergraduate and postgraduate degree programmes are similarly organized, with the proportions 0.2 SFTE for the planning and 0.8 SFTE for the specialist activities.

At first sight the above may appear to be complicated. In practice it is simple to operate and has survived the vagaries of 12 years' turbulent polytechnic history. It has enabled the school to grow without compromising its educational principles. Timetabling is a relatively minor problem. It has to be to accommodate over 700 distinctive programmes of study. Students are allocated to tutors, and between them they arrange their own times to suit themselves. In this way student control is respected and preserved.

Institutions considering introducing independent study hold back mainly because of uncertainties about resource issues. Circumstances vary and our solutions may not so easily transfer. However, the birth, growth, survival, and scale of the School for Independent Study should give reassurance that it is actually possible. We didn't know how to do it when we set out in 1974. In the best independent study tradition, we knew what we wanted and we learned how to do it as we went along. One of our guiding principles has been that our resource and administrative arrangements should derive from our educational principles, ie in response to student needs, and not the other way round. This has often meant that we have had to devise arrangements different from those prevalent in other parts of the polytechnic, as in timetabling, and have had to resist pressure for administrative conformity. Our advice to those who wish to follow would be to start from the proposition that students are in control of their own programmes, and they should devise and establish only those procedures and controls which enable students to plan what they want to do, gain approval for their intentions, secure access to resources and tutorial help, and gain credit for their achievements.

Conclusions

Our experience has been that it is possible within the constraints of a modern large institution of higher education to introduce the maximum amount of student autonomy of learning to the personal benefit of students, the advantage of the institution and the interests of the staff, and with the support of student sponsors.

As we have grown from fringe experimental status to be a major established unit, we have pushed to see how many ways independent study can be used. We have built up a network of access courses organized on an independent study basis, we are helping schools experiment with independent study as an alternative way of pupils' using their last years at school, and we are beginning to address the issue of professional recognition in traditional occupations. Experiments are under way for using independent study to facilitate international credit tranfer and to improve staff development. The applications seem endless. The success of independent study is that potential students, of all kinds, can see how it would help them to get a better education. We have no difficulty in selling the idea to students, only to some academics and professions.

Most encouraging is what we have learned about the programme's educational value. It seems to 'reach those parts of the person that other courses miss'. It puts the development of personal qualities and attributes on to centre stage, rather than being something to be picked up on the side. As one former student put it:

> There is an awful truth about independent study. It is about yourself and there is no escaping it.

(The International Newsletter for Independent Study (INIS) aims to bring together people interested in independent study. It appears three times a year and contains details of ideas and schemes from all over the world as well as news items, articles and points of view. Details of subscriptions and back numbers are available from INIS, School for Independent Study, North East London Polytechnic, Holbrook Road, Plaistow, London E15.)

Chapter 14

On Leadership, Change and Autonomy

Richard Bawden, *Dean, Faculty of Agriculture,*
Hawkesbury Agricultural College, Richmond, New South Wales

For a significant part of my professional life as an agricultural educator I have been grappling with a single paradox: how does one provide leadership in a system geared to encouraging its participants to be both autonomous and interdependent? As a lecturer at university my challenge was confined to encouraging students enrolled in my courses to accept increasing responsibility for their own learning while working cooperatively together. In this I achieved enough success to encourage me to expand my efforts. Later, as elected Dean of the same faculty in which I had been a lecturer, I tried to extend the challenge of the autonomy/interdependent duality. Encouraging autonomy among academics was easy. Interdependency, on the other hand, was almost impossible to achieve, particularly when it came to shared intellectual visions, and integrated research activities.

In 1978 I left that university and moved as Head of the School of Agriculture to Hawkesbury Agricultural College. I did this because of the avowed aim of many of the academics at that institute to encourage students to become more autonomous as learners.

So with a sympathetic climate I could now pursue the noble dream of helping people associated with our School to become autonomous learners while concurrently encouraging interdependency between them: between all of us, actually, as the dream extended to being a community of people dedicated to the improvement of agriculture and of people in the rural sector of this country at large.

The early days

Experimenting with innovative strategies such as contract learning and self-directed individual and small group projects within my single discipline of parasitology had been one thing. But here, on Monday, 10 July 1978, was I, charged in my new position with providing leadership for change across a whole

227

faculty of agriculture. My terms of reference as Head of School were succinct yet daunting:

To assume responsibility for the overall:
– academic development and
– administration of the School. And
– to provide professional leadership to staff and students, and
– promote the activities of the School in the community.

Hadn't I just spent a decade trying to introduce innovation into a baccalaureate degree programme at my previous institution? Hadn't I suffered the wrath of my faculty colleagues who had labelled my courses superficial and non-rigorous and mickey mouseish and psychological clap-trap? And latterly, as Dean of that venerable faculty, hadn't I failed abjectly to even achieve consensus on the need to review the curriculum?

What was going to be so different about being a Head of School (= Faculty Dean) at Hawkesbury Agricultural College that would enable me to succeed where, at my previous university in the same position, I had been so manifestly unsuccessful?

Reference to my diary reveals that there were four factors uppermost in my mind as I sat at my new desk in my new office in my new position at my new institution.

First, there was the issue of power. In the university faculty, structured as it was around discipline-based research departments, a non-professorial elected Dean interested essentially in learning and coherent curricula had little power of sanction beyond friendly persuasion! The appointed Deanship at Hawkesbury with its budget responsibilities was the opposite story altogether.

Secondly, there was the issue of involvement in practical agriculture. Faculty members at the Agricultural College were sustaining a century-long commitment to the everyday problems of Australian farmers and held a primary concern for teaching; two concerns my university colleagues had not shared!

Thirdly, there was a clear concern at Hawkesbury about the need for a new approach to the increasingly complex issues of contemporary technological agriculture including some of its negative impacts on social and physical environments: a far cry from the science for production orientation of my university days.

Finally, there certainly seemed to be a climate of acceptance of innovation in curriculum at the College. Indeed Malcolm Knowles was visiting the College just at that time and his words, quoted from his then recent book, were ringing around the campus loud and clear: 'What we are talking about is a basic human competence – the ability to learn on one's own – that has suddenly become a prerequisite for living in this new world' (Knowles, 1975).

The challenge that I faced was to facilitate the development of a system that would facilitate the development of the autonomous learner! And here I was addressing the issue of academics as autonomous learners as well as their students. Clearly there was no way that we could effectively design and facilitate strategies for autonomous learning if we ourselves were not behaving autonomously. Upon reflection I was also thinking about the organization itself as a learner, although this did not become clear to me until reading the insights of Chris Argyris and Donald Schön (1980) just a couple of years later. The work of these two writers strongly reinforced my long cherished belief that entire groups could learn together by creating and sharing tentative models and maps and metaphors of common experiences. In other words, groups of people in organizations such as ours could share common understandings about issues in ways which would enable the whole group to adjust to changes in its environment. In this way, groups would act as individual learners do, fluctuating between experiences and actions in the concrete world, and conceptualizations and reflections in the abstract. My belief in these dichotomies of the learning process in individuals had been developed from reading about the construct notions of George Kelly (1955), the cognitive ideas of Dewey (1910), Piaget (1970) and Bruner (1966), the experiential theories of Lewin (1951) and Kolb and his associates (1974) and the systems theories of von Bertalanffy (1968) and Ackoff (1974) and Gregory Bateson (1972). Indeed, the very model of leadership that I had adopted as a basis for my style, that of Lieberman and his colleagues (Lieberman *et al*, 1973), combined meaning attribution with executive action (in a climate set by empathy and emotional stimulation). Leadership then became equivalent in my mind to the process of facilitation of group learning. As Dean my role would be to help in the development of a climate where theories and models of learning and facilitating and change would be as high on the agenda as those of agriculture itself. We would need to be as thoughtful about the process as we would about the content. Our educational practices would need to reflect our theories of learning, and these in turn would need to be sensitive to our practical experiences. As an effective collaborator I would have to be in there, boots and all, developing and sharing my own models and experiences as an educator yet in a way which encouraged others to develop and share theirs too.

Here I was confronting several of the major paradoxes in the development of an environment to encourage autonomy in learning. What if my 40 academic peers rejected all of my models out of hand and, in the name of their own autonomy, each developed individual models of education? Or what if they all accepted the notion of autonomy for students but failed to accept it for themselves? Or what if they accepted the ideas and together developed strategies to allow the students to develop autonomously only to have the students reject the idea in turn? And perhaps above all, how could the debate about conflict between the need for essential knowledge for agriculturalists be reconciled with the notion of autonomy as a desirable competency?

Well, one obvious approach was to encourage small initiatives in curricular innovation which could be tried and evaluated; new experiences used as a source of our learning; new situations based on new constructs of the learning process and the idea of competency. As long as we were absolutely explicit about our intentions, then this seemed both appropriate and ethical.

Curriculum development as action research

For our curricular initiatives we would adopt an experiential, action-research approach to our own development. Under these circumstances, 'theory leads to practice; but the practice is itself the source of the theory; neither is prime; the process generates itself' (Checkland, 1985). Our theories and practices in the faculty would be developed through joint experiences, and shared models and maps would be developed from our understanding of those experiences. Argyris and Schön (1980) refer to 'the theory of action constructed from observation of actual behaviour as theory-in-use' (p 129). They go on to submit that 'Organisational learning occurs when members of the organisation (faculty in our case) act as learning agents for the organisation by detecting and correcting errors in organisational theory-in-use, and embedding the results of their inquiry in private images and shared maps of organisation' (p 137).

Academic leadership under these circumstances would be to facilitate organizational learning through the process of collaborative action research. The key to effective change would be participation. For the first month following my appointment as Head of School I did as the conventional newcomer – I listened. I visited faculty and students, technical and farm staff, farmers and researchers, extension people and agri-politicians. I was greatly encouraged by what I heard: the 'espoused theories', and most impressed by the commitment to education in general and to learning in particular within Hawkesbury. I then conducted a series of seminars and colloquia attempting to synthesize my maps with others I had encountered. Concern for the state of agriculture and for people in rural communities was shared by a large cohort of faculty. So too was concern for the inadequacies of the Hawkesbury graduates to deal with the emerging complexity of such issues. Finally, there was a high degree of agreement with the need to help students (and other clients) to learn how to learn; how to gain autonomy in order to become people capable of interdependency!

When the details of the extant curricula were examined it was obvious that although the above notions were generally accepted across the Faculty, the processes and strategies of the educational practices were not consistent with their achievement. The espoused theories were not congruent with the theories-in-use.

Taking the opportunity of starting a new course in animal production (A.P.), we decided late in 1978 to go for radical reform. As 'he-with-the-power', I appointed from among the faculty a coordinator to select and lead a course planning team. The mandate I gave the coordinator, who did not hold a senior academic rank but was a highly respected educator, was to design a programme around notions of self-direction, competency and problem-solving. This would be one of the small innovative experiential initiatives which would allow us to test our espoused theories in practice and to provide experiences which would encourage new theories.

The themes that emerged from the deliberations of the AP planning team which were subsequently developed into the documentation for accreditation included:

> The graduate will understand and be able to manipulate the essential processes in commercially sound animal production systems. The (four semester) course will emphasise the self-development of the individual within a problem-solving context which will ensure adaptation to change and an attitude of sensitivity and self-evaluation.
>
> Graduates will understand that education is a lifelong process and that they will have merely begun a period of continued independent learning. Above all they will be adaptable and useful citizens with a strong social awareness and a sense of community responsibility.

Noble sentiments indeed, and though couched in terms that now seem extraordinarily naive and pedantic they were certainly far removed from the objectives of conventional courses in agriculture which stressed subjects and examinations and formal hours of study and pedagogy. The aims of this new programme far transcended the emphasis on knowledge and skills acquisition of traditional courses by groping towards notions of competencies and learning as a creative, investigative process involving the whole person.

The strategies to be used in this new programme included self-directed projects based on a learning contract system, problem-based workshops directed by academics, and hands-on experience by the students themselves as managers of actual mini-farms on the College's farm estate. Both individual and group projects would be facilitated by academics. The programme also included a period to be spent on an actual full-scale commercial property of a cooperating farmer.

The course programme was hastened through the processes of accreditation over just three months (from School Board of Studies to College Academic Board to College Council Academic Planning Committee to College Council itself to the outside body of the State's Higher Education Board). The first students were enrolled in February 1979 on the course by now controlled by a course management team. I deliberately chose not to become a member of either of these teams, preferring instead to act as a consultant facilitator to the team itself. The outline of the programme is displayed in Figure 1.

The structure of the AP course that was proposed in the accreditation documents was one based on three phases:

Phase I

This occurs during Semester I and is aimed at

(a) Development of a common frame of reference among students.
(b) Experience in the real world of commercial animal production in those areas appropriate to each individual. These areas may include:

   (i) Basic animal orientation and skills in handling animals.

continued

WELSH COLLEGE OF MUSIC & DRAMA LIBRARY

235

(ii) Basic animal science and management knowledge relevant to the particular animal enterprise.

(iii) An appreciation of the technical, economic and social factors which may affect an animal production enterprise.

(iv) The basis of an ability to critically observe and record relevant data in an animal production system as a first step in evaluation.

(v) A developing ability to communicate with farmers, farm workers, farm advisers and commercial service people, and an appreciation of the role of attitudes in this communication.

(c) Ability to recognize problems and critical resource areas in an animal production enterprise.

Phase II

This phase occurs during Semesters II and III and is aimed at providing the necessary experiences to solve animal production enterprise problems. This will involve three different activities, the main one of which will be small-group activities based on solving inter-disciplinary problems actually constructed by resource people but based on Phase I experiences.

A second activity will be the operation of an on-College animal enterprise to allow consolidation of Phase I experiences and to allow for the continual identification of real problems and their resolution. This will involve realistic decision-making and opportunities for evaluation of decision consequences.

The third activity will be individual learning units contracted by each individual to suit his own needs, talents and interests. This will allow for considerable in-depth study in basic areas relevant to the course. An increasingly variable and sophisticated range of programmes will be available as resource people continue to develop these in response to demand.

Phase III

This will occupy Semester IV. During this phase the student will be given the opportunity to study in depth an area of his own choosing. This will enable a distinct vocational orientation to develop. This will be achieved by way of a project that will have both a practical and academic content. This project will be subject to a learning contract between the student, course director and resource supervisor, and again will be variable in form to suit the individual needs consistent with overall course aims.

Figure 1

For all the enthusiasm of the Team and its undoubted resources, and for all the endeavours of its members to learn how to facilitate this experiential learning process, problems there were aplenty. Reflecting on our experiences three years later, we were to conclude that:

The one constant feature of innovative educational systems is the ever-presence of unpredicted situations and problems. Many, of course, are of a minor organizational nature, but failure to respond appropriately can create a more serious situation threatening the trust between the student and his <sic> facilitator. Bawden *et al* (1981)

By responding appropriately we meant new learning, the questioning of the adequacies of our old models and practices and the quality of our response to new experiences.

We recognized deficiencies in our own abilities to facilitate autonomous learning, being never sure when to retain control and when to let go. In fact we were still pretty unsure about what we really meant by autonomous learning: our models were vague and ambiguous. Our one-to-one counselling skills and group facilitation capabilities, both features of the new programme, ranged from the tentative to the downright inadequate. The often apparent unwillingness of the students to accept responsibility for their own learning, and their manifest discomfort in group situations, exacerbated anxieties arising from our own performances. We were also often confused between the aims and processes of formative or feedback assessments and summative ones. We felt constrained by the use of behavioural objectives as basic competencies to be mastered. The intellectual maps that we were developing of systems approaches to agriculture were too abstract to be of apparent utility, yet we were most anxious to project the notions of the benefit of studying the whole. Finally we were very conscious of an overall environment in the school, and especially the college, which ranged from somewhat hesitant support to overt hostility. The vast majority of the students after all were progressing through the extant conventional courses, and most of the school's academics were conventionally 'teaching' them.

These concerns notwithstanding, the experience of participation in the course was a source of considerable learning for all concerned. An early feature of the AP course was the openness with which problems in the programme were discussed among all the participants. Course councils between members of the management team and the students were a regular event, and the problematic issues became sources of learning for all concerned. I attended these spasmodically and was also often involved in discussions with academics about their experiences and the adequacies or otherwise of the models-in-use. And there was clear evidence of change in expectation by the students. From early cries of 'What are you going to do about it?', the students soon shifted their position to 'What can we all do to improve our situation?'

In response to the new roles which the students were developing, the staff began to assume the role of consultants to their client-learners in an open and honest atmosphere of co-learning. Problem-solving workshops were adopted as an important medium for student learning, and they soon also became important media for staff-development activities. Outside facilitators were brought in to conduct workshops on facilitation, assessment, evaluation and other topics. The members of the team greatly increased their competencies through this experiential combination of experience through running the programme with concept-based workshops.

Clearly the need to reflect on their experiences, to conceptualize improvements and to act accordingly were becoming normative behaviours by those in the team. Yet, somewhat surprisingly to me, the individuals in this course management group were not keen to share their experiences and/or conceptual maps with others outside the AP group. In fact, far from being seen as harbingers of further reform, they became somewhat besieged and were accused of being secretive and elitist.

In retrospect I did little to assuage these divisions, for I was up and away with a new and more ambitious curricular project: to facilitate the development of a novel undergraduate degree programme. This would be a more difficult challenge than the associate diploma programme in a number of important respects. The main issue was associated with the fact that as a degree programme there were expectations about essential knowledge known by graduate professionals which was less applicable to diplomate para-professionals.

The planning of this course programme would involve many more staff than its AP predecessor. It would, after all, be the major programme on offer in the school, being in the direct lineage of almost a hundred years of development of equivalent courses in the college. Once again I appointed a coordinator for a course planning team, and he in turn selected his interdisciplinary team from within the faculty. Keen to encourage the continued trend towards increasing autonomy by the academics acting across their disciplinary boundaries, I elected again not to become a full member of that group but chose instead the role of consultant to it.

My role as itinerant consultant to this group was to have a fairly negative impact. In fact the evolution of this programme I believe was markedly impeded by the unintended misuse of my power position. As this new programme would be the central one in our emerging family of courses, I was anxious to directly influence its development to a much greater extent than the associate diploma initiative. To this end I presented to the team a model which I believe embraced the triumvirate of notions I had brought to Hawkesbury with me. I had continued to develop and expose these ideas to my colleagues since my arrival, and felt confident that I had a sound conceptual map which integrated autonomous, experiential learning with systems theories.

As it transpired, the model which I injected into the proceedings was not conceptually sound and in fact was downright misleading as a guide to curricular development. Although this became clear fairly early on in the deliberations of the group, there was a reluctance to amend or reject it. In later discussions with the coordinator of the planning group he admitted that this was because I had appeared very defensive of it. This was not only a misuse of power on my part but was also anti-intellectual in the extreme. Once my model was abandoned, a new and much more appropriate one was generated within the group (in my absence) and it in turn has spurned generations of new models to which many of us have contributed. Individual autonomy paradoxically brings a synergy to group creativity.

This incident not only illustrates another major turning point in our collegial development but it also emphasizes the importance that models and metaphors have assumed in our learning environment as manifestations of our theories-in-use.

However, it was one thing to share our learning within the faculty and to achieve consensus on curricula based on our shared maps and models. It was quite another situation beyond the faculty. As we had predicted, there was marked opposition to our proposed degree programme, and it came from many sources. For many months I found myself on a never-ending circuit – from one group of sceptics to another: beyond the faculty but within the college; beyond the college within agriculture and its multitude of industries, professions and communities; beyond the college-present and into the college-past via the alumni; beyond agricultural education and into higher education itself through other institutions and bureaucracies. At every turn I found more hostile reactions than supportive ones (and after every experience I reflected on the incremental increase in my assertiveness since the previous occasion!). On all of these occasions the exposure to our maps and models was brief and this possibly served more to confuse than to clarify. First, many people were unaccustomed to actually addressing the issue of processes of learning, expecting instead to enter the usual fray about balance of content. Secondly, there were very few people who seemed comfortable with the basic assumptions about conceptual mapping, or the creation of metaphors and models as a basis for learning how to change. And thirdly, there was the group of people who could see no reason at all for change from what currently existed. This latter group gained a disappointing number of supporters from among the alumni doggedly still calling itself (as it does to this day) the Old Boys Union!

All of these experiences, uncomfortable though they often were, provided me with ample opportunities to validate our emerging theories. They also provided impetus for continued refinement of the theories-in-use we were developing. It was also very important that I shared as much of these experiences with my colleagues as possible.

By now it was 1981 and I among others had read and had been markedly influenced by the theories of organizational learning proposed by Argyris and Schön. Debates about our theories-in-use as models became common, and we instituted a series of vehicles such as regular open forums, broadsheets and seminars to facilitate collaboration. This climate for sharing concepts and experiences continues to this day and is certainly one of the great strengths of our organization.

Literally dozens of models have been developed and shared as the basis for changes in our practices, just as shared experiences in practice have led to the generation of new models. Four major themes in particular recur in these interactions, and models that incorporate their messages have persisted through the years. Over time there have been many amendments and refinements to them, but they remain the maps to our territory. They represent:

(a) the idea of learning as a rhythmic, recurring process akin to problem tackling, and involving the concrete and the abstract, reflection and action;
(b) the idea of a methodology being a set of activities representing this cyclic learning process and the notion that different but related methodologies are appropriate for different levels of learning or problem tackling;

235

(c) the representation of agriculture as a human activity system involving transactions between people and their environments; and

(d) the desired outcome of learning modelled as a matrix of competencies combining, on the one hand, confluent development of the learner across the three domains of knowledge (cognitive), skills (conative) and attitudes (affective) with, on the other, particular attributes such as effective communication, autonomous/interdependent learning behaviour, and systems agriculture.

We have defined capable systems agriculturalists as those who:

1. Approach real world agricultural situations, experiences, events and problems with a sense of their 'wholeness'.

2. Appreciate that a convenient way of examining such 'wholeness' is to view it as a dynamic system of interrelated physical, biological and human parts.

3. Can differentiate purposeful (goal setting) systems from purposive (goal seeking) ones and demonstrate problem identification in each, using analytical strategies from systems-based ones to technological and scientific reductionist approaches when appropriate.

4. Can use appropriate analytical skills to describe the essential features of such systems including their purposes, environmental forces, behaviour, transformations, dynamics, cybernetics and regulations, relevant subsystems and components, management and measures of performance.

5. Are able to use appropriate methods of analysis and synthesis to identify and help effect feasible and desirable improvements in problem situations within systems, contingent upon the nature of the situation and systems involved.

6. Are able to design and desirably manage novel farming systems which are stable, sustainable and equitable.

7. Can clearly define their roles in relation to any problem and be conscious of the impact of those roles in the functioning of the system under review.

8. Are able to communicate effectively with a wide spectrum of people involved with agricultural and related systems and help them learn more about the systems with which they are involved.

9. Are aware of, and can optimize, the confluency of their three domains of abilities (intellectual, affective and conative or behavioural) and, through continued experiential and autonomous learning activities, maintain their usefulness into the future.

(Bawden and Valentine, 1984)

Graduates with these characteristics certainly have approaches to problematic situations which are very different from those of their counterparts with conventional degrees in agricultural science. They are competent at a range of methodologies, all of which essentially reflect the experiential process and their professional ethic as one of helping.

We did not start out with the intention of creating the systems agriculturalist.

The early documentation of the curricula makes no mention of the concept. But the construct emerged as we practised our own learning about agricultural and rural development, about theories of intelligence and learning, about learning from experience and autonomy, about learning styles and individuality, about intuition and rationality and about cognitive psychology and epistemology. And as we have learnt and adapted our environment to fit emerging needs and adapted ourselves to emerging environmental forces, so we have become increasingly autonomous as individuals.

In essence, then, each academic as an individual learner is encouraged to explore his or her own experiences in agriculture and/or educational practice, utilizing the common maps – the organizational theories-in-use.

Reflections on these actions lead to further personal insights, new meanings if you will, and possible suggested modifications to the theories and models. These suggestions in turn are presented to colleagues for debate in task-force groups, course-management groups or across the entire faculty, as seems appropriate and comfortable. In this manner we are at once autonomous and interdependent, using our colleagues as sources of meanings as well as validators of meanings we ourselves have created.

Through this process of participation, then, we manage changes in both 'territory' and 'maps'. Yet while there is the imperative to innovate in the face of change, there is also the need to maintain a stability about the organization. Increasingly we are able to see these two features of change and stability as two faces of the same phenomenon of development: we are stable because we change!

It is our view that our students, our outreach clients, our visitors and our administrators all enter our learning system as active participants, as co-learners. From the beginning we share our models and maps, not just of agriculture but of our ways of learning. Our aim with all of these people is, as with ourselves, to help them become more effective autonomous learners and to encourage their interdependency. Rather than as a classroom for *diffusing* knowledge we see our faculty as a network of learners *creating* both new knowledge and new ways of knowing.

The spirit of this is captured in the extract from our handbook describing the overview of the undergraduate degree programme (refer to Figure 2).

Course overview

The emphasis throughout the program is on developing the students' ability to take effective action in tackling agricultural problems. Learning-by-doing is the way this is done. Problem-based learning projects replace the conventional approach of studying subjects. The learning process is active and controlled by the learner.

Phase Themes

Although described as discrete phases the program is regarded as a continuum with the common focus of the competencies of the systems agriculturalist.   *continued*

Phase I – Semester 1 and 2

The key emphasis of this Phase is discovery of the systems nature of agriculture, the interaction of ecosystems and social systems, and analysis of problem situations and an introduction to problem-solving methodologies. Group tasks are a feature of the Phase and the group is a learning laboratory for development of communication skills.

Phase II – Semester 3,4,5

This Phase is centred on an off-campus experience, usually living and working on a cooperator's farm. The first semester of the Phase concentrates on introducing students to issues associated with manipulation of farming systems by managers and encouraging them to prepare for the off-campus experience. The second semester of the Phase is spent off-campus in a 'real-world' agricultural situation and allows students to develop competencies in problem-solving and situation-improving in agricultural situations. Students utilise their earlier learning to understand and participate in the dynamics and management of the situation. There is also opportunity to study the place of the system in the regional socio-economic environment and assess the impact of agriculture on the physical environment and on wider systems.

The third semester of the Phase allows students to use College resources and their off-campus experience to complete projects related to their off-campus situation and their own learning.

Phase III – Semester 6 and 7

The purpose of this phase is to allow students the opportunity to further develop their learning skills and to gain specialised competencies in an area or areas of agriculture of particular relevance to them, especially as it relates to their immediate employability. They do this by developing a profile of the competencies needed by a graduate in their chosen career area and by initiating and carrying out situation-improving and problem-solving projects that will enable the competencies to develop. They are encouraged to carry out projects in actual career settings during the Phase and a trend is developing in which students work on projects in conjunction with potential employers.

Learning strategies

While the relative balance between them varies as students progress through the program, there are essentially three types of learning strategies used:

1. Sequenced learning experiences, designed by staff around problems associated with various aspects of farming systems and the social and environmental forces that shape and affect them.
2. Unsequenced but staff-structured learning experiences, generally designed to meet students' needs for specific knowledge or skills.
3. Unsequenced, self-structured learning experiences.

With the increasing development of autonomy in learning as a student progresses throughout the program, there is decreasing emphasis placed on staff-initiated learning strategies and increasing emphasis on student-initiated experiences. Phase Two, in the pre-farm semester, has predominantly unsequenced, staff-initiated experiences and in the farm and post-farm semesters has mainly student-initiated learning experiences. Phase Three has a predominance of student-initiated learning experiences.

Assessment and progression

Assessment takes two forms, summative and formative.

Summative assessment occurs at the end of the phases and assesses a student's eligibility to progress to the next phase of the program and to graduate. The assessors are looking for evidence that the student's competencies as a systems agriculturalist have developed to the point where they can avail themselves of the learning opportunities of the next phase (progression) or are eligible to practise as a professional systems agriculturalist (graduation).

Formative assessment is the assessment of the learning projects which are the means by which the student develops his/her competencies. Formative assessment takes many forms – quizzes, self-assessment questions, written feedback on assignments and projects, feedback on performance in seminars and group activities, feedback on problem-centred projects by clients and resources and people, written comments on competency development by staff, peers and clients. The evidence accruing from formative feedback is incorporated into summative assessment submissions by students and is considered by summative assessment interview panels.

Satisfactory and unsatisfactory grades only are awarded for phases 1 and 2. Graduation with Merit may be awarded to students who demonstrate an outstanding level of competency development.

Figure 2

Further details of this particular course have been published elsewhere (Bawden and Valentine, 1984) as have details of our spiralling model of experiential learning (Bawden, 1985) and our approach to systemic methodologies of learning (Bawden *et al*, 1984). If all of these developments in our functions remain areas of fertile debate, within the faculty, so too do notions about and actions for change in our organizational structures. This perforce includes the role of leadership and in particular the role of the Dean.

Reflections on leadership

The notion of the designated leader as the sole functional decision-maker, strategist, change agent or illuminator has long been abandoned by the majority in this faculty. As autonomous beings we are all functional leaders from time to time, depending on circumstances. In fact one of the powers endowed by autonomy is to choose the roles one wishes to play in any group situation.

These may be different leadership roles or styles contingent upon the needs of the situation, and Joy Higgs expands on this concept of situational leadership in her chapter in this book. Or they may be roles where one concedes to others the function of leadership as source of influence and actions. The attributes one seeks in a person as a leader must therefore be cognizant of these dimensions. Equally the personal competencies one seeks to improve as a leader in this context are multidimensional.

Mention has already been made of the concept of leadership of Lieberman and his colleagues which I adopted as a useful model to guide my actions in my early days as Dean at Hawkesbury. Like all my conceptual maps, this one, too, was eternally tentative. It has been greatly amended by my subsequent experiences and by my reconstructions of the basic idea of leadership as a source of influence and power. Key ideas in this reinterpretation have included those relating to factors and styles of leadership (Bolman, 1976; Hersey and Blanchard, 1982; Lieberman *et al*, 1973) to styles and group roles (Belbin, 1981), to powers of influence (Luke, 1972; Smith, 1980), to types of interventions (Heron, 1975) and to the facilitation of learning (Brundage and MacKeracher, 1980; Burgess, 1977; Rogers, 1969). Of particular importance have been the notion of power and its relationships with authority. Ruth Elliott (1980) has made the elegant distinction between two approaches to the concept of power: power over and power to. Thus,

> One approach is concerned to analyse power as a relationship between individuals or groups which enables one individual or group to impose its will on the other. The emphasis here is on the power of A, as an individual or group, *over* B. The second approach is concerned to analyse power as a 'system property', rather than as a property of individuals or groups which enables the successful realisation of 'system' goals. The emphasis here is on power *to*, in the sense of the capacity to achieve certain goals or objectives.

As I reflect on the past nine years of my Deanship at Hawkesbury I recognize a marked transition in my style of leadership. In spite of rationalization and self-protestation to the contrary, there is ample evidence to suggest that my early days as Dean were characterized by authority through a power-over model: from the injection of inappropriate models into curriculum-development initiatives to the centralization of decisions concerning tenure, promotions and sabbatical leave; from recommendations effectively abolishing discipline-based depart-ments to decisions to terminate contracts of senior academics; from the commercial reorientation of the college farms to the retrenchment of farm staff; from persistence with models of autonomous learning to insistence on the merits of systemic approaches. All of these initiatives revealed what Weber (1947) has defined as 'the probability that one actor within a social relationship will be in a position to carry out his own will despite resistance, regardless of the basis on which this probability rests' (p 321).

As the years have progressed, I believe that I have learnt from my experiences and from the mistakes that such an authority-laden approach has brought. As a consequence I have consciously adopted strategies that are much more reflective of the model of power to, enabling the system to generate and achieve its own purposes and express its own learning. The response, as could be predicted by those who support the benefits of interdependence through autonomy, has been overwhelmingly constructive.

A comprehensive and participative systems analysis of the school, led by two colleagues, Bob Macadam and Roger Packham (1984, 1985), has enabled the development of clear and concise purposes and functions. Extensive debate

240

around the functional models developed by these colleagues has led to immeasurable improvement in the quality of our educational strategies and in the overall climate of the organization. It has also led to an organizational structure based on a management matrix with responsibility and authority spread across the entire faculty. We have moved from a bureaucratic school structure to a collegial faculty one and, through participation, now represent an actively learning system.

Conclusion

I am not sure which is cause and which is effect, but in designing a system to encourage the development of autonomy in student learning we have created a system which has encouraged the development of autonomy all round! And in liberating the components of the system to be autonomous we have heightened their interdependency. One of the neatest ways to express the transition from a teacher-centred learning system of dependent students to one centred on interdependent learners is captured by the change from power over to power to. This shift authority from teacher to learner or learning group, dictates the adaptation of leaders to facilitators.

At Hawkesbury we are led to conclude that fiddling with curricula to encourage student self-direction can eventually result in a major transformation of the entire organization itself. We are also led to believe that although this has led to a marked improvement in the quality of education we offer, 'there still has to be a better way of doing this'! Without putting too fine a point on it, democracy in a society is a function of the autonomy of its people. It behoves us as educators to develop educational environments which encourage its acquisition! In doing so we must be prepared to innovate and change the way we do things.

Chapter 15

Putting it into Practice: Promoting Independent Learning in a Traditional Institution

Malcolm Cornwall,
Department of Physical Sciences, Brighton Polytechnic

Introduction

The arguments and case studies presented so far in this book provide a persuasive – one would like to think convincing – argument for the introduction of more opportunities for independence in learning within the general framework of tertiary education. Let us assume that you, a typical reader, are persuaded or perhaps even convinced by them, and have now decided that you would like to go ahead and introduce much more independent learning into your own courses. There remains the problem of putting the idea into practice in *your* particular course, with your kind of students and within the constraints of your particular department and institution, all of which are, of course, not quite like those of anyone else.

Are there therefore any general lessons to be learned from the case studies and from the general experience of others which can help you in your particular circumstances? I think there are.

The case studies illustrate several widely different ways in which one may convert innovative enthusiasm for the general ideas into practical and successful concrete realities. But through all the case studies, there runs the common strand of a carefully thought out organizational structure or framework within which students can develop and exercise independence in their learning. The need for such structuring is, I believe, the major lesson that can be learned from the diverse experience of earlier innovators. And it is the main topic of this chapter.

There are, too, among the case studies, several hints of the inevitability of institutional resistance to change and the problems of educational innovation. When we are faced with proposals for new approaches, or simply with new ideas, which challenge some of our most cherished beliefs about the 'right' way that teaching and learning should take place, not surprisingly we will be inclined to argue against them and resist their implementation. For the proponents of independence in learning these reactions can create very severe problems. Some of these problems and possible ways in which they can be tackled are dealt with later in this chapter.

All innovators in the field of independent learning will, however, find that their initial problems are not so much practical ones, but are those related to the misunderstandings, anxieties and straightforward prejudices of their colleagues. In the final section of this chapter, therefore, I consider some of the more familiar arguments against independent learning, attempt to analyse them and outline some of the counter-arguments that might be deployed.

But before we can properly discuss the organizational and innovative issues and problems, it seems to me that we must first define in 'operational' terms what we mean by 'independence' in learning. As a preliminary to my later discussion, I will first consider one approach – a tentative and rather simplified one – to the problem of definition. My suggestion is that a measure of the degree of independence in learning that a course provides can be indicated by the amount of *choice* that a student is allowed within the curriculum.

Degrees of independence in learning

In higher education our methods of teaching are notoriously ill-defined and loosely described (Atherton, 1972). Even the lecture, the ubiquitous workhorse of the academic world, describes a wide variety of activities and is by no means a unanimously agreed set of procedures. It is therefore not surprising that the much richer concept of 'independent learning' can materialize in such a variety of organizational formats, as illustrated in the case studies. All the contributors would be very likely to subscribe to the general definition of 'independent learning' proposed by John Heron in Chapter 4 and endorsed and discussed in the chapter by John Powell. But what in *practical* terms have each of these (and many other) approaches to independence in learning in common? One such characteristic, perhaps the most crucial, is that they all provide the learner with *some degree of personally significant choice* in one or more aspects of the course of studies. After all, 'independence', in common parlance, implies that the individual has a large degree of choice, considerable autonomy, in decision-making affecting his or her aims and activities, and the values he or she puts on them.

Some of the factors in the curriculum, in terms of which we might 'measure' the degree of choice with which a course of study provides a student, are suggested in Figure 1.

In this diagram I have also attempted to indicate an approximate ordering or 'hierarchy' of these factors. My criterion for the suggested order of the 'steps' is the extent to which the provision of choice in each of these aspects of the curriculum is likely to require reorganization of a conventional 'teacher pre-scribed, teacher-presented, teacher-paced and teacher-assessed' course. For example, allowing students choice of their specific objectives is likely to have more impact on the conventional curricular pattern than, say, allowing only the

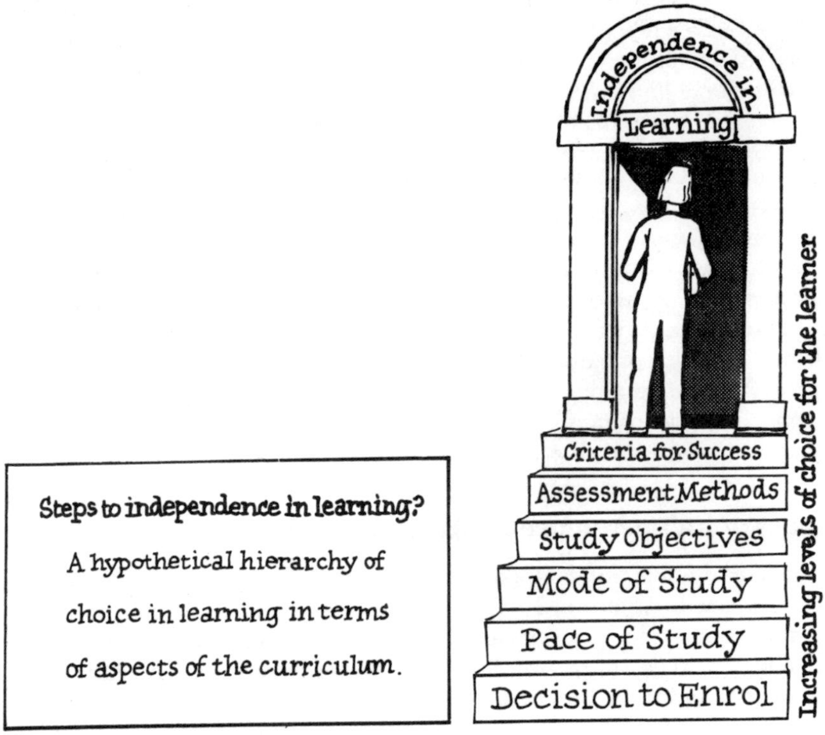

Independence in Learning

Increasing levels of choice for the learner

Criteria for Success
Assessment Methods
Study Objectives
Mode of Study
Pace of Study
Decision to Enrol

Steps to independence in learning?

A hypothetical hierarchy of choice in learning in terms of aspects of the curriculum.

Figure 1

choice of the ways in which learning takes place. But allowing students to choose assessment methods and criteria may create the need for even more profound reorganization of the 'normal' course pattern.

It is worth emphasizing that the suggested hierarchy is based more on practical organizational and innovative considerations than on any logical interrelationships. The factors I have indicated are simply those that, *in practice*, are aspects of the curriculum within which students can be given more or less freedom of choice.

In practical terms, as the student moves up the 'steps' he is in effect being required successively to ask him or herself questions such as: 'Shall I join this course?'; 'When and how fast will I study?'; 'In what way will I study?'; 'What books or other resources shall I use?'; 'What specific objective shall I pursue in my studies?'; 'What particular knowledge, skills or attitudes do I wish to acquire?'; 'How do I wish these to be assessed?'; 'What should be the criteria for my success or failure?'.

It will be obvious that defining any course of study in such a one-dimensional way is a gross oversimplification of the true range of variability which can exist between courses which seem to offer the same degree of 'independence' to the learner. Nevertheless, there does seem to be some relationship between the extent to which a course allows choice in the sense I have outlined, and the organizational and innovative problems it raises. The further your course is, or you would like it to be, up the hierarchy, the more radical are the issues that are raised and the bigger are the problems of implementation and organization.

One might add in passing that in the present context, it is the relaxation of the prescriptive and controlling influence of the teacher and of the education system that is our concern. Individuals are still subject to the pressures, coercions and inducements of the 'real' world, and to the constraints and limitations of their own abilities and character, no matter how 'free' they are allowed to be within the sometimes rather cosy educational world. We might even interpret our advocacy of 'independence' in learning in higher education as an attempt to remove, or at least reduce, the mediation of the teacher between the learner and the 'real' world of unformulated problems, non-predigested information, personal decision-making and value judgements.

Providing a framework: some prerequisites for success

The case studies illustrate the fact that giving independence to students does not mean abandoning one's responsibilities as a teacher; that giving up the rigidly teacher-centred structure of the traditional course in tertiary education does *not* mean having no structure.

Certainly, a move towards independence in learning and a relaxation of some conventional constraints must be associated with greater freedom of choice for the learner; but, as seems to be the case for freedom more generally, one may well create more genuine autonomy by imposing a well-defined and agreed set of 'rules of the game'. Occasionally, the 'rules' can be minimal or even just taken for granted. Thus there have been some successful examples of courses of independent study in which students have been given nothing but the general indication of what it is they are expected to do, and a final deadline.

The School of Independent Studies at Lancaster University (Percy and Ramsden, 1980) has used a minimal framework along these lines for several years. Likewise in most colleges and universities in the USA students can earn academic credit by 'independent study', in which a small section of a course is given over to the private study of self-selected topics, on which 'term papers' must be submitted for assessment. Approaches like these certainly seem to work for some students, but they do tend to put a premium on the almost unaided efforts of students to learn by themselves.

It is not accidental that options of this kind, whether formally offered or not, are often taken by mature students, who already possess some of the necessary skills for working in this way. For the typical 18-year-old entrant into tertiary education sudden immersion into this sort of independence is more likely to lead to sinking rather than learning to swim. Independence, like freedom, needs a framework to nurture and support it.

The general features of a framework or structure for independent learning are as follows:

1. clearly defined goals
2. availability of the necessary material and human resources
3. an understanding of the roles and responsibilities of both the teacher and the students
4. arrangements by which both parties can be prepared for the new demands to be imposed on them and can acquire some of the appropriate skills in a 'fail-safe' way
5. means by which the success of the course can be checked as it proceeds and if necessary changed without bureaucratic snags.

These, it seems to me, are the minimum requirements of 'structuring' that it is desirable to include in any innovative course. For courses which aim to promote independence in learning they are essential.

But can we go beyond these generalities? Unfortunately, the reader expecting any neat recipe or blueprint for promoting independence in his or her own course will be disappointed. This is not only because there are obviously a large number of varieties and degrees of 'independence', nor only because there is also an infinite variety of local conditions and constraints. Even if other things were equal, the educational environment and, above all, people, are never quite the same from place to place or time to time. Ultimately the minor and often unexpected details of an educational situation can make or break an innovation. Most important is probably the accidental and largely uncontrollable mix of personalities, interests, motivations and aspirations to be found among the participants in the average course – most important, the teacher him/herself. There is no neat formula for dealing with these variables. However, it is worth saying a little more about two of the aspects of structuring listed above, as they are particularly important. One is the need for *careful preparation* and induction of both students and teachers; the other is the desirability of careful 'quality control' or *evaluation* of the processes and the outcome of the course. I will also discuss briefly some of the possible implications for structuring of the differences between 'regular' and mature students.

Preparing students and teachers

Too often, it seems, students and their teachers are plunged into new ways of teaching and learning on the assumption that they can pick up the new skills needed. Sudden and unprepared imposition of the demands and responsibilities of extensive autonomy in learning can be counter-productive. As John Powell emphasizes in Chapter 6, both students and teachers need to learn to cope with the new kinds of role they will be expected to play. This process cannot be rushed and time for adjustment is very important. It is not simply a matter of acquiring new technical skills: long-standing assumptions about the function and behaviour of an academic teacher may need to be changed.

Telling students or teachers in talks or in introductory notes about the new pressures and roles is not enough. Gradual and controlled introduction of the actual experience of working within the new framework should be built in as part of the innovation itself. The need for gradualism in this respect has been emphasized in a different context by Kelly (1955) as quoted by Gibbs (1981). Kelly describes the process of acceptance of new ideas as one of cautious negotiation. He emphasizes the great importance of the existing way in which people construct their personal worlds. This personal construct cannot be lightly abandoned on the say-so of another or because of the sudden appearance of new kinds of demands. Change must come about in a gradual and piecemeal way.

Throughout the process of weaning students into greater autonomy and responsibility, a major role of the teacher and of the course structure must be to provide guidance and support. Learners must be assured that a 'safety net' exists and that they are not entirely dependent on their own (probably initially rather meagre) resources. One of the problems for teachers, like parents, is to judge correctly when and to what extent to let go of the hand of those for whom they have a responsibility. There is no way, unfortunately, in which this can be done without taking *some* risks. It is particularly in this respect that a gradual approach may be necessary.

There are examples among the case studies of ways in which students may be prepared for independence in the educational context. There are also descriptions elsewhere of other ways in which students and teachers can learn some of the skills involved using various forms of workshops, games, simulations and group sessions (eg; Gibbs, 1981; Cornwall *et al*, 1977; Jaques, 1984). Certainly there should be no serious organizational (or innovative) problems in most institutions about introducing small components of independence into otherwise conventional courses. For example, students in small groups can be asked to prepare over several weeks short reports on a subject of their own choice (within the subject area of the course) and to present a talk on it to a full session of their fellow students; or students can be asked to study a part of a course independently, using the teacher as a consultant. These minor innovations are undoubtedly trivial when compared with the more full-blooded approaches to independent learning described in the case studies. Nevertheless, they can provide a very useful first taste of independence for many students and their teachers. Even a small component of such activities within an otherwise closely prescribed and directed curriculum seems to loom very large in the perceptions of most students, when they first experience it.

A final innovative tip concerns the need to use what might be called the Jesuit approach; get them early and they are yours for life! In the present context this is not as sinister as it may sound. It means simply that the skills and attitudes appropriate to independent study are likely to be best promoted by allowing students to experience *some* autonomy as early as possible during a course of study. The attitudes and expectations of students about what is expected of them and what are the usual methods of teaching and learning, seem to be firmly established quite soon after they enter the new and unfamiliar world of higher education. If part of that normal pattern of activity includes elements of independent study, the later introduction of 'real' independence is likely to be much easier, and will not be so likely to be regarded as deviant.

Innovative problems

Innovation – the introduction of the new or unfamiliar – is difficult in any field. In tradition-bound higher education it is more difficult than in most other fields. The introduction of independent learning is likely to provoke more resistance than many other innovations, because it challenges some of the more fundamental preconceptions about how learning can and should take place. However, during the 1980s, a colder climate of financial cuts, staff reductions, higher student-staff ratios has enveloped higher education in many countries, often creating low staff morale and insecurity. In this climate proposals for introducing independent learning can create an ambivalent response. On one hand there appears the promise of a relaxation of the increasing pressures on teachers through a reduction in 'contact hours'; on the other the threat that a reduction in apparent 'teaching loads' (a telling phrase) by administrators could lead to even further cuts in staffing. In both cases the fallacy lies in the confusion of teaching *efficiencies* as measured by student-staff ratios and unit costs, and *effectiveness* of learning as measured by the professional and personal development of students. These very practical concerns for professional survival and institutional efficiency tend to override pedagogic objections that can be raised against independence in learning. I will return to them later. Nevertheless, even when institutional problems are resolved there remain numerous arguments against change in general (see, for example, Astin, 1976). These arguments may take the form of the 'not-invented-here' syndrome, or the 'we haven't done it before' response or, perhaps, the many variants on the theme of deference to potentially disapproving higher authority of the 'mother-wouldn't-like-it' type. Among such institutions are one's academic board or senate, the accrediting bodies like the Council for National Academic Awards in the UK, the various professional bodies like the Council for Engineering Institutions or, more diffusely, 'Industry'. Such arguments must be treated seriously, if not always with respect. At the very least they force innovators to reassess their own arguments, to build in safeguards, to plan and prepare the ground more carefully than they otherwise would. It is not unknown for over-eager innovators to allow their enthusiasm to carry them across the logical gaps in their arguments or organizational proposals. The rationale and the organizational plans may look impeccable on paper but the reality will not be anything like as neat.

Those who put some form of independent learning into practice as the basis for a whole course must be prepared for special difficulties. Roughly speaking, the amount of innovative effort necessary will be proportional to the location of the innovation up the 'steps' in Figure 1. How much you can 'get away with' depends to a great extent on how much you want to rewrite the conventional script for the roles of teacher and student.

New approaches in teaching and learning have rarely in the past been initiated by institutions at a formal level: the so-called 'top down' approach. The initiative usually arises by a 'bottom up' movement from the enthusiastic and energetic efforts of a few individual teachers.

The pioneering spirit seems to be an essential ingredient in carrying through an innovation, especially if it challenges cherished notions of what is possible, right or proper. But this brings dangers. We can probably all think of exciting new developments in our own departments or institutions which flourished briefly but were too closely associated with one or two individuals to survive their disappearance from the scene, or the flagging of their interest and enthusiasm for their own brainchild. For an innovation to stick it must become properly institutionalized; it must become a new tradition. That means that the successful innovator, having proved the feasibility of the new approach, must attempt to get the institutional regulations, especially the procedures for the allocation of resources and the decision-making mechanism, amended so as to provide formalized support for the new approach. This may sound over-legalistic, but when the going gets tough, for example when there is a financial pruning exercise, the innovation which is tolerated as an act of institutional goodwill or simply tacked on to the departmental organization is the easiest to dispense with.

The hard realism that has been imposed on us in the bleak eighties has paradoxically promoted the possibility of quite radical change. Savage reductions in staffing in which have been imposed in many areas, and demands for increasing efficiency have led to searches for more flexible and cost effective methods of teaching. Under the pressure of maintaining perceived standards with diminishing numbers of teachers and other support staff, independent learning has been 'discovered' by some institutions (and sometimes by the staff themselves) as a partial remedy for their problems. The motivation may be educationally suspect and the response sometimes less than enthusiastic, for reasons mentioned earlier. Nevertheless, in pedagogic terms, the newly discovered enthusiasm does offer long frustrated innovators an unprecedented opportunity for genuine educational change. Even though they may ostensibly encourage new approaches that appear to increase efficiency and the use of limited staff resources, an approach which reduces the class contact hours by substituting autonomous activity on the part of the student is a very attractive proposition – fewer staff, equal or improved output. Unfortunately, the implicit model is simply one in which formal teaching is reduced and the student is expected to make up the loss by private study.

It is clear from the rest of this book, reducing class contact hours is *not* synonymous with the reduction of the time the teacher spends in teaching, except in the narrow sense of formal lecturing. The enthusiasm for autonomous study engendered by institutional and national demands for increased productivity must be tempered by the recognition that reduced contact hours can easily be matched or exceeded by the increased hours of preparation, guidance, assessment and management of 'independent' study. However, North East London Polytechnic (see Chapter 13) has found ways of maintaining the educational integrity of their approach within a limited budget.

Some barriers to change

The 'authority', especially at the national level, often tends to be thought of as an inhibitor of change and a reactionary maintainer of tradition. In fact, it may be eager itself to stimulate and nurture educational innovation and sometimes in over-cautious hidebound institutions and not always for narrowly economic motives. The most dominant and immediate resisters of change are much more likely to be one's colleagues whose motives are many and varied (and certainly not always unreasonable!). Administrators, too, are likely to frown upon deviations from convention which threaten to upset the system.

For example, in science and technology departments used to the idea that student attainment can and always should be quantitatively measurable in quasi-precise examination percentages, it is not surprising that there might be suspicion of courses which place emphasis on difficult-to-measure skills and attitudes. The administration also usually demands neat ranking of students according to exact numerical criteria of performance, with pass-fail decisions sometimes dependent on one or two percentage points. It is as if Lord Rayleigh's dictum, which may be paraphrased: 'If you can't measure it, you don't know much about it', has been taken seriously beyond the realms of classical physics itself.

The system is also likely to be thrown into confusion by attempts to schedule a course of independent study in other than the conventional way, ie with teaching hours divided neatly and periodically into one, two or three hour slots once or twice a week for a particular course. Attempts by a teacher to use larger blocks of time or to plan a teaching schedule flexibly according to the likely demands of students at different stages of a course require considerable negotiation with academic colleagues and administrators who may be unwilling to be so flexible. Administrators in particular are very sensitive to any blurring of the apparently well-defined 'contact hours' criterion which in many institutions is the primary index used to calculate the all-important student-staff ratio for the department and the institution. These are just a few of the many organizational problems.

I have given several examples of what might be called structural sources of resistance to change. Anyone advocating or trying to initiate independent learning on a significant scale will usually experience a wealth of objections and

Figure 2
© Sue Curtiss, Malcolm Cornwall, 1977

criticism related to more fundamental educational issues. In the last section of this chapter I have tried to produce a short compendium of arguments against independence in learning (based on actual conversations and discussion), together with an indication of some of the responses that one might make.

Seven arguments against independent study

Left to themselves students would work at a low level and standards would drop
A common and natural concern of academics is that standards will fall on the introduction of a new and unfamiliar method of teaching and learning. There is, however, much evidence to suggest that the level and standard of work is more often higher in independent study than we would expect from students on conventional courses at comparable stages. Yes, there are students who perform poorly when learning to study independently. But the weak student is to be found whatever approaches we adopt to teaching and learning, and we do not (or should not) judge the effectiveness of a new approach in terms of the performance of the least successful. On average, standards even in conventional terms are certainly not necessarily lower.

Lurking behind this criticism, too, is the assumption that level and standard are to be judged only in terms of the almost exclusive criterion of most conventional courses, namely in terms of the coverage of the standard content of a predigested and conventionally acceptable syllabus.

The outcome of independent learning must be judged at least as much in terms of the acquisition of skills and abilities as of the acquisition of factual knowledge. Not least among these abilities is that of learning autonomously. Moreover, one might question whether conventional courses can inculcate in students the range of intellectual skills which are usually referred to in the statements of aims and objectives of courses. The emphasis, in practice, on the production of 'right' answers would seem to mitigate against any real intellectual relationships between students and the material studied. Students become concerned with satisfying the expectations of particular teachers rather than adopting a critical attitude to the subject matter.

It has to be accepted, however, that if independent learning were adopted more widely, the ability to reproduce given areas of content in conventional examinations might decline. This would be more than compensated for by an improvement in other abilities of much longer term importance, not least the ability to plan and manage one's own learning. And although the assessment of these abilities is not amenable to the quasi-precise methods we employ in general in higher education, there are various ways in which we can monitor and evaluate their development.

Finally, the criticism presupposes that the independent learner would be 'left to himself'. But independent learning is not synonymous with learning in isolation. Students have a tutor or tutors (as with research students) and probably a group with whom work can be planned and discussed. The tutor acts as a resource, a counsellor, and maybe even a devil's advocate, who helps students towards reaching their own ends in their own ways, rather than as a prescriber of given goals and means, as he or she is in the conventional approach. The function of tutors is to be a sounding board or sympathetic ear, and their reactions can stimulate students to explore more deeply or investigate alternative strategies.

Students are not capable of working independently
This objection is usually based on the assumption that students lack the basic knowledge and skills from which to begin to work independently. After at least 18 years of life in general and 13 years of formal education, students are seemingly unable to take any initiative for deciding what and how they will learn and the task remains the sole responsibility of the teacher. Nevertheless, approximately three or four years later, raw graduates entering the professions or becoming research students are regarded as being capable of a very high degree of autonomy, especially with respect to being responsible for their own learning. Should we conclude that this is the result of a process of maturation which occurs at approximately 21 years of age during the rather sharp transition between student and graduate status? It does not seem at all obvious why three more years of an education almost identical in its approach to that already experienced in school should succeed in creating people capable of continuing to learn efficiently and independently where the previous 13 years have failed. In reality, it is of course the necessity to learn independently which produces the ability. Clearly, the only way to learn to swim is to get into the water, and it is patently better to do this in the presence of someone who can rescue you when you sink and can encourage you to try again, rather than when you are alone and in danger of drowning. From the moment of taking one's feet off the bottom and clumsily splashing about, expertise will develop through a combination of advice from the instructor and watching other people, but mainly through hard practice. So, too, with learning to learn independently. To expect the student to have the skills to operate successfully in the very early stages is an unrealistic as expecting a child to swim on his or her first day at the seaside. Some students will need to be encouraged into the water, others restrained from rushing in headlong. All will need help in developing their skills over time. But, just as the child of an overprotective parent is unlikely to learn to swim, so the student of an overprotective teacher will not learn to be an independent learner.

It is more efficient and much quicker to use teacher-directed learning than to allow students to find out for themselves
In terms of a set syllabus it is probably, but not necessarily, the case that the independent learner will not so quickly cover the ground. However, if the formulation of problems, the development of approaches to learning and of research techniques, and several other intellectual skills are considered to be at least as important as the acquisition of a body of knowledge, then it will not be time wasted.

At a more fundamental level, the implied 'efficiency' of conventional approaches is questionable. Even in terms of content-centred aims, the economy of teacher-directed learning seems illusory. Academic teachers approach their subject matter from a position of in-depth knowledge. Their teaching is a summary of complex material which by its condensation has, inevitably, lost many of its original subtleties. The process of oversimplification continues as the teacher's comments are transformed into students' notes. Students thus learn to 'know', for example, that the working classes are linguistically inept, and repeat it endlessly in examination scripts. In science courses, too, the artificially neat and closed character of a conventional syllabus belies the real nature of science and its methodology. Teacher-directed learning can easily cover a lot of ground; I doubt that students are necessarily gaining much familiarity with the scenery *en route*. To some critics the 'finding out for themselves' character of independent learning seems to have been misinterpreted as akin to an advanced form of 'discovery learning'. It is, of course, nothing of the sort. There is no suggestion that present knowledge should be kept hidden from students. On the contrary, through the necessity of using a wide range of media they will be likely to explore well beyond the scope of what any individual teacher might reasonably be expected to offer. It could be argued that learning restricted only to that knowledge which is prescribed by the teacher is potentially far more limited than resource-based learning, and is therefore less efficient.

In a highly structured subject it is essential that students be given a firm foundation of basic facts on which they can build
This objection can be approached at two levels. First, given that the students with whom we deal have already acquired some of the basic material through their school courses, it would not be unreasonable to expect that they have reached a point where they might become independent learners. But it is often claimed that students have not, in fact, mastered the basics sufficiently well to move on by themselves. If that is indeed the case, we need to ask the question already posed: will further instruction of a similar kind succeed where it has failed before?

It might, on the other hand, be claimed that the relevant basic facts are different from those met in a school syllabus. Students will be ignorant of their existence so that even if they are literate and numerate in the broadest sense they will not be aware that the facts are there to be acquired. They will therefore attempt to solve problems without the benefit of relevant knowledge. But this is, of course, the situation of research students, especially at the start of their work. In this case we seem prepared to accept that the areas of existing knowledge required to solve a problem will become evident with the analysis of the problem, and that the nature of the project will force them to learn at the appropriate levels. If a text proves too difficult they will be forced back down the knowledge hierarchy until they reach a point which relates to their existing knowledge and level of understanding. In this way, the hierarchical and lateral connections will become apparent through the research activity itself, and the relevant part of the map of knowledge will be brought vividly to their attention. Why is it that this process should not be thought to be possible for the learner on other levels in higher education?

At a second and more basic level one might question the fundamental assumption concerning the way we learn which is implied in this criticism. This assumption is revealed by the metaphor in terms of which the objection is expressed, viz, that learning a subject is akin to building a house; first we must have the foundations (prescribed basic knowledge), and then we can build on this brick by brick (*quanta* of knowledge), each neatly fitting within the existing structure. Clearly, with such a model of learning, it is nonsense to attempt to build the second floor until the foundations and first floor are complete; that is, to expect students to fit in blocks of advanced knowledge before they have consolidated the lower levels. A reflection of this model of learning can be found in the rigidly hierarchical format of most scientific textbooks, where there is an assumed identity between the formal structure of knowledge and the form in which that knowledge is taught and learned.

An alternative, and more appropriate metaphor for learning, if we are to remain in the field of construction, is that of building a steel-framed structure in outer space – an interconnected network of potentially infinite extent, to which it is possible to add pieces in almost any order as long as they interconnect in some way, and form a pattern which makes sense to the builder. In this model there is nothing to prevent us completing the whole structure in outline before filling in the finer detail, or indeed starting at one place rather than another. I do not suggest that this analogy is necessarily consistent with all that is known about the learning process. But there is, of course, some support from the well-known work of Piaget, and of Bruner (eg 1966) for such a model of learning. The information processing school of cognitive psychology (Norman, 1973; Lindsay and Norman, 1977; Rumelhart, 1977) has also developed models of memory and of the cognitive processes more generally, based on much empirical evidence, which are consistent with the sort of network model referred to above.

As with any analogy, implicit or explicit, it is tempting but unwise to elaborate it beyond its intended purpose. Here that purpose is simply to attempt to show that the conventional assumption that there is a uniquely definable predetermined body of knowledge which is necessarily a prerequisite for any independent study, does not seem to be in accord with our experience of learning, nor with our growing knowledge of the learning process.

Students don't know what they ought to study
This objection is closely related to the previous one. It assumes that only when, like the teacher, you have a superior knowledge of the subject, can you see what knowledge it is appropriate to acquire at each stage. This aspect has already been discussed.

There are, however, other implications behind the criticism, involving what is seen as the educationalists' responsibility towards the professions and society at large. It may be argued that employers need to be sure that their employees have covered an agreed area of knowledge which they can then take for granted (though employers themselves rarely seem to adopt such a view – see, for example, Jevons and Turner, 1972). These agreed areas are often negotiated with professional bodies consisting of people who have been through traditional courses themselves and who are mainly concerned with the status of their profession. They are people whose central interests are, quite properly not only different from those of educationalists, but also, it could be argued, different from those of employers. The curriculum dictated by these bodies is not therefore necessarily related to the real needs of the job. Unfortunately the influence of the professional bodies cannot be ignored, whatever our views are as professional educationalists of the validity of their requirements.

Most students prefer to be taught

This is probably true. Being taught is a more comfortable, less threatening situation than learning independently. It is mainly a matter of finding out what you ought to know and how best to regurgitate this back to the teacher.

It is also true that many teachers enjoy the didactic lecturing situation. Although both students and tutors might have private doubts about the effectiveness of this approach as the most common mode of teaching, this mode is still the dominant one. Its dominance can be ascribed to a process of mutual seduction in which each party, while recognizing the undesirability of the situation, is egged on by the apparent willingness of the other.

It would, of course, be inconsistent with my central argument to disregard the preference of students concerning the methods by which they are taught, but preference implies choice, and choice is only real when, firstly, one is aware and has some experience of the alternatives and, secondly, the opportunity to choose is actually offered. In our present system neither condition seems in general to hold. Students, like the people in the advertisement for a famous brand of stout, can claim 'I don't like it because I've never tried it'. Usually they can go further and add, 'In any case it's not available'.

It would be fair to argue, however, that to substitute one approach to learning – independent study – for another is hardly going to increase choice. But even supposing one were to advocate the replacement of the existing approach by independent learning, rather than its introduction alongside the traditional, one would not limit student choice. Independent learning, as this book aims to show, is an aim and not simply a method. To become an independent learner is to attain an ability to use a wide variety of ways of learning including, if available and appropriate, a course of lectures.

You can't properly assess flexibility, adaptability and other such qualities

This view has already been discussed briefly earlier in this chapter. So often in education the assessment tail wags the curriculum dog. Certainly assessment is important. And the assessment of the skills and abilities which independent study claims to foster are often much more difficult to assess than the acquisition of factual knowledge and the ability of students to manipulate this knowledge in a fairly simple way. But the difficulty of assessment should not prevent us from structuring our courses in such a way as to develop other skills and abilities if we consider them to be important. Even within most existing courses the apparent objectivity and precision of our formal examination procedure belies the reality of how, ultimately, our judgements of students are actually made. No matter how many sophisticated statistical techniques we import into assessment, at the heart of the matter is a professional judgement based on a largely intuitive understanding of what we are trying to achieve. In project gradings, evaluation is often an ill-defined compromise between the differing professional judgements of various examiners.

Nevertheless, we can and should strive to improve and develop the means by which we assess the less objectifiable outcomes of our educational processes. In the meantime, we ought to recognize that we *do* make such assessments in the course of our roles as teachers, in assessing project work, in examiners' meetings, in writing references. And, whether we can assess them accurately or not, the skills and abilities which we all accept as important goals for higher education can clearly be more effectively promoted by certain educational approaches than others. I have no doubt that independent learning is one such approach.

The teacher's knowledge and expertise would not be properly used ...
Most teachers would not be able to work in this way

These are two separate but closely related criticisms. The first reflects an understandable anxiety that to allow and encourage independent learning is to devalue the present skills and capabilities of teachers. In blunter terms it implies that if we are not careful we will make ourselves redundant. It is possible to reassure critics that far from devaluing their technical knowledge and skills, their independent learners are likely to recognize and value highly the expert guidance which the teacher can provide in helping them with their learning difficulties. The second statement has been discussed briefly earlier in this chapter and it is based on a recognition that the acceptance of independent learning requires the teacher to adopt a new and unfamiliar role. Instead of expert interpreters and dispensers of specialist knowledge, teachers need to be guides to resources, consultants. Instead of being overseers of the progress of students through a prescribed syllabus, they need to be guides and advisers on their learning problems as they develop an increasing degree of self-direction. As emphasized earlier, the provision of advice, guidance and, frequently, direct assistance, is crucial to the development of autonomy in learning. Unfortunately, teachers in higher education are not necessarily going to possess the skills or experience appropriate to this non-didactic role. But if one accepts the need to move in a small way towards the development of greater independence in learning, then the onus is on us to acquire some of these skills. Staff retraining and development programmes are obviously part of the answer; 'learning on the job' by introducing or extending the degree of independent learning in existing courses in a limited and controlled way, is another. Above all, the continued use of our own skills as independent learners in order to extend our competence in appropriate ways, seems not only the most apt but also the most effective way of enabling us to help students to become more effective independent learners themselves.

Postscript

These, then, are just some of the arguments and counter-arguments that the enthusiast for independent learning should be aware of. You will no doubt hear many other reasons why it 'can't be done'. You might well have thought of a few others yourself. Only a little imagination is needed to generate many possible difficulties and problems. But if, nevertheless, you believe it is worthwhile to go ahead with your own innovations based on independent learning, it is encouraging to be reminded of Mark Twain's comments: 'I've foreseen many problems in my life. Luckily many of them never turned up!'

References

Abe, D Henner-Stanchina, C and Smith, P (1975) *New Approaches to Autonomy: Two Experiments in Self-Directed Learning*, Mélanges Pédagogiques – 1975, Nancy, France: Centre de Recherches et d'Applications Pédagogiques en Langues, Université de Nancy.

Abercrombie, M L J (1960) *The Anatomy of Judgement*, London: Hutchinson; Harmondsworth: Penguin (1969).

Abercrombie, M L J (1981) Changing basic assumptions about teaching and learning, in Boud D J (ed) *Developing Student Autonomy in Learning*, 1st Edn. London: Kogan Page, 38-54.

Ackoff, R L (1974) *Redesigning the Future*, New York: John Wiley.

Adams, J D (1974) *Phases of Personal and Professional Development*, unpublished manuscript, NTL Institute for Applied Behavioural Science.

Ali, M A, Thomas, E J Hamilton, J D and Brain, M D (1977) Blood and guts: one component of an integrated program in biological sciences as applied to medicine, *Canadian Medical Association Journal*, **116**, 59-61.

Allport, G (1960) *Personality and Social Enounter*, Boston:Beacon Press.

Argyris, C and Schön, D (1980) What is an organisation that it may learn?, in Lockett M, and Spear, R (eds) *Organisations as Systems*, Milton Keynes: Open University Press, 128-37.

Astin, J (1976) *Academic Gamesmanship: Student-Orientated Change in Higher Education*, New York: Praeger.

Atherton, C (1972) Lecture, discussion and independent study: instructional methods revisited, *Journal of Experimental Education*, **40**, 4, 24-8.

Audemars, D, Borel, M and Jacot, J (1977) *Le Petit Guide du Parrain*, Lausanne: EPFL-CPD (1974), October.

Ausubel, D P (1968) *Educational Psychology: A Cognitive View*, New York: Holt, Rinehart & Winston.

Bagnall, R G (1987) Enhancing self-direction in adult education: a possible trap for enthusiasts, *Discourse: the Australian Journal of Educational Studies*, **8**, 1, 90-100.

Barrows, H S and Mitchell, D L M (1975) An innovative course in undergraduate neuroscience: experiment in problem-based learning with 'problem boxes'. *British Journal of Medical Education*, **9** (4), 223-30.

Barrows, H S and Tamblyn, R (1977) The portable patient problem pack (P4): a problem based learning unit, *Journal of Medical Education*, **52**, 1002-4.

Barrows, H S and Tamblyn, R (1980) *Problem-based Learning: An Approach to Medical Education*, New York: Springer.

Bateson, G (1972) *Steps to an Ecology of Mind*, New York: Ballantine.

Bawden, R J (1985) Problem-based learning: An Australian perspective, in Boud D J (ed) *Problem-based Learning in Education for the Professions*, Sydney Higher Education Research and Development Society of Australasia, 43-57.

Bawden, R J and Valentine, I (1984) Learning to be a capable systems agriculturalist, *Programmed Learning and Educational Technology*, **21**, 273-87.

Bawden, R J, Drinan J P and Lundie-Jenkins, D G (1981) Curriculum design by objectives: case studies in innovative education at Hawkesbury, *Research and Development in Higher Education*, **4**, 109-27.

Bawden, R J, Macadam, R D, Packham, R G and Valentine, I (1984) Systems thinking and systems practices in the education of agriculturalists, *Agricultural Systems*, **13**, 205-25.

Beck, J E (1979) Changing construing by experiential learning methods: a framework for research, *Paper presented at the Third International Congress on Personal Construct Psychology*, Breukelen, The Netherlands, July 1979.

Becker, H S, Geer, B and Hughes, E C (1968) *Making the Grade: the Academic Side of Academic Life*, New York: John Wiley.

Belbin, R M (1981) *Management Teams: Why They Succeed or Fail*, London: Heinemann.

Bell, D (1967) Notes on the post-industrial society, *The Public Interest*, No. 6.

Bernard, D and Papagiannis, G J (1983) Educational diversification in less industrialized countries: a sociolinguistic approach in the study of nonformal education, in Bock, J C and Papagiannis, G J (eds) *Nonformal Education and National Development*, New York: Praeger, 184-204.

Bernstein, B (1977) *Class, Codes and Control, Vol.3*, 2nd Edn. London: Routledge & Kegan Paul.

Bertalanffy, L von (1968) *General Systems Theory: Foundation, Development, Applications*, New York: Braziller.

Biggs, J B (1979) Individual differences in study processes and the quality of learning outcomes, *Higher Education*, 8 (4), 381-93.

Biggs, J B (1982) Student motivation and study strategies in university and college of advanced education populations, *Higher Education Research and Development*, 1, 33-55.

Biggs, J B (1987) *Student Approaches to Learning and Studying*, Melbourne: Australian Council for Educational Research.

Biggs, J B and Telfer, R (1987) *The Process of Learning*, 2nd Edn, Sydney: Prentice-Hall of Australia.

Bilorusky, J and Butler, H (1975) Beyond contract curricula to improvisational learning, in Berte, N R (ed) *Individualizing Education Through Contract Learning*, Alabama: University of Alabama Press, 144-72.

Bloom, B S *et al* (1956) *Taxonomy of Educational Objectives I: The Cognitive Domain*, New York: Longmans Green.

Blumberg, P, Sharf, B F and Sinacore, J M (1982) Impact of independent-study programme upon professional careers, *Medical Education*, 16, 156-60.

Bolman, L (1976) Group leader effectiveness, in Cooper C C (ed) *Developing Social Skills in Managers*, London: Macmillan.

Boud, D J (1981) Toward student responsibility for learning, in Boud D J (ed) *Developing Student Autonomy in Learning*, 1st Edn, London: Kogan Page, 21-37.

Boud, D J (1983) Self and peer assessment in higher and continuing professional education: an annotated bibliography, in Boud, D J and Lublin, J (eds) *Self Assessment in Professional Education*, Kensington: Tertiary Education Research Centre, University of New South Wales, 35-55.

Boud, D J (1985) Problem-based learning in perspective, in Boud, D J (ed) *Problem-based Learning in Education for the Professions*, Sydney: Higher Education Research and Development Society of Australasia, 13-18.

Boud, D J (1986) *Implementing Student Self-assessment*, Sydney: Higher Education Research and Development Society of Australasia.

Boud, D J and Griffin, V R (eds) (1987) *Appreciating Adults Learning: From the Learner's Perspective*, London: Kogan Page.

Boud, D J and Prosser, M T (1980) Sharing responsibility: staff–student cooperation in learning, *British Journal of Educational Technology*, 11 (1),24-35.

Boyd, H R and Cowan, J (1985) A case for self-assessment based on recent studies of student learning, *Assessment and Evaluation in Higher Education*, 10 (3).

Boyd, H R, Adeyemi-Bere, A and Blackhall, R F (1984) Acquiring professional competence through learner-directed learning – an undergraduate perspective, in *Royal Society of Arts Education for Capability Occasional Paper No.7.*

Boydell, T (1976) *Experiential Learning*, Manchester Monographs No.5, Manchester: Department of Adult and Higher Education, University of Manchester.

Brookfield, S D (1981) Independent adult learning, *Studies in Adult Education*, 13 (1), 15-27.

Brookfield, S D (1984) Self-directed adult learning: a critical paradigm, *Adult Education*

Quarterly, **35** (2), 59-71.

Brown, C (1983) Confessions of an autodidact, *Adult Education (UK)*, **56** (3), 227-32.

Brown, W F *et al* (1971) Effectiveness of student-to-student counselling on the academic adjustment of potential college dropouts, *Journal of Educational Psychology*, **62**, 285-9.

Brun, J (1976) *La Parrainage à l'EPFL en 1973–74 et en 1975–75: Résultats d'une Première Enquête auprès des Parrains et des Filleuls*, Lausanne: EPFL-CPD.

Brundage, D H and MacKeracher, D (1980) *Adult Learning Principles and their Application to Program Planning*, Toronto: Ontario Ministry of Education.

Bruner, J S (1957) Going beyond the information given, in Bruner, J S *et al* (eds) *Contemporary Approaches to Cognition*, Cambridge, Mass: Harvard University Press, 41-67.

Bruner, J S (1966) *Toward a Theory of Instruction*, Cambridge, Mass: Harvard University Press.

Burgess, T (1977) *Education After School*, Harmondsworth: Penguin.

Cameron, S W (1983) The Perry scheme: a new perspective on adult learners, *Proceedings of the 24th Annual Adult Education Research Conference*, 8-10 April, 1983, University of Montreal, 38-43.

Campbell, V N (1964) Self-direction and programmed instruction for five different types of learning objectives, *Psychology in the Schools*, **1** (4), 348-59.

Candy, P (1987a) Evolution, revolution or devolution: increasing learner-control in the instructional setting, in Boud, D J and Griffin, V R (eds) *Appreciating Adults Learning: From the Learner's Perspective*, London: Kogan Page, 159-78.

Candy, P C (1987) *Reframing Research into 'Self-Direction' in Adult Education: A Constructivist Perspective*. Unpublished Doctoral Dissertation, The University of British Columbia.

Candy, P C, Harri-Augstein, E S and Thomas, L F (1985) Reflection and the self-organized learner: a model of learning conversations, in Boud, D J, Keogh, R and Walker, D (eds) *Reflection: Turning Experience into Learning*, London: Kogan Page, 106-16.

Carnegie Foundation (1972) *The Fourth Revolution: Instructional Technology in Higher Education*, New York: McGraw Hill.

Chaire de Pédagogie et Didactique (1976a) *Le Parrainage à l' EPFL: Enquête auprès des Parrains et des Filleuls, faite au Semestre d'Eté 1976*, Lausanne: EPFL-CPD, September.

Chaire de Pédagogie et Didactique (1976b) *Enquête auprès des Parrains et des Filleuls sur la Formation Pédagogique des Etudiants, faite au Semestre d'Eté 1976*, Lausanne: APFL-CPD, September.

Champagne, M (1976) *Le Parrainage à l'EPFL: Expérience de 1975. Rapport Résumé de l'Enquête faite auprès des Parrains et des Filleuls et Recommandations à l'Inention des Nouveaux Parrains et des Counseillers de Classe de Première Année*, Lausanne: APFL-CPD, October.

Checkland, P B (1985) From Optimizing to Learning: A Development of Systems Thinking for the 1990s, *Journal of the Operations Research Society*, **36**, 757-67.

Chené, A (1983) The concept of autonomy in adult education: a philosophical discussion, *Adult Education Quarterly*, **34** (1), 38-47.

Chickering, A W (1969) *Education and Identity*, San Francisco: Jossey-Bass.

Chickering, A W and Associates (1981) *The Modern American College*, San Francisco: Jossey-Bass.

Coles, C R (1985) Differences between conventional and problem-based curricula in their students' approaches to studying, *Medical Education*, **19**, 308-9.

Combs, A W and Snygg, D (1959) *Individual Behaviour*, 2nd Edn, New York: Harper.

Combs, A W, Avila, D L and Purkey, W W (1971) *Helping Relationships*, Boston, Mass: Allyn & Bacon.

Cornwall, M G (1979) *Students as Teachers: Peer Teaching in Higher Education*, Cowo-Publicatie 7906-01, Amsterdam: University of Amsterdam.

Cornwall, M, Schmithals, F and Jaques, D (1977) *Project-Orientation in Higher Education*, Brighton: Brighton Polytechnic.

Cowan, J (1978) Freedom in the selection of course content: a case-study of a course without a syllabus, *Studies in Higher Education*, **3** (2) 139-48.

Cowan, J (1984) Acquiring professional competence through learner-directed learning – a lecturer's view, in *Royal Society of Arts Education for Capability Occasional Paper No. 7.*

Crittenden, B (1978) Autonomy as an aim of education, in Strike, K A and Egan,K (eds) *Ethics and Educational Policy*, London: Routledge & Kegan Paul, 105-26.

Crockett, W H (1965) Cognitive comlpexity and impression formation, in Maher, B A (ed) *Progress in Experimental Personality Research* Vol.2, New York: Academic Press, 47-90.

Curran, C A (1976) *Counseling–learning in Second Languages*, Apple River, I11: Apple River Press.

Danis, C and Tremblay, N (1985) The self-directed learning experience: major recurrent tasks to deal with, *Proceedings of the Fourth Annual Conference of the Canadian Association for the Study of Adult Education*, 28-30 May, 1985, Montreal, Quebec, 283-301.

Davie, L (1987) Evolving perspectives of learning, in Boud, D J and Griffin, V R (eds) *Appreciating Adults Learning: From the Learner's Perspective*, London: Kogan Page, 197-208.

Dearden, R F (1972) Autonomy and education, in Dearden, R F, Hirst, P F and Peters, R S (eds) *Education and the Development of Reason*, London: Routledge & Kegan Paul, 448-65.

Dearden, R F (1975) Autonomy as an educational ideal, in Brown, S C (ed) *Philosophers Discuss Education*, London: Macmillan, 3-18.

Dearden, R F (1984) *Theory and Practice in Education*, London: Routledge & Kegan Paul.

Dewey, J (1910) *How We Think*, New York: Heath.

Dittman, J (1976) Individual autonomy: the magnificent obsession, *Educational Leadership*, **33** (6), 463-7.

Donald, J G (1976) Contracting for learning, *Learning and Development*, **7** (5).

Dressel, P L and Thompson, M M (1973) *Independent Study: A New Interpretation of Concepts, Practices and Problems*, San Francisco: Jossey-Bass.

Dunlop, F (1986) The education of the emotions and the promotion of autonomy: are they really compatible?, *British Journal of Educational Studies*, **34** (2), 152-60.

Elbaz, F (1983) *Teacher Thinking: A Study of Practical Knowledge*, London: Croom Helm.

Elliott, R (1980) Conceptual Approaches to Power and Authority, in Lockett, M and Spear, R (eds) *Organisations as Systems*, Milton Keynes: Open University Press, 138-47.

Elton, L R B and Laurillard, D M (1979) Trends in research on student learning, *Studies in Higher Education*, **4**, 87-102.

Entwistle, N J and Percy, K A (1974) Critical thinking or conformity? an investigation of the aims and outcomes of higher education, in *Research into Higher Education – 1973*, London: Society for Research into Higher Education.

Entwistle, N J and Ramsden, P (1983) *Understanding Student Learning*, London: Croom Helm.

Eraut, M, MacKenzie, N and Papps, I (1975) The mythology of educational development: reflections on a three-year study of economics teaching, *British Journal of Educational Technology*, **6** (3),20-34.

Erickson, G L (1987) Constructivist epistemology and the professional development of teachers, *Paper presented at the annual meeting of the American Educational Research Association*, 20-24 April 1987, Washington, DC.

Farnes, N (1975) Student-centred learning, *Teaching at a Distance*, **3**, 2-6.

Faure Report (1972) *Learning to Be: The World of Education Today and Tomorrow*, Report of the International Commission on the Development of Education, Paris: UNESCO.

Feldman, D H (1980) *Beyond Universals in Cognitive Development*, Norwood, New Jersey: Ablex.

Ferrier, B M and Hamilton, J D (1977) A preparatory course for medical students who lack a conventional academic background,*Journal of Medical Education*, **52**, 390-5.

Ferrier, B M, McAuley, R D and Roberts, R S (1978) Selection of medical students at McMaster University, *Journal of the Royal College of Physicians*, **12** (4) 365.

Ferrier, B M and Woodward, C A (1987) Career choices of McMaster University medical graduates and contemporary Canadian medical graduates, *Canadian Medical Association Journal*, **133**, 39-44

Fleming, W and Rutherford, D (1984) 'Recommendations for Learning': rhetoric and reaction, *Studies in Higher Education*, **9** (1), 17-26

Fransson, A (1979) On qualitative differences in learning: IV – Effects of motivation and test anxiety on process and outcome, *British Journal of Educational Psychology*, **47**, 244-257.

Furedy, C and Furedy, J J (1985) Critical thinking: toward research and dialogue, in Donald, J G and Sullivan, A M (eds) *Using Research to Improve Teaching*, New Directions for Teaching and Learning No.23, San Francisco: Jossey-Bass, 51-69.

Gentry, N D (1974) Three models of training and utilization, *Professional Psychology*, **5**, 207-14.

Gibb, J R (1964) Climate for trust formation, in Bradford, L P *et al* (eds) *T-Group Theory and Laboratory Method*, New York: John Wiley, 279-309.

Gibbons, M, Bailey, A, Comeau, P, Schmuck, J, Seymour, S and Wallace D (1980) Towards a theory of self-directed learning: a study of experts without formal training, *Journal of Humanistic Psychology*, **20** (2), 41-56.

Gibbs, B (1979) Autonomy and authority in education, *Journal of Philosophy of Education*, **13**, 119-32.

Gibbs, G (1981) *Teaching Students to Learn*, Milton Keynes: The Open University Press.

Gibran, K (1923) *The Prophet*, New York: Alfred A Knopf.

Gilligan, C (1981) Moral development, in Chickering, A W and Associates, *The Modern American College*, San Francisco: Jossey-Bass, 139-57.

Gindes, B C (1973) *New Concepts of Hypnosis*, Hollywood, Cal: Wilshire.

Goldman, R M, Wade, S and Zegar, D (1974) Students without harness: the 'SUM' experiment in self-paced learning, *Journal of Higher Education*, **45**, 197-210.

Goldschmid, B and Goldschmid, M L (1976a) Peer teaching in higher education: a review, *Higher Education*, **5**, 9-33.

Goldschmid, B and Goldschmid, M L (1976b) Enabling students to learn and participate effectively in higher education, *Journal of Personalized Instruction*, **1** (2), 70-5.

Goldschmid, M L and Burckhardt, C (1976) Expérience de parrainage dans une école polytechnique, *European Journal of Engineering Education*, **1**, (2), 108-12.

Griffin, V R (1982) Self-directed adult learners and learning, in Herman, R (ed) *The Design of Self-Directed Learning: a Handbook for Teachers and Administrators*, Toronto: The Ontario Institute for Studies in Education Press.

Griffin, V R (1987) Naming the processes, in Boud, D J and Griffin, V R (eds) *Appreciating Adults Learning: From the Learner's Perspective*, London: Kogan Page, 209-21.

Gross, R D and Gross, B (1983) *Independent Scholarship: Promise, Problems and Prospects*, New York: College Entrance Examination Board.

Guglielmino, L M (1977) *Development of the Self-directed Learning Readiness Scale*, Doctoral Thesis, University of Georgia.

Hamilton, J D (1976) The McMaster curriculum: a critique, *British Medical Journal*, **1**. 1191-6.

Harber, C and Meighan, R (1986) A case study of democratic learning in teacher education, *Educational Review*, **38** (3), 273-82.

Häyrynen, Y-P (1980) Aesthetic activity and cognitive learning: creativity and orientation of thinking in new problem situations, *Adult Educatioin in Finland*, **17** (3), 5-16.

Heiney, W F Jr (1977) 'Less Practising what you preach': a plan for helping freshmen psychology majors get off to a good start, *Teaching of Psychology*, **4** (2), 73-6.

Henner-Stanchina, C (1976) *Two years of Autonomy: Practice and Outlook,*, Mélanges Pédagogiques – 1976, Nancy, France: Centre de Recherches et d'Applications Pédagogiques en Langues, Université de Nancy.

Herman, R (ed) (1982) *The Design of Self-directed Learning: A Handbook for Teachers and Administrators*, Toronto: The Ontario Institute for Studies in Education Press.

Heron, J (1974) *The Concept of a Peer Learning Community*, Guildford: Human Potential Research Project, University of Surrey.

Heron, J (1975) *Six Category Intervention Analysis*, Guildford: Human Potential Research

Project, University of Surrey.

Heron, J (1979a) *Behaviour Analysis in Education and Training*, University of London: British Postgraduate Medical Federation.

Heron, J (1979b) *Peer Review Audit*, University of London: British Postgraduate Medical Federation.

Heron, J (1981) Experiential research methodology, in Reason, P and Rowan, J (eds) *Human Inquiry: A Sourcebook of New Paradigm Research*, Chichester: John Wiley, 153-66.

Hersey, P and Blanchard K, (1982) *Management of Organizational Behavior* 4th Ed, New Jersey: Prentice-Hall.

Higgs, J (1987) Program structure and self-direction in independent study programs, in Miller, A H and Sachse-Akerlind (eds) *Research and Development in Higher Education*, **9**, Sydney: Higher Education Research and Development Society of Australasia, 258-61.

Hodgson, V and Reynolds, M (1987) The dynamics of the learning community: staff intentions and student experience, in Boud, D J and Griffin, V R (eds) *Appreciating Adults Learning: From the Learner's Perspective*, London: Kogan Page, 149-58.

Hunt, D E and Sullivan, E V (1974) *Between Psychology and Education*, Hinsdale, Ill: Dryden Press.

Jackins, H (1965) *The Human Side of Human Beings*, Seattle: Rational Island.

Jankovic, V, Beauvallet-Caillet, E, Beigbeger, I *et al.* (1979) *European Expert Meeting on the Forms of Autodidactic Learning*, Paris, 16-19 October 1979, Final Report and Recommendations, Paris: Division of Structures, Contents, Methods and Techniques, Unesco.

Jaques, D (1984) *Learning in Groups*, London: Croom Helm.

Jevons, F R and Turner, H D L (eds) (1972) *What Kinds of Graduates Do We Need?*, Oxford: Oxford University Press.

Kelly, G A (1955) *The Psychology of Personal Constructs*, New York: Norton Press.

Klemp, G O (1977) *Three Factors of Success in the World of Work: Implications for Curriculum Planning in Higher Education*, Boston: McBer and Company.

Knapper, C K (1980) *Evaluating Instructional Technology*, London: Croom Helm.

Knapper, C K and Cropley, A J (1985) *Lifelong Learning and Higher Education*, London: Croom Helm.

Knowles, M S (1975) *Self-directed Learning: A Guide for Learners and Teachers*, New York: Association Press.

Knowles, M S (1978) *The Adult Learner: A Neglected Species*, 2nd Edn, Houston: Gulf Publishing Company.

Knowles, M S (1980) *The Modern Practice of Adult Education: From Pedagogy to Andragogy*, Chicago: Follett.

Knowles, M S (1986) *Using Learning Contracts*, San Francisco: Jossey-Bass.

Koetting, J R (1984) Foundations of naturalistic inquiry: developing a theory base for understanding individual interpretations of reality, *Media and Adult Learning*, **6** (2), 8-18.

Kohlberg, L (1972) Humanistic and cognitive – developmental perspectives on psychological education, in Purpel, R E and Belanger, M (eds) *Curriculum and Cultural Change*, Berkeley, Cal: McCutchan, 394-402.

Kolb, D A, Rubin, L M and McIntyre, J M (1974) *Organisational Psychology: an Experiential Approach*, New Jersey: Prentice-Hall.

Kubler-Ross, E (1970) *On Death and Dying*, New York: Macmillan.

Kuhn, D (1981) The role of self-directed activity in cognitive development, in Sigel, I E, Brodzinsky, D and Golinkoff, R M (eds) *New Directions in Piagetian Theory and Practice*, Hillsdale, New Jersey: Lawrence Erlbaum Associates, 353-7.

Kuhn, T S (1970) *The Structure of Scientific Revolutions*, 2nd Edn, Chicago, Ill: University of Chicago Press.

Lawson, K H (1982) *Analysis and Ideology: Conceptual Essays on the Education of Adults*, Nottingham Studies in the Theory and Practice of the Education of Adults, Nottingham: Department of Adult Education, University of Nottingham.

WELSH COLLEGE OF MUSIC & DRAMA LIBRARY

Lehman, T (1975) Educational outcomes from contract learning at Empire State College, paper presented at the 30th National Conference on Higher Education, Chicago, Ill.

Levitan, H (1981) Science education: an experiment in facilitating the learning of neurophysiology, *The Physiologist*, **24**, 19-27.

Lewin, K (1951) *Field Theory in Social Sciences*, New York: Harper & Row.

Lewis, B N (1977) The rationale of adaptive teaching machines, in Goldsmith, M (ed) *Mechanisation in the Classroom: An Introduction to Teaching Machines and Programmed Instruction*, London: Souvenir Press, 83-119.

Lewis, H A (1978) A teacher's reflections on autonomy, *Studies in Higher Education*, **3** (2), 149-59.

Lieberman, M A, Yalom, I D and Miles, M B (1973) *Encounter Groups: First Facts*, New York: Basic Books.

Lindsay, P H and Norman, D A (1977) *Human Information Processing*, 2nd Edn, London: Academic Press.

Little, G (1970) *The University Experience: An Australian Study*, Melbourne: Melbourne University Press.

Little, G (1975) *Faces on the Campus: A Psycho-Social Study*, Melbourne: Melbourne University Press.

Loevinger, J (1976) *Ego Development: Conception and Theories*, San Francisco: Jossey-Bass.

Luke, R A (1972) The internal normative structure of sensitivity training groups, *Journal of Applied Behavioural Science*, **7**, 689-708.

Macadam B, (1985) Introducing problem-based learning into a curriculum, in Boud D J (ed) *Problem-based Learning in Education for the Professions*, Sydney: Higher Education Research and Development Society of Australasia, 199-206.

Macadam, R D and Packham, R G (1984) *A Systems Analysis of the School of Agriculture, Part I*, Internal Document, Hawkesbury Agricultural College.

Macadam, R D and Packham, R G (1985) *A Systems Analysis of the School of Agriculture, Part II*, Internal Document, Hawkesbury Agricultural College.

Maclean, H (1987) Linking person-centred teaching to qualitative research training, in Boud, D J and Griffin, V R (eds) *Appreciating Adults Learning: From the Learner's Perspective*, London: Kogan Page, 127-36.

Martin, E (1987) Adaptation to university learning and the school experience, in Miller, A H and Sachse-Akerlind, G (eds) *Research and Development in Higher Education*, **9**, Sydney: Higher Education Research and Development Society of Australasia, 319-29.

Martin, W B (1976) *The Negotiated Order of the School*, Toronto: MacMillan of Canada.

Marton, F (1981) Phenomenography: describing conceptions of the world around us, *Instructional Science*, **10**, 177-200.

Marton, F, Hounsell, D and Enwistle, N J (1984) *The Experience of Learning*, Edinburgh: Scottish Academic Press.

Marton, F and Säljö, R (1976a) On qualitative differences in learning: I Outcome and process, *British Journal of Educational Psychology*, **46**, 4-11.

Marton, F and Säljö, R (1976b) On qualitative differences in learning: II Outcome as a function of the learner's conception of the task, *British Journal of Educational Psychology*, **46**, 115-27.

Marton, F and Säljö, R (1984) Approaches to learning, in Marton, F, Hounsell, D and Entwistle, N J (eds) *The Experience of Learning*, Edinburgh: Scottish Academic Press, 36-55.

McKenzie, J, O'Reilly, D and Stephenson, J K (1985) Independent study and professional education, *Studies in Higher Education*, **10** (2),187-97.

Meighan, R and Harber, C (1986) Democratic learning in teacher education: a review of experience at one institution, *Journal of Education for Teaching*, **12** (2), 163-72.

Meisler, R (1984) *Trying Freedom: The Case for Liberating Education*, San Diego: Harcourt Brace Jovanovich.

Merriam, S B and Simpson, E (1984) *A Guide to Research for Educators and Trainers of Adults*, Malabar, Florida: Krieger.

Millar, C., Morphet, T and Saddington, T (1986) Curriculum negotiation in professional adult education, *Journal of Curriculum Studies*, **18** (4) 429-43.

Miller, C M L and Parlett, M (1974) *Up to the Mark: A Study of the Examination Game*, London: Society for Research into Higher Education.

Morgan, A (1983) Theoretical aspects of project based learning in higher education, *British Journal of Educational Technology*, **14** (1), 66-78.

Neufeld,V R (1983) Adventures of an adolescent: curriculum change at McMaster University, in Friedman, C P and Purcell, E F (eds) *The New Biology and Medical Education*, New York: Macy Foundation, 256-286.

Neufeld, V R and Barrows, H S (1974) The 'McMaster Philosophy': an approach to medical education, *Journal of Medical Education*, **49** (11), 1040-50.

Newble, D I and Clarke, R M (1986) The approaches to learning of students in a traditional and in an innovative problem-based medical school, *Medical Education*, **20**, 267-73.

Newsom, R and Foxworth, C L (1980) A study of impact of specific teaching strategies on locus of control of adult students: July 1979 to June 1980, unpublished paper, Denton College of Education, North Texas State University.

Nolan, R E (1981) Dependency versus autonomy in adult second language learning, *Proceedings of the 22nd Annual Adult Education Research Conference*, 1-3 April, 1981, Northern Illinois University, De Kalb, 140-5.

Norman, D A (1973) Memory, knowledge and the answering of questions, in Solso, R L (ed) *Contemporary Issues in Cognitive Psychology*, New York: Wiley.

Novak, J D and Gowin, D B (1984) *Learning How to Learn*, New York: Cambridge University Press.

Nuffield Foundation Group for Research and Innovation in Higher Education (1975) *Towards Independence in Learning*, London: Nuffield Foundation.

Nystedt, L and Magnusson, D (1982) Construction of experience, in Mancuso, J and Adams-Webber, J (eds) *The Construing Person*, New York: Praeger.

Pallie, W and Brain, E (1978) 'Modules' in morphology for self study: a system for learning in an undergraduate medical programme, *Journal of Medical Education*, **12**, 107-13.

Paskow, A (1974) Are college students educable?, *Journal of Higher Education*, **45**, 184-96.

Percy, K and Ramsden, P (1980) *Independent Study: Two Examples from English Higher Education*, Guildford: Society for Research into Higher Education.

Perry, W G (1970) *Forms of Intellectual and Ethical Development in the College Years: A Scheme*, New York: Holt, Rinehart & Winston.

Perry, W G (1981) Cognitive and ethical growth: the making of meaning, in Chickering, A W and Associates. *The Modern Amercan College*, San Francisco: Jossey-Bass. 76-116.

Peters, R S (1966) *Ethics and Education*, London: Allen & Unwin.

Phillips, D C (1975) The anatomy of autonomy, *Educational Philosophy and Theory*, **7** (2). 1-12.

Phillips, D Z (1973) Democratization: some themes in unexamined talk, *British Journal of Educational Studies*, **21** (2), 133-48.

Phillips, E M (1980) Education for research: the changing constructs of the postgraduate, *International Journal of Man-Machine Studies*, **13**, 39-48.

Piaget, J (1970) *Genetic Epistemology*, New York: Columbia University Press.

Piaget, J (1972) *The Principles of Genetic Epistemology*, New York: Viking.

Polanyi, M (1967) *The Tacit Dimension*, London: Routledge & Kegan Paul.

Powell, J P (1981) Helping and hindering learning, *Higher Education*, **10**, 103-17.

Powell, J P (1985) Autobiographical learning, in Boud, D J, Keogh, R and Walker, D (eds) *Reflection: Turning Experience into Learning*, London: Kogan Page, 41-51.

Quine, W V and Ullian, J S (1978) *Web of Belief*, New York: Random House.

Quinton, A M (1971) Authority and autonomy in knowledge, *Proceedings of the Annual Conference of the Philosophy of Education Society of Great Britain*, **5**, 2, Supplement, 201-215.

Ramsden, P (1979) Student learning and perceptions of the academic environment, *Higher Education*, **8**, 411-27.

Ramsden, P (1984) The context of learning, in Marton, F, Hounsell, D and Entwistle, N J (eds) *The Experience of Learning,* Edinburgh: Scottish Academic Press, 144-64.

Ramsden, P (1985) Student learning research: retrospect and prospect, *Higher Education Research and Development,* **4** (1), 51-69.

Ramsden, P (1987) Why and how to study student learning, in Miller, A H and Sachse-Akerlind, G (eds) *Research and Development in Higher Education,* 9, Sydney: Higher Education Research and Development Society of Australasia, 141-54.

Ramsden, P and Entwistle, N J (1981) Effects of academic departments on students' approaches to studying, *British Journal of Educational Psychology,* **51**, 368-83.

Ramsden, P, Beswick, D and Bowden, J (1987) Learning processes and learning skills, in Richardson, J, Eysenck, M and Warren-Piper, D (eds) *Student Learning: Research in Education and Cognitive Psychology,* Milton Keynes: Society for Research into Higher Education and The Open University Press, 168-76.

Riesman, D (1950) *The Lonely Crowd,* New Haven, Conn: Yale University Press.

Rogers C R (1961) *On Becoming a Person,* Boston, Mass: Houghton-Mifflin.

Rogers, C R (1969) *Freedom to Learn: A View of What Education Might Become,* Columbus, Ohio: Charles E Merrill.

Rogers, C R (1983) *Freedom to Learn in the 80s,* Columbus, Ohio: Charles E Merrill.

Rowan, J (1981) A dialectical paradigm for research, in Reason, P and Rowan, J (eds) *Human Inquiry: a Sourcebook of New Paradigm Research,* Chichester: John Wiley, 93-112.

Rowan, J and Reason, P (1981) On making sense, in Reason, P and Rowan, J (eds) *Human Inquiry: a Sourcebook of New Paradigm Research,* Chichester: John Wiley, 113-37.

Rumelhart, D E (1977) *An Introduction to Human Information Processing,* New York: Wiley.

Säljö, R (1975) Qualitative differences in learning as a function of the learner's conception of the task, *Gothenburg Studies in Educational Sciences* Number 14, Gothenburg, Sweden: University of Gothenburg.

Säljö, R (1982) Learning and understanding: a study of differences in constructing meaning from a text, *Gothenburg Studies in Educational Sciences* Number 41, Gothenburg, Sweden: University of Gothenburg.

Sarason, S B, Davidson, K S, Lighthall, F F, Waite, R R and Ruebush, B K (1960) *Anxiety in Elementary School Children,* New York: Wiley.

Schön, D A (1983) *The Reflective Practitioner: How Professionals Think in Action,* New York: Basic Books.

Schön, D A (1987) *Educating the Reflective Practitioner: Toward a New Design for Teaching and Learning in the Professions.* San Francisco: Jossey-Bass.

Schramm, W (1977) *Big Media, Little Media: Tools and Technologies for Instruction,* Los Angeles: Sage.

Schutz, W C (1967) *Joy: Expanding Human Awareness,* New York: Grove Press.

Schwartz, D (1971) *The Magic of Thinking Big,* New York: Cornerstone.

Sibley, J C (1978) Faculty of Health Sciences, McMaster University, Canada – the 1977 perspective, *Medical Education,* **12** (5) 15-18.

Sloan, M and Schommer, B T (1975) The process of contracting in community nursing, in Spradley, B W (ed) *Contemporary Community Nursing,* Boston: Little, Brown & Co.

Smith, P B (1980) The T-group Trainer – Group Facilitator or Prisoner of Circumstance? *Journal of Applied Behavioural Science,* **14**, 63-77.

Soltis, J F (1984) On the nature of educational research, *Educational Researcher,* **13** (10), 5-10.

Spearman, C (1923) *The Nature of Intelligence and Principles of Cognition,* London: Macmillan.

Spradley, B W (1981) *Community Health Nursing: Concepts and Practice,* Boston: Little, Brown & Co.

Stalker-Costin, A J (1986) 'Threatening the Priesthood': the potential for social transformation through nonformal education, *Proceedings of the 27th Annual Adult Education Research Conference,* 23-25 May, 1986, Syracuse University, New York, 273-8.

Stanton, H E (1975a) Weight loss through hypnosis, *American Journal of Clinical Hypnosis,* **18**, 34-8.

Stanton, H E (1975b) The treatment of insomnia through hypnosis and relaxation,

Australian Journal of Clinical Hypnosis, **3**, 4-8.

Stanton, H E (1975c) Ego enhancement through positive suggestion, *Australian Journal of Clinical Hypnosis* **3**, 32-6.

Stanton, H E (1977) Test anxiety and hypnosis: a different approach to an important problem, *Australian Journal of Education*, **21**, 179-86.

Stanton, H E (1978a) *Helping Sudents Learn: The Improvement of Higher Education*, Washington, DC: University Press of America.

Stanton, H E (1978b) Therapy and teaching, *Proceedings of the British Society of Medical and Dental Hypnosis*, **4**, 5-13.

Stanton, H E (1978c) A one-session hypnotic approach to modifying smoking behaviour, *International Journal of Clinical and Experimental Hypnosis*, **25**, 22-9.

Stanton, H E (1979) *The Plus Factor: a Guide to Positive Living*, Sydney: Collins/Fontana.

Stephenson, J (1980) The use of statements in North East London Polytechnic, in Adams, E and Burgess, T (eds) *Outcomes of Education*, London: Macmillan, 132-49.

Strike, K A (1982) *Liberty and Learning*, Oxford: Martin Robinson.

Strong, M (1977) *The Autonomous Adult Learner: the Idea of Autonomous Learning, the Capabilities and Perceived Needs of the Autonomous Learner*, unpublished M Ed thesis, University of Nottingham.

Svensson, L (1976) Study skill and learning, *Gothenburg Studies in Educational Sciences*, Number 19, Gothenburg, Sweden: University of Gothenburg.

Sweeney, G D and Mitchell, D L M (1975) An introduction to the study of medicine: phase 1 of the McMaster MD Program, *Journal of Medical Education*, **50**, 70-7.

Talbot, R (1978) *Résultants de l'Enquête sur le Parrainage 1977-78*. Lausanne: EPFL-CPD, September.

Taylor, M (1986) Learning for self-direction in the classroom: the pattern of a transition process, *Studies in Higher Education*, **11** (1), 55-72.

Taylor, M (1987) Self-directed learning: more than meets the observer's eye, in Boud, D J and Griffin, V R (eds) *Appreciating Adults Learning: From the Learner's Perspective*, London: Kogan Page, 179-96.

Thomas, L F and Harri-Augstein, E S (1985) *Self-organised Learning: Foundations of a Conversational Science for Psychology*, London: Routledge & Kegan Paul.

Torbert, W R (1976) *Creating a Community of Inquiry: Conflict, Collaboration, Transformation*, London: John Wiley.

Torbert, W R (1978) Educating toward shared purpose, self-direction and quality work: the theory and practice of liberating structure, *Journal of Higher Education*, **49** (2), 109-35.

Tough, A (1971) *The Adult's Learning Projects*, Second Edition 1979, Toronto: Ontario Institute for Studies in Education.

Tuckman, B W (1965) Developmental sequence in small groups, *Psychological Bulletin*, **63**, 384-99.

von Glasersfeld, E (1974) Piaget and the radical constructivist epistemology, in Smock, C D and von Glasersfeld, E (eds) *Epistemology and Education: The Implications of Radical Constructivism for Knowledge Acquisition*, Mathemagenic Activities Program – Follow Through, Research Report Number 14, Athens, Georgia: University of Georgia, 1-26.

von Glasersfeld, E (1984) An introduction to radical constructivism, in Watzlawick, P (ed) *The Invented Reality: How Do We Know What We Believe We Know? Contributions to Constructivism*, New York: W W Norton.

von Glasersfeld, E and Smock, C D (1974) Introduction, in Smock, C D and von Glasersfeld, E (eds) *Epistemology and Education: The Implications of Radical Constructivism for Knowledge Acquisiton*, Mathemagenic Activities Program – Follow Through, Research Report Number 14, Athens, Georgia: University of Georgia, xi-xxiv.

Walsh, W (1978) The McMaster Programme of Medical Education, Hamilton, Ontario, Canada: developing problem-solving abilities, in Katz, F M and Fulop, T (eds) *Personnel for Health Care: Case Studies of Educational Programmes*, Public Health Papers, 70, Geneva: World Health Organization.

Wang, M C (1983) Development and consequences of students' sense of personal control, in Levine, J M and Wang, M C (eds) *Teacher and Student Perceptions: Implications for Learning*, Hillsdale, New Jersey: Lawrence Erlbaum Associates, 213-47.

Wasserman, C W, McCarthy, B W and Ferree, E H (1975) Student paraprofessionals as behavior change agents, *Professional Psychology*, **6**, 217-23.

Watkins, D (1984) Student perceptions of factors influencing tertiary learning, *Higher Education Research and Development*, **3**, 33-50.

Watson, H J, Vallee, J M and Mulford, W R (1981) *Structured Experiences and Group Development*, Canberra: Curriculum Development Centre.

Weathersby, R P (1981) Ego development, in Chickering, A W and Associates, *The Modern American College*, San Francisco: Jossey-Bass, 51-75,

Weber, M (1974) *The Theory of Social and Economic Organisation*, New York, Free Press.

White, J P (1982) *The Aims of Education Restated*, London: Routledge & Kegan Paul.

Woodward, C A and Ferrier, B M (1982) Perspectives of graduates two or five years after graduation from a three-year medical school, *Journal of Medical Education*, **57**, 294-302.

Wrenn, R L and Mencke, R (1972) Students who counsel students, *Personnel and Guidance Journal*, **50**, 687-9.

Index

269